CGAP®
CERTIFIED GOVERNMENT AUDITING PROFESSIONAL

Exam Study Guide
4th Edition

Thomas F. O'Connor, CIA, CGAP, CGFM, CDFM, CPA, CMA, CFE, MPA

Stephen L. Morgan, CIA, CGAP, CGFM, CFE, MPA

Contributing Editor

Sam M. McCall, CIA, CGAP, CPA, CGFM, PhD

Published by The Institute of Internal Auditors Research Foundation
247 Maitland Avenue
Altamonte Springs, Florida 32701-4201

The Institute of Internal Auditors' (IIA's) International Professional Practices Framework (IPPF) comprises the full range of existing and developing practice guidance for the profession. The IPPF provides guidance to internal auditors globally and paves the way to world-class internal auditing.

The IIA and The IIARF work in partnership with researchers from around the globe who conduct valuable studies on critical issues affecting today's business world. Much of the content presented in their final reports is a result of IIARF-funded research and prepared as a service to The IIARF and the internal audit profession. Expressed opinions, interpretations, or points of view represent a consensus of the researchers and do not necessarily reflect or represent the official position or policies of The IIA or The IIARF.

ISBN-13: 978-0-89413-722-8
18 17 16 15 14 13 12 1 2 3 4 5 6 7 8 9

CONTENTS

DETAILED CONTENTS

LIST OF TABLES

REVIEWERS AND CONTRIBUTORS

The authors wish to acknowledge The Institute of Internal Auditors (IIA) for permission to use various IIA publications, as well as the authors of the third edition who gave us a solid base from which to update and refine the manual.

We are much indebted to Sam McCall, city auditor of Tallahassee, Florida, and now a member of the Federal Accounting Standards Advisory Board. We are privileged to be the beneficiaries of Sam's in-depth knowledge of government auditing and accounting gained from many years in prominent roles, including past national president of the Association of Government Accountants (AGA) and Deputy State Auditor of Florida. As the primary content editor in developing the initial draft, Sam's comments were invaluable for enhancing the final product. We thank him mightily.

Additional professional members of The IIA and The IIA Research Foundation (IIARF) were kind and wise in their counsel and advice. For example, Urton Anderson, Joe Bell, and Susan Driver from the IIARF Committee of Research and Education Advisors (CREA) gave generously of their time to make this manual better than it ever would have been without their help.

Also, Lillian McAnally, Deborah Poulalion, and the late Dinah Wallace were professional and thorough in their detailed edits. We would be remiss not to mention the encouragement and support offered by additional IIA members and friends — notably Margie Bastolla, Judy Burke, Christie O'Loughlin, Ronell Raaum, Colleen Waring, and Robert Black — all of whom have a long history of support for enhancing the internal audit function in the public sector, as well as advancing the CGAP program.

Last, on a personal note, both authors wish to express gratitude for the support and inspiration gained from their beloved family members. Tom dedicates the manual to his wife, Gail, his four children and his 10 grandchildren — Heather, Brooke, Raleigh, Jake, Hannah, Leah, Olivia, Arthur, Shraddha, and Vi. Steve dedicates the manual to his wife, Debra, and two sons, Garrett and Frank. We both chose to work on the manual at times when we would rather have spent time with them. We love them for enduring those lost times.

ABOUT THE AUTHORS

Thomas F. O'Connor, CIA, CGAP, CGFM, CDFM, CPA, CMA, CFE, is a self-employed consultant and trainer. He has 34 years' experience as a governmental auditor, investigator, and evaluator. His career included 30 years at the U.S. Government Accountability Office (U.S. GAO); three years at the U.S. Agency for International Development (USAID); and approximately one year at the Peace Corps. He has experience in all aspects of governmental auditing, and has extensive foreign experience. As an adjunct to his audit work, he has presented more than 1,000 training classes. His educational background includes a BA in accounting from St. Ambrose University, and a master's in public administration from the University of Oklahoma.

Mr. O'Connor has been an avid supporter and contributor to the growth of The IIA's Certified Government Auditing Professional (CGAP) program. Starting shortly after that program was established, he presented CGAP exam preparation courses to approximately 75 audiences at all levels of government in the United States and a few overseas, resulting in several hundred new CGAPs. He is the author of *CGAP Exam Study Questions* published by The IIA Research Foundation in March 2010. In the world of governmental auditing, he has become known as "Mr. CGAP."

Stephen L. Morgan, CIA, CGAP, CGFM, is president of EGAPP, Inc., Excellence in Government Accountability and Performance Practices, a company that specializes in training government auditors and managers. He is the former city auditor of Austin, Texas, where he directed a full scope audit office that conducts performance audits, fraud investigations, and consulting engagements. Mr. Morgan played a critical role in helping the City of Austin evolve its performance measurement and management system into an accepted model for other government organizations. Before joining the City Auditor's Office, he was an evaluator in the U.S. GAO's National Productivity Office. For more than 20 years, Mr. Morgan has designed and delivered courses in performance measurement, management, and audit. He has co-authored three IIA textbooks, including *Performance Auditing: A Measurement Approach,* 1st and 2nd editions.

Mr. Morgan holds a BA in pre-law (government) and a master's in public administration, both from the University of Texas. In May 2009, he received the Victor Z. Brink Memorial Award, The IIA's highest award for leadership and service to the global internal audit profession. In May 2007, Mr. Morgan accepted the National Intergovernmental Audit Forum's Excellence in Government Performance and Accountability from the Comptroller General of the United States. Also, in March 2002, he became the fourth annual recipient of the Harry Hatry Distinguished Performance Measurement Practice Award from the American Society of Public Administration. Mr. Morgan holds certificate number 1 as a CGAP.

PREFACE

The purpose of this guide is primarily to help prepare you to pass the Certified Government Auditing Professional (CGAP) examination. The guide can be used for self-study or in conjunction with a formal training class, available from various sources. In either case, it is critical that you tailor your exam preparation to your own background and experience, which may dictate additional study to fill in any individual gaps. While intended primarily to help prepare readers for the CGAP examination, the manual also offers a comprehensive overview for any interested parties, of governmental auditing in the public sector in an era of heightened accountability and transparency, coupled with budgetary constraints and related debates.

The guide is based on the CGAP Exam Topic Outline established by The IIA. The four domains of the manual parallel the four domains of the CGAP examination.

Domain I describes four sets of audit standards and other guidance to which government auditors may be subject, depending on their location and role. These standards have undergone revisions — some significant — in the past few years, so auditors must stay abreast of the latest changes. The section also highlights the growing recognition of the auditor's role of addressing governance in the public sector. Last, domain I highlights the recent strong emphasis on risk assessment, internal control and ethics in the public sector, and how auditors need to respond.

Domain II includes three major topics — management of the audit function, the many types of audit services and areas of current emphasis, and the processes that are critical to effective delivery of those services. As in other functions, managers of government audit activities benefit from staying informed and properly applying current management theories to their area of responsibility. The range and diversity of government audit services is extensive and varies greatly among audit organizations, dependent on a number of factors, including laws, regulations, the nature of programs to be audited, and changing environments and expectations of citizens. This section pinpoints the key points in the process — from planning to reporting and follow-up — that lead to effective audit service. On a broader level, domain II explains how the standards and guidance discussed in domain I are related to each of the three major topics.

Domain III elaborates on domains I and II by providing insight into the methodologies, techniques, skills, and critical thinking that governmental auditors need in today's environment. First, a few specific management concepts and techniques are discussed, although government auditors recognize that the need for knowledge in this area expands as auditors move up "in the ranks." Second, domain III places heavy emphasis on the crucial need for auditors to have the skills and techniques needed to assess performance measurement and management — an area of explosive and relentless growth and visibility in the public sector in recent years. Third, important audit tools (such as statistics and analytical tools) are presented as well as a call to auditors to harness the power of technology and analytics to improve their effectiveness. Fourth, audit approaches to integrity issues, such as fraud prevention and detection, always of great interest to the public, are explored. Last, auditors are called upon to avoid logical fallacies.

Domain IV provides a perspective on the unique nature of the government environment when assigned to auditing in that environment. It should be noted that domain IV has a distinctly United States orientation, although some concepts and theories apply in other countries, particularly in the Western part of the world. Domain IV includes specifics of performance management initiatives at different levels of government in the United States — although many other countries have their own similar initiatives. Discussion of accounting practices at the national, state, and local level are esoteric to the United States. The unique role of governmental budgeting (likely similar to some other countries) and several specific approaches used in the United States are discussed. Service delivery methods, such as directly by government personnel or indirectly by contractors or grantees, are explored. Other areas where the approach in the public sector differs from the private sector include procurement and human resource management.

As stated elsewhere, The IIA has designated the CGAP examination to be closed, meaning that actual test questions are not publicly available. However, two sources should be of significant benefit to those preparing for this examination. Appendices A and B provide 15 actual past test questions and explanatory answers. In addition, *CGAP Exam Study Questions,* published by The IIA, includes 237 questions and explanatory answers. Those questions are not actual but have been deemed plausible after review by The IIA.

One last point: The reader is likely aware that the CGAP examination is offered in two versions —United States and international. This manual should be valuable for either version with two caveats: domain I includes coverage of the Generally Accepted Government Auditing Standards (GAGAS) (the Yellow Book), whereas the international version does not include specific questions on GAGAS. As stated above, domain IV has a heavy U.S. emphasis, so those taking the international examination may wish to expand their preparation related to domain IV of the examination.

We have sought to make this study guide as user friendly as possible. These approaches include incorporating the current information and trends, explanatory examples, tables (where possible), and digestible language. We hope it fully meets your needs, whether you seek to become a CGAP or for another purpose.

DOMAIN I
Standards, Governance, and Risk/Control Frameworks

Primary topics of interest and importance to government audit professionals include:

- Standards.
- Governance.
- Risk/control frameworks.
- IIA Code of Ethics.

I.A Standards

I.A.1 Role of a Comprehensive Set of Auditing/Evaluation Standards

Many professions have established standards to guide their practitioners and to create a basis for third-party review. Auditing has also established standards that are general specifications that delineate the essential attributes required for a quality audit. They establish the characteristics that should be met in planning, conducting, and reporting an audit. If the work satisfies audit standards, it provides a basis for ensuring and promoting audit quality.

Audit standards usually address the following areas:

- Audit staff qualifications.
- Independence.
- Due professional care.
- Quality control.
- Audit planning.
- Fieldwork.
- Reporting.

The IIA's *International Standards for the Professional Practice of Internal Auditing* (*Standards*) also addresses management of the internal audit activity.

Audit standards are developed and followed to:

- Provide uniform guidance to auditors.
- Build credibility and confidence in the auditing profession.
- Inform customers (the public, public officials, management, stakeholders, etc.) about the role of auditing.
- Establish a basis for conducting internal and external reviews of quality audits.

I.A.2 Application of Appropriate Standards in All Assignments

Governmental auditing is distinctive. The standards that apply specifically to government audits include:

- IIA *Standards.*
- Generally Accepted Government Auditing Standards (GAGAS) (the Yellow Book) of the U.S. Government Accountability Office (U.S. GAO).
- International Organization of Supreme Audit Institutions (INTOSAI) Standards.
- International Standards on Auditing (ISA).

The four sets of audit standards contain similar principles but have some conceptual differences, as well as differences in terminology. Also, there are various degrees of interaction among the proponents of these sets of standards, as well as recognition among the standards of the others. In some instances, one set acknowledges that that set may be used in conjunction with one or more other sets of standards.

The application of the appropriate audit standards is dependent on a myriad of issues, such as laws, regulations, audit requirements, and even the policies of the audit organization. Furthermore, the application of appropriate standards depends on 1) the objective of the engagement, 2) other mandates or local requirements relevant to the audit organization and the engagement itself, and 3) availability of information. In most cases, the guideline to follow is that if you cannot follow the relevant/appropriate standard and are unable to decline the engagement, the constraint must be disclosed in the report.

Statutes, laws, and mandates at all government levels often dictate the type and frequency of audit activities. Thus, when planning a government audit, research should be performed to ascertain which standards apply to specific audit engagements. Due to the complexity of the financial relationships between federal, state, and local government, detailed guidance has been developed to identify the total amount of financial assistance an entity actually receives. The need for thorough research in the planning process cannot be overemphasized and is critical to the audit process.

Additionally, certain countries, regions, or local governments may have developed specific standards that apply. Often, these take the form of audit manuals or other publications designed to supplement auditing standards already in place.

The Institute of Internal Auditors' (IIA) *Standards*[1]

Established in 1941, The Institute of Internal Auditors (IIA) is an international professional organization headquartered in Altamonte Springs, Florida, USA. The IIA considers itself "the internal auditor's global voice, recognized authority, acknowledged leader, chief advocate, and principal educator. Members work in internal auditing, risk management, governance, internal control, information technology audit, education, and security" (The IIA's International Professional Practices Framework [IPPF]). As of early 2012, The IIA had a membership of more than 170,000 professionals worldwide, performing audits in diverse environments and within organizations that vary in purpose, size and complexity. These organizations include both governmental and private sector environments.

The IPPF is the conceptual framework that organizes authoritative guidance promulgated by The IIA. The IPPF consists of six elements:

Mandatory Guidance

1. Definition of Internal Auditing
2. Code of Ethics
3. *Standards*

Strongly Recommended Guidance

4. Position Papers
5. Practice Advisories
6. Practice Guides

The IIA also issues another category called Supplemental Guidance. The IIA encourages conformance with this guidance *to the extent applicable to the practitioner's organization and the internal audit functions* (italics added). Examples of Supplemental Guidance topics are Public Sector Definition, Role of Audit in Public Sector Governance, and Red Book-Yellow Book Comparison.

In general, a framework provides a structural blueprint of how a body of knowledge and guidance fits together. As a coherent system, it facilitates consistent development, interpretation, and application of concepts, methodologies, and techniques useful to a discipline or profession. Specifically, the purpose of the IPPF is to organize the full range of internal audit guidance in a manner that is readily accessible on a timely basis. No information contained within the IPPF should be construed in a manner that conflicts with applicable laws or regulations. If a situation arises where information contained within the IPPF may be in conflict with legislation or regulation, internal auditors are encouraged to contact The IIA or legal counsel for further assistance.

The Three Mandatory Elements of the IPPF

Mandatory guidance in the IPPF means that The IIA considers conformance with the principles as required and essential to the professional practice of internal auditing. The three mandatory elements of the IPPF are discussed below.

The IIA's Definition of Internal Auditing

"Internal auditing is an independent, objective *assurance* and *consulting* activity designed to add value and improve an organization's operations. It helps an organization accomplish its objectives by bringing a systematic, disciplined approach to evaluate and improve the effectiveness of *risk management, control, and governance processes*" (emphasis added).

Assurance services involve the internal auditor's objective assessment of evidence to provide an independent opinion or conclusions regarding an entity, operation, system, or other subject matter. The nature and scope of the assurance engagement are determined by the internal auditor. *Consulting* services are advisory in nature at the specific request of an engagement client; the nature and scope of the consulting engagement are subject to agreement with the engagement client. The IIA states that, in performing consulting services, the internal auditor should maintain objectivity and not assume management responsibility.

The IIA's Code of Ethics

These standards are presented and discussed later in this chapter.

International Standards for the Professional Practice of Internal Auditing (Standards)

According to The IIA, the purpose of the *Standards* is to:

- Delineate basic principles that represent the practice of internal auditing as it should be.
- Provide a framework for performing and promoting a broad range of value-added internal audit activities.
- Establish the basis for the evaluation of internal audit performance.
- Foster improved organizational processes and operations.

The IIA notes that, if the *Standards* is used in conjunction with standards issued by other authoritative bodies, internal audit communications may cite use of the other standards, as appropriate. In such a case, if inconsistencies exist between the *Standards* and other standards, internal auditors and the internal audit activity *must* conform with the *Standards,* and *may* conform with the other standards if they are more restrictive.

> **Note:** Many local governments in the United States follow both the *Standards* and the U.S. GAO's GAGAS, discussed below.

Internal audit activities are performed in diverse legal and cultural environments; within organizations that vary in purpose, size, and structure; and by persons within or outside the organization. While differences may affect the practice of internal auditing in each environment, compliance with the *Standards* is essential if the responsibilities of internal auditors are to be met. If internal auditors are prohibited by laws or regulations from complying with certain parts of the *Standards*, they should comply with all other parts of the *Standards* and make appropriate disclosures.

The *Standards* are principles-focused, mandatory requirements consisting of:

- Statements of requirements.
- Interpretations.

The *Standards* uses the word "must" to specify an unconditional requirement, and the word "should" where conformance is expected unless, when applying professional judgment, circumstances justify deviation.

The *Standards* includes three types of audit standards:

1. ***Attribute standards*** address the attributes of organizations and individuals performing internal audit services.
2. ***Performance standards*** describe the nature of internal audit services and provide quality criteria against which the performance of these services can be measured. The Attribute and Performance Standards apply to all internal audit services.
3. ***Implementation standards*** expand upon the Attribute and Performance Standards by providing the requirements applicable to assurance or consulting activities.

Attribute Standards

Following is a list of The IIA's Attribute Standards as of the 2012 update of the IPPF:

1000 – Purpose, Authority, and Responsibility
1010 – Recognition of the Definition of Internal Auditing, the Code of Ethics, and the *Standards* in the Internal Audit Charter

1100 – Independence and Objectivity
1110 – Organizational Independence
1111 – Direct Interaction with the Board
1120 – Individual Objectivity
1130 – Impairment to Objectivity or Objectivity

1200 – Proficiency and Due Professional Care
1210 – Proficiency
1220 – Due Professional Care
1230 – Continuing Professional Development

1300 – Quality Assurance and Improvement Program
1310 – Requirements of the Quality Assurance and Improvement Program
1311 – Internal Assessments
1312 – External Assessments
1320 – Reporting on the Quality Assurance and Improvement Program
1321 – Use of "Conforms with the *International Standards for the Professional Practice of Internal Auditing*"
1322 – Disclosure of Nonconformance

Performance Standards

Following is a list of The IIA's Performance Standards as of the 2012 update of the IPPF:

2000 – Managing the Internal Audit Activity
2010 – Planning
2020 – Communication and Approval
2030 – Resource Management
2040 – Policies and Procedures
2050 – Coordination
2060 – Reporting to Senior Management and the Board
2070 – External Service Provider and Organizational Responsibility for Internal Auditing

2100 – Nature of Work
2110 – Governance
2120 – Risk Management
2130 – Control

2200 – Engagement Planning
2201 – Planning Considerations
2210 – Engagement Objectives
2220 – Engagement Scope
2230 – Engagement Resource Allocation
2240 – Engagement Work Program

2300 – Performing the Engagement
2310 – Identifying Information
2320 – Analysis and Evaluation
2330 – Documenting Information
2340 – Engagement Supervision

2400 – Communicating Results
2410 – Criteria for Communicating
2420 – Quality of Communications
2430 – Use of "Conducted in Conformance with the *International Standards for the Professional Practice of Internal Auditing*"
2431 – Engagement Disclosure of Nonconformance
2440 – Disseminating Results
2450 – Overall Opinions

2500 – Monitoring Progress

2600 – Resolution of Senior Management's Acceptance of Risks

Examples of an Attribute and a Performance Standard are presented below:

Attribute Standard 1000 – Purpose, Authority, and Responsibility. The purpose, authority, and responsibility of the internal audit activity must be formally defined in an internal audit charter, consistent with the Definition of Internal Auditing, the Code of Ethics, and the *Standards.* The chief audit executive must periodically review the internal audit charter and present it to senior management and the board for approval.

1000.A1 – The nature of assurance services provided to the organization must be defined in the internal audit charter. If assurances are to be provided to parties outside the organization, the nature of these assurances must also be defined in the internal audit charter.

1000.C1 – The nature of consulting services must be defined in the internal audit charter.

Performance Standard 2010 – Planning. The chief audit executive must establish risk-based plans to determine the priorities of the internal audit activity, consistent with the organization's goals.

2010.A1 – The internal audit activity's plan of engagements must be based on a documented risk assessment, undertaken at least annually. The input of senior management and the board must be considered in this process.

2010.A2 – The chief audit executive must identify and consider the expectations of senior management, the

board, and other stakeholders for internal audit opinions and conclusions.

2010.C1 – The chief audit executive should consider accepting proposed consulting engagements based on the engagement's potential to improve management of risks, add value, and improve the organization's operations. Accepted engagements must be included in the plan.

> **Note:** This publication includes information on the Attribute and Performance Standards, and related Interpretations, and Implementation Standards, as they existed at the time of the 2011 IPPF. Current information on the Attribute, Performance, and Implementation Standards is available on The IIA's website (theiia.org).

The Three Strongly Recommended Elements of the IPPF

Strongly recommended guidance means The IIA has endorsed the guidance through a formal approval process. This guidance describes practices for effective implementation of the three elements of mandatory guidance. The three elements of strongly recommended guidance are discussed below.

Position Papers

The IIA intends Position Papers to assist a wide range of interested parties, including those not in the internal audit profession, in understanding significant *governance, risk, or control issues* and delineating related roles and responsibilities of internal auditing.

Two examples of issued Position Papers are: 1) The Role of Internal Auditing in Enterprise-wide Risk Management, and 2) The Role of Internal Auditing in Resourcing the Internal Audit Activity. Current Position Papers can be accessed at The IIA's website or by contacting The IIA directly.

Practice Advisories

The IIA intends Practice Advisories to assist internal auditors in applying the Definition of Internal Auditing, the Code of Ethics, and the *Standards* and promoting good practices. They address internal audit's approach, methodologies, and consideration but do not detail processes or procedures. They include practices relating to international, country, or industry-wide issues; and legal or regulatory issues.

Practice Guides

The IIA's Practice Guides provide detailed guidance for conducting internal audit activities. They include detailed processes, such as tools and techniques, programs, and step-by-step approaches, including examples of deliverables.

As of mid-2012, The IIA had issued the following Practice Guides (a partial list):

- Auditing Executive Compensation and Benefits.
- Auditing External Business Relationships.
- CAEs – Appointment, Performance Evaluation, and Termination.
- Evaluating Corporate Social Responsibility/Sustainable Development.
- Formulating and Expressing Internal Audit Opinion.
- Internal Auditing and Fraud.
- Update to The Role of Auditing in Public Sector Governance.
- Definition of Public Sector.
- Value of IA and IA Capability Model-Public Sector.
- Implementing a new Internal Audit Function in the Public Sector.

At about the same time, The IIA had issued 16 Global Technology Audit Guides and a four-part Guide to the Assessment of IT Risk (GAIT).

The above brief discussion is intended to provide a basic understanding of The IIA's audit guidance. A more comprehensive understanding of the IPPF with all of its elements, including the *Standards,* can be gained by reading the entire IIA references. Also, readers are encouraged to keep current with revisions of any parts of the IPPF by visiting the IIA website (theiia.org) and/or contacting The IIA.

GAO's Generally Accepted Government Auditing Standards (GAGAS)[2]

> **Note:** Those preparing to take the CGAP exam may want to keep in mind that The IIA states that the specifics of GAGAS are not tested on the international version of the exam. However, GAGAS is a very important set of audit standards for government auditors in the United States, and is well recognized as a valuable model in several other countries.

In 1921, the Accounting and Budget Act established the U.S. General Accounting Office (now the U.S. Government Accountability Office) (U.S. GAO). The GAO is situated in the legislative branch at the federal level of the U.S. government. The GAO's role in auditing and other functions has evolved and changed over the years. In 1972, the GAO issued the initial publication of the Generally Accepted Government Auditing Standards (GAGAS), which is also referred to as the Government Auditing Standards (GAS) and commonly as the Yellow Book. In December 2011, the GAO issued the sixth major revision of the Yellow Book.

Who follows GAGAS? The GAO states the following: "Provisions of laws, regulations, grant agreements and policies frequently require audits be conducted in accordance with GAGAS. In addition, many auditors and audit organizations voluntarily choose to perform their work in accordance with GAGAS. The requirements and guidance apply to audits of government entities, programs, activities, and functions, and of government assistance administered by contractors, nonprofit entities, and other nongovernmental entities when the use of GAGAS is required or is voluntarily followed." Examples of federal audit organizations required to follow GAGAS are the GAO itself and the Offices of Inspector General in federal agencies. Many government audit organizations at the state and local level in the United States have legally adopted or voluntarily chosen to follow GAGAS. Moreover, other audit organizations in the United States and other countries have adopted key concepts and principles from GAGAS.

The July 2007 version of GAGAS was revised in 2011. The December 2011 version of GAGAS is lengthy — a body of 177 pages, plus three appendices addressing 1) supplemental guidance, 2) a conceptual framework for independence, and 3) the Comptroller General's Advisory Council on Government Auditing Standards. A brief description of the 2011 GAGAS is presented in the following pages. A more comprehensive understanding of GAGAS can be gained by reading the entire text. Also, readers are advised that they can keep current on any GAGAS updates or revisions by the GAO by visiting the GAO website (www.gao.gov).

GAGAS defines the following terms:

- An "auditor" is any individual performing work in accordance with GAGAS (including audits and attestation engagements), regardless of job title;
- An "audit organization" refers to government audit organizations as well as public accounting or other firms that perform audits and attestations in accordance with GAGAS (audit organizations can be external or internal or "hybrids"); and
- The term "audit" refers to *financial audits, attestation engagements, and performance audits* conducted in accordance with GAGAS. Chapter 2 of this publication discusses these terms in more detail.

GAGAS does not cover nonaudit services, defined as professional services other than audits or attestation engagements. If these are performed, independence issues may arise, and this is discussed later.

GAGAS uses two categories of requirements:

1. Unconditional requirements (the word *must* is used.)
2. Presumptively mandatory requirements (the word *should* is used.)

In addition, GAGAS includes "explanatory material" where the words *may, might,* or *could* are used.

I.A.3 Role and Impact of Other Auditing Standards and Their Relationship with the Above Standards

Auditors may use GAGAS in conjunction with professional standards from other authoritative bodies.

For financial audits and attestation engagements:

- Certain American Institute of Certified Public Accountants (AICPA) standards are incorporated by reference.
- Auditors may elect to use the standards from the International Auditing and Assurance Board (IAASB), and related International Standards on Auditing (ISAs) and International Standards on Assurance Engagements (ISAEs) in conjunction with GAGAS.
- Auditors may elect to use the Public Company Accounting Oversight Board (PCOAB) standards in conjunction with GAGAS.

For performance audits, the Yellow Book does not incorporate other standards by reference but recognizes that auditors may use or be required to use other standards, such as:

- The IIA's *Standards*.
- Guiding Principles for Evaluators, American Evaluation Association.
- The Program Evaluation Standards, Joint Committee on Standards for Education Evaluation.
- Standards for Educational and Psychological Testing, American Psychological Association.
- IT Standards, Guidelines, and Tools and Techniques for Audit and Assurance and Control Professionals, ISACA.

Stating Compliance with GAGAS in the Auditor's Report

Auditors should include one of the following types of compliance statements: 1) *unmodified,* stating that the auditor performed the audit in accordance with GAGAS, or 2) *modified,* stating that (a) some specific applicable requirements were not followed, or (b) because of significant departures, the auditor was unable to and did not perform in accordance with GAGAS. When auditors do not comply, professional judgment is to be used to decide the type of GAGAS compliance statement is appropriate.

General Standards in GAGAS

The general standards apply to all three types of audits, as identified in GAGAS. The four general standards relate to independence, professional judgment, competence, and quality control and assurance.

1. *Independence.* In all matters relating to the audit work, the audit organization and the individual auditor, whether government or public, must be independent.

GAGAS includes extensive discussion of the independence standard. In part, GAGAS states that independence:

- Is a state of mind, and also involves appearances.
- Applies to both auditors and audit organizations.
- Needs to consider time periods.
- Consists of (a) a conceptual framework, (b) requirements for audit organizations structurally located within the entities they audit, (c) requirements if nonaudit services are performed, and (d) documentation requirements.

Internal audit organizations are encouraged to use The IIA's *Standards* in conjunction with GAGAS. Also, GAGAS sets forth criteria to be considered independent when internal auditors work under the direction of the audited entity's management.

GAGAS includes extensive discussion on considerations regarding independence if an audit organization performs nonaudit services. GAGAS states that "If an auditor were to assume management responsibility for an audited entity, the management participation threats could be so significant that no safeguards could reduce them to an acceptable level." However, the facts and circumstances need to be considered to determine whether an activity is a management responsibility. GAGAS provides many examples of how certain activities should be viewed, and how to assess threats to independence if nonaudit services are performed. GAGAS also contains specific requirements for documentation of such conclusions on independence considerations.

*2. **Professional judgment.*** Auditors must use professional judgment in planning and performing audits and in reporting the results.

The professional judgment standard includes such concepts as reasonable care and professional skepticism. Professional judgment and competence are interrelated because judgments made are dependent on the auditors' competence. This standard relates to all aspects of auditors' professional responsibilities, including the need for independence and consideration of the risk level of each audit. The standard does not imply unlimited responsibility or infallibility.

3. Competence. The staff assigned to perform the audit must collectively possess adequate professional competence needed to address the audit objective and perform the work in accordance with GAGAS.

The competence standard includes 1) technical knowledge, 2) additional qualifications for financial audits and attestations, 3) and the continuing professional education (CPE) requirements. Technical knowledge includes knowledge of GAGAS, general knowledge of the environment in which they audit, communication skills, and other skills appropriate for the work being performed. Auditors who perform financial audits should be knowledgeable of the generally accepted accounting principles and applicable AICPA standards. Likewise, auditors performing attestation engagements should be knowledgeable of the applicable standards. Auditors are required to obtain at least 80 hours of CPE every two years, with at least 20 hours in any one year.

4. Quality control and assurance. Each audit organization performing audits in accordance with GAGAS must:

- Establish and maintain a system of quality control that is designed to provide the audit organization with reasonable assurance that the organization and its personnel comply with the professional standards and applicable legal and regulatory requirements.
- Have an external peer review performed by reviewers independent of the audit organization being reviewed at least once every three years.

The audit organization should establish policies and procedures in its system of quality control that collectively address:

- Leadership responsibilities for quality.
- Independence, legal, and ethical requirements.
- Initiation, acceptance, and continuance of audits.
- Human resources.
- Audit performance, documentation, and reporting.
- Monitoring of quality.

The peer review team should include:

- Review of the audit organizations' quality control policies and procedures.
- Consideration of the adequacy and results of the audit organization's internal monitoring procedures.
- Review of selected auditors' reports and related documentation.
- Review of other documents as necessary.
- Interviews with a selection of the reviewed audit organization's professional staff at various levels.

The peer review team should prepare one or more written reports. These reports may include one of three types of results — pass, pass with deficiencies, and fail.

Standards for Financial Audits in GAGAS

For financial statement audits, GAGAS incorporates by reference the AICPA's Statements on Audit Standards (SAS). All sections of the SAS are incorporated, including the introduction, objectives, definitions, application, and other explanatory material. In addition, GAO has added other requirements.

For *performing* financial audits, the additional GAGAS requirements relate to:

- Auditor communication.
- Previous audit and attestation engagements.
- Fraud, noncompliance with provisions, contracts and grant agreements, and abuse.
- Developing elements of a finding.
- Audit documentation.

Auditor communication. The auditors should communicate pertinent information that needs to be communicated to individuals contracting for or requesting the audit, and to cognizant legislative committees when auditors perform the audit pursuant to a law or regulation, or they conduct the work for the legislative committee that has oversight of the audited entity. There is an exception where this requirement does not apply.

Previous audit and attestation engagements. Auditors should evaluate whether the audited entity has taken appropriate correction action where there could be a material effect on the statements or other financial data

significant to the audit objective. Auditors should consider this information in assessing risks and in planning how to do the audit.

Fraud, noncompliance with provisions of laws, regulations, contracts, and grant agreements, and abuse. Compliance with contracts and grant agreements is an extension of the auditor's consideration. Abuse involves deficient or improper behavior, or misuse of authority for personal financial interests or of those of an immediate or close family member or business associate. Abuse does not necessarily involve fraud or noncompliance, and, because subjectivity is involved, auditors are not required to detect abuse. Auditors are not to interfere with investigations or legal proceedings, and it may be appropriate for auditors to work with investigators or legal authorities.

Developing elements of a finding: For findings of internal control deficiencies and noncompliance, the auditors should develop the elements of the findings that are relevant and necessary. The four traditional elements of a finding are:

- *Criteria,* e.g., a law that identifies the required or desired state of expectation (what should be).
- *Condition,* a situation that exists (what is).
- *Cause,* the reason/explanation (why) for the difference between the condition and the criteria.
- *Effect,* the impact of the difference (so what?).

Audit documentation. In addition to the AICPA requirements for audit documentation, auditors should comply with the following additional requirements:

- Document supervisory review, before the report release date, of the evidence that supports findings, conclusions, and recommendations.
- Document departures from GAGAS requirements and the impact on the audit and conclusions reached in certain circumstances.

Audit documentation is to be made available to others as appropriate.

For *reporting* on financial audits, the additional GAGAS requirements relate to:

- Reporting auditor's compliance with GAGAS.
- Reporting on internal control and compliance with provisions of laws, regulations, contracts, and grant agreements.
- Communicating deficiencies in internal control, fraud, compliance with provisions of laws, regulations, contracts, and grant agreements, and abuse.
- Reporting views of responsible officials.
- Reporting confidential or sensitive information.
- Distributing reports.

Reporting compliance with GAGAS. When auditors comply with all applicable GAGAS requirements, they should make a statement to that effect. A statement on compliance with the AICPA standards is unnecessary because GAGAS incorporates the AICPA standards by reference.

Reporting on internal control and compliance. Auditors should include a description of the scope of the auditors' testing of internal control over financial reporting and of compliance with provisions of laws, regulations, contracts, and grant agreements. Auditors should also state whether their tests provided sufficient, appropriate evidence to support opinions on the effectiveness of internal control and on compliance. In a financial audit, the objective differs from an examination of internal control in accordance with the AICPA's Statements of Attestation Standards (SSAEs), which is to express an opinion on the design or the design and operating effectiveness of an entity's internal control, as applicable. If the auditors report separately on internal control and compliance, the report containing the opinion should contain a reference to the separate reports.

Communicating deficiencies in internal control, fraud, noncompliance with provisions of laws, regulations, contracts, and grant agreements, and abuse. Based on the work performed, the auditors should communicate 1) significant deficiencies and material weaknesses in internal control (using AICPA definitions), 2) instances of fraud and noncompliance that have a material effect on the audit and any other instances that warrant the attention of those charged with governance, 3) noncompliance with contracts or grant agreements that have a material effect on the audit, and 4) abuse that has a material effect on the audit. Auditors should develop the elements of a finding to the extent necessary. GAGAS provides two criteria for when findings should be presented directly to parties outside the audited entity.

Reporting views of responsible officials. The auditors should obtain and report these views and any planned corrective actions. GAGAS provides specifics on how to do this, and states that, if the audited agency refuses or is unable to do so in a timely manner, the auditor may issue the report without the comments.

Distributing reports. Report distribution depends on the relationship of the auditors to the audited entity and the nature of the information in the report. GAGAS cites three categories:

1. Distribute to those charged with governance and oversight.
2. Internal audit organizations may follow The IIA's *Standards* after considering potential risks, consulting with senior management or legal counsel, and citing distribution in the report.
3. Contracted public accounting firms should clarify distribution.

Additional GAGAS considerations for financial audits. GAGAS discusses two considerations that *may* apply: 1) materiality levels, considering lower levels than in non-GAGAS audits, and 2) early communication of control deficiencies and noncompliance, if important due to relative significance and urgency.

Standards for Attestation Engagements in GAGAS

Auditors performing attestation engagements should comply with the AICPA general attestation standard on criteria, the fieldwork and reporting attestation standards, and the corresponding SSAEs, which are incorporated in GAGAS by reference. Auditors should also comply with additional standards included in GAGAS. Attestation engagements can provide one of three levels of service (examination, review, or agreed-upon procedures), and applicable requirements vary depending which of the three levels is being performed.

For examination engagements. These are similar (not exactly the same) to the additional requirements in performing financial audits. For fieldwork, the additional requirements relate to 1) auditor communication; 2) previous audits and attestation engagements; 3) fraud, noncompliance with laws, regulations, contracts, and grant agreements, and abuse; 4) developing elements of findings; and 5) examination engagement documentation.

For reporting, the additional requirements relate to 1) reporting auditors' compliance with GAGAS; 2) reporting deficiencies in internal control, fraud, noncompliance with provisions of laws, regulations, and grant agreements, and abuse; 3) reporting views of responsible officials; 4) reporting confidential or sensitive information; and 5) distributing reports. GAGAS also includes two additional matters of consideration — materiality levels and early communication of deficiencies.

For review engagements. GAGAS additional fieldwork requirement relates to communicating significant deficiencies, material weaknesses, instances of fraud, noncompliance with provisions of laws, regulations, contracts, or grant agreements, or abuse that come to the auditor's attention.

The additional reporting requirements relate to reporting auditors' compliance with GAGAS, and distributing reports. GAGAS also includes two additional considerations — establishing an understanding regarding services to be performed, and reporting on review engagements.

For agreed-upon engagements. The additional fieldwork requirement and the two additional reporting requirements are essentially the same as that for review engagements. Also, the two additional considerations are the same as for review engagements.

Performance Audits: Fieldwork Standards in GAGAS

The purpose of fieldwork standards in performance audits is to establish an overall approach for auditors to apply in obtaining reasonable assurance that the evidence is *sufficient* and *appropriate* to support the auditors' findings and conclusions. The concept of *significance* assists auditors throughout the performance audit; *significance* is defined in GAGAS as the relative importance of a matter within the context in which it is being considered,

including quantitative and qualitative factors. (Significance is comparable to the term material in financial statement engagements.) Auditors try to reduce *audit risk,* defined as the possibility that the auditors' findings, recommendations, or assurance may be improper or incomplete, based on factors such as evidence that is not *sufficient* and/or *appropriate,* or other factors. GAGAS cites ways that auditors can reduce audit risk. These concepts of reasonable assurance, significance, and audit risk form a framework for applying fieldwork requirements.

Fieldwork requirements for performance audits relate to:

- Planning the audit.
- Supervising staff.
- Obtaining sufficient, appropriate evidence.
- Preparing audit documentation.

Planning the audit. Auditors must adequately plan and document the planning of the work necessary to address the audit objectives. Planning is critical, as indicated by the significant coverage in GAGAS. Some key factors in planning are listed below.

- Auditors must plan the audit to reduce audit risk to an appropriate level to obtain reasonable assurance that the evidence is sufficient and appropriate to support the findings.
- An *objective(s)* is essentially the question(s) the audit is intending to answer. The *scope* sets the boundary of the audit (e.g., time period, etc.). The *methodology* describes the nature and extent of audit procedures.
- The auditors should assess audit risk and significance by gaining an understanding of:
  - The nature and profile of the programs and needs of potential users.
  - Internal control as it relates to the specific objectives and scope.
  - Information systems control within the context of the audit objective.
  - Provisions of laws, regulations, contracts, and grant agreements, and potential fraud and abuse that are significant within the context of the audit objectives.
  - Ongoing investigations or legal proceedings within the context of the objectives.
  - The results of previous audits and attestation engagements that directly relate to the current audit objectives.
- The auditors also should:
  - Identify potential criteria to evaluate matters subject to audit.
  - Identify sources of evidence and identify the amount and type of evidence needed.
  - Evaluate whether to use the work of other auditors and specialists.
  - Assign staff and specialists with adequate collective professional competence.
  - Communicate about planning and performing the audit to management officials, those charged with governance, and others as applicable.
  - Prepare a written audit plan.

Supervision. Audit supervisors or those designated to supervise auditors must properly supervise staff. This involves staying informed of significant problems, reviewing work performed, and providing on-the-job training. The nature and extent varies, based on a number of factors.

Obtaining sufficient, appropriate evidence. Auditors must obtain sufficient, appropriate evidence to provide a reasonable basis for their findings and conclusions. Sufficiency is a measure of quantity (would a knowledgeable person be persuaded?). Appropriateness is a measure of quality and involves relevance, validity, and reliability. Evidence may be obtained by observation, inquiry, or inspection. GAGAS discusses how sources and techniques used can affect the reliability of the evidence. Further, GAGAS states, "Auditors should perform and document an overall assessment of the collective evidence to support findings and conclusions..."

Auditors should plan and perform procedures to develop the elements of a finding necessary to address the audit objectives. The four classical elements of a finding are condition, cause, criteria, and effect. However, GAGAS states the following: "Thus, a finding or set of findings is complete to the extent that the audit objectives are addressed and the report clearly relates those objectives to the elements of a finding." (Note: This view — permissible under GAGAS — means that a complete audit finding can include one, two, three, or four elements, even though most government auditors usually identify all four.)

In considering evidence, GAGAS also states that early communication of deficiencies (relating to internal control, fraud, noncompliance, or abuse) to those charged with governance or management may be important because of their relative significance and the urgency for corrective action.

Audit documentation. Auditors must prepare audit documentation related to planning, conducting ,and reporting for each audit. Auditors should prepare audit documentation in sufficient detail to enable an experienced auditor, having no previous connection to the audit, to understand from the audit documentation the nature, timing, extent, and results of audit procedures performed, the audit evidence obtained, and its source and the conclusions reached, including evidence that supports the auditors' significant judgments and conclusions.

Audit documentation serves to 1) provide the principal support for the auditors' report, 2) aid auditors in conducting and supervising the audit, and 3) allow for the review of audit quality. GAGAS discusses what should be documented and the need for supervisory review. The quantity, type, and content of audit documentation are a matter of the auditors' professional judgment.

Performance Audits: Reporting Standards in GAGAS

Reporting. Auditors must issue audit reports communicating the results of each completed performance audit. The *form* should be appropriate for the intended use and in writing, or in some other retrievable form. Forms include written reports, letters, briefing slides, or other presentation materials. The purposes are to 1) communicate the results of audits to those charged with governance, the appropriate officials of the audited entity, and appropriate oversight officials, 2) make the results less susceptible to misunderstanding, 3) make results available to the public, unless specifically limited, and 4) facilitate follow-up to determine whether appropriate corrective actions have been taken. GAGAS discusses actions to be taken if, after the report is issued, auditors discover they did not have sufficient, appropriate evidence to support the reported findings or conclusions.

Report contents. Auditors should prepare reports that contain:

- The objectives, scope, and methodology of the audit.
- The audit results, including findings, conclusions, and recommendations, as appropriate.
- A statement about the auditors' compliance with GAGAS.
- A summary of the views of responsible officials.
- (If applicable) the nature of any confidential or sensitive information omitted.

Distributing reports. The GAGAS standard for report distribution for performance audits is essentially the same as for financial audits.

Supplemental Guidance in GAGAS

The supplemental guidance does not establish additional requirements but instead is intended to facilitate auditor implementation of GAGAS requirements. The supplemental guidance is divided into 1) overall guidance, and 2) guidance related to standards for financial audits, attestation engagements, and performance auditors.

The overall supplemental guidance addresses internal control and provides examples of deficiencies in internal control, abuse, and fraud risk. Regarding internal control, GAGAS cites *Internal Control – Integrated Framework* published by the Committee of Sponsoring Organizations of the Treadway Commission (COSO). In addition, GAGAS cites two GAO publications — 1) the *Standards for Internal Control in the Federal Government,* which incorporates the concepts developed by GAO, and 2) the related *Internal Control Management and Evaluation,* which includes a process for assessing internal control.

The guidance also includes examples of 1) deficiencies in internal control, 2) abuse, and 3) indicators of fraud risk. Further, the guidance discusses how to determine whether laws, regulations, and provisions of contracts and grant agreements are significant in the context of the audit objectives.

The guidance cites examples of laws, regulations, and other authoritative sources that require the use of GAGAS, such as:

- The Inspector General Act of 1978, as amended, requires statutorily appointed federal inspectors general to comply with GAGAS and to assure that work performed by nonfederal auditors complies with GAGAS.
- The Chief Financial Officers (CFO) Act of 1990, as amended in 1994, and the Accountability for Tax Dollars Act of 2002 require that financial audits of most federal entities be complete in accordance with GAGAS.
- The Single Audit Act Amendments of 1996 require that GAGAS be followed in audits of state and local governments and nonprofit entities that receive federal awards. OMB Circular A-133 provides government-wide guidelines and policies.
- Auditors at state and local levels of government may be required by state and local laws and regulations to follow GAGAS.

Many audit organizations, both in the United States and other countries, voluntarily follow GAGAS even when not formally required to do so.

The guidance discusses the roles of 1) those charged with governance, and 2) management.

GAGAS identifies three types of audits/engagements: financial audits, attestation engagements, and performance audits. Of these, GAGAS provides examples of objectives for:

- ***Attestation engagements.*** Includes "an entity's internal control over financial reporting" and "the accuracy and reliability of reported performance measures."
- ***Performance audits.*** Subdivided into 1) program effectiveness and results, 2) internal control, 3) compliance, and 4) prospective analysis.

The guidance includes more than 10 pages of discussion on the General Standard of Independence.

Regarding fieldwork standards for Performance Audits, the guidance discusses:

- Eight examples of "criteria."
- Types of evidence and the strengths and weaknesses of each type.
- Determining the "appropriateness" of evidence.
- Issues concerning the "cause" and "effect" elements of audit findings.

Regarding reporting standards for Performance Audits, the guidance presents seven quality elements:

1. Accurate.
2. Objective.
3. Complete.
4. Convincing.
5. Clear.
6. Concise.
7. Timely.

Comparison of The IIA's *Standards* and the GAO's GAGAS[3]

An IIA publication available from the IIA website compares the two sets of standards discussed above (commonly known as the Red Book and the Yellow Book). The publication states the following: "The U.S. Government Accountability Office (GAO) and The Institute of Internal Auditors (IIA) are recognized nationally and internationally as leaders in promoting high quality audit work through the issuance of professional auditing standards." As indicated above, many government auditors use one or both of these two sets of standards. The IIA publication is intended to identify similar principles and key differences and to provide suggestions should a governmental internal audit organization be required or elect to follow both.

The U.S. Government Accountability Office (GAO) and The Institute of Internal Auditors (IIA) are recognized nationally and internationally as leaders in promoting high quality audit work through the issuance of professional auditing standards. Professional auditing standards provide a framework for conducting high quality audits. Both organizations are committed to working together to develop standards that are complimentary and can be used to perform high quality government audits.

The purpose of the IIA comparison is to identify similar principles and key differences between each organization's standards and to provide suggestions for consideration should a government internal audit organization be required to or elect to comply with both organizations' standards in conducting audit work.

For IIA members, the document may be accessed through the IIA home page, the Guidance and Resources tab, the Standards and Guidance option, the "Red Book-Yellow Book Comparison." For those who are not IIA members, the IIA publication can be purchased through the IIA Bookstore. The publication is of great value to CGAP candidates.

International Standards of Supreme Audit Institutions (ISSAIs)[4]

The International Organization of Supreme Audit Institutions (INTOSAI) operates as an umbrella organization for the external government audit community. INTOSAI was founded in 1953 and has grown from the original 34 countries to having 190 full members and four associate members in 2012.

INTOSAI has endorsed an ISSAI framework that contains the standards and guidance on good governance (INTOSAI GOVs). INTOSAI standards are intended as a "model" for government audit standards, established and endorsed by the INTOSAI organization, but which must be adopted and/or modified by the Supreme Audit Institution (SAI) of any specific country in order to be used. The actual requirements and practices of individual SAIs vary widely around the INTOSAI "model."

The ISSAI Framework

The ISSAI framework, adopted in 2007, includes four levels:

1. Founding principles.
2. Codes for SAIs.
3. Fundamental audit principles (including auditing standards).
4. Auditing guidelines.

As of August 2011, under its framework, the INTOSAI has adopted approximately 70 standards and guidelines. Thus, INTOSAI has issued a large amount of reference material, most of which can be accessed via INTOSAI's website (www.intosai.org) or through direct communication with INTOSAI. For purposes of this manual, presented below is a basic description of Level 3 and a very limited discussion of Level 4.

INTOSAI 's Basic Principles and Audit Standards (Level 3)

The INTOSAI auditing standards consist of four parts:

1. Basic Principles in Government Auditing (ISSAI 100).
2. General Standards in Government Auditing and Standards with Ethical Significance (ISSAI 200).
3. Field Standards in Government Auditing (ISSAI 300).
4. Reporting Standards in Government Auditing (ISSAI 400).

Basic Principles in Government Auditing

The 10 basic principles relate to:

1. Consideration of ***materiality*** in applying auditing standards.
2. Application of ***judgment*** to diverse situations.
3. The need for ***accountability*** in using public resources.
4. The need for ***information, control, evaluation, and reporting***, and management's role.
5. Promulgation of ***accounting standards*** and ***performance targets.***
6. Fair presentation of ***financial position and results of operations.***
7. ***Internal control systems*** to minimize errors and irregularities.
8. ***Legislative enactments*** for auditor access.
9. ***All audit activities*** should be within the SAI's audit mandate.
10. Improving techniques for ***auditing the validity of performance measures.***

General Standards in Government Auditing

The general auditing standards describe the qualifications of the auditor and/or the auditing institution so that they may carry out the tasks related to field and reporting standards in a competent and effective manner.

The general auditing standards are that the SAI should have policies and procedures to:

- Recruit personnel with suitable qualifications.

- Develop and train personnel to perform their tasks effectively, and to define the basis for advance of auditors and other staff.
- Prepare manual and other written guidance and other written guidance and instructions concerning the conduct of audits.
- Support the skills and experience available within the SAI and identify the skills that are absent (further details omitted herein).
- Review the efficiency and effectiveness of the SAI's internal standards and procedures. (While there is not a specific requirement for "external quality control [peer] reviews," the ISSAI does state: "The quality of the work of the SAI can be enhanced by strengthening internal review and probably by independent appraisal of its work.")

General Standards with Ethical Significance

The general audit standards with ethical significance include:

- *The auditor and the SAI* must be independent.
- *SAIs* should avoid conflicts of interest between the auditor and the entity under audit.
- *The auditor and the SAI* must possess the required competence (this does not mandate a specific number of hours of continuing professional education [CPEs]).
- *The auditor and the SAI* must exercise due care and concern in complying with the INTOSAI auditing standards (further details not provided herein).

Field Standards in Government Auditing

The purpose of field standards is to establish the criteria or overall framework for the purposeful, systematic, and balanced steps or actions that the auditor has to follow. These steps and actions represent the rules of research that the auditor, as a seeker of audit evidence, implements to achieve a specific result.

The field standards establish the framework for conducting and managing audit work. They are related to the general auditing standards, which set out the basic requirements for undertaking the tasks covered by the field standards. They also are related to the reporting standards, which cover the communication aspect of auditing, as the results from carrying out the field standards constitute the main source for the contents of the opinion or report.

The field standards applicable to all types of audits are:

- The auditor should plan the audit in a manner which ensures that an audit of high quality is carried out in an economic, efficient, and effective way and in a timely manner.
- The work of the audit staff at each level and audit phase should be properly supervised during the audit; and documented work should be reviewed by a senior member of the audit staff.
- The auditor, in determining the extent and scope of the audit, should study and evaluate the reliability of internal control.
- In conducting *regularity (financial) audits*, a test should be made of compliance with applicable laws and regulations. The auditor should design audit steps and procedures to provide reasonable assurance of detecting errors, irregularities, and illegal acts that could have a direct and material effect on the financial statement amounts or the results of regularity audits. The auditor also should be aware of the possibility of illegal acts that could have an indirect and material effect on the financial statements or results of regularity audits.
- In conducting *performance audits,* an assessment should be made of compliance with applicable laws and regulations when necessary to satisfy the audit objectives. The auditor should design the audit to provide reasonable assurance of detecting illegal acts that could significantly affect audit objectives.

> **Note:** Further details from INTOSAI on this standard are not included herein.

- Competent, relevant, and reasonable evidence should be obtained to support the auditor's judgment and conclusions regarding the organization, program, activity, or function under audit.
- In regularity (financial) audits, and in other types of audits when applicable, auditors should analyze the financial statements to establish whether acceptable accounting standards for financial reporting and disclosure are complied with. Analysis of financial statements should be performed to such a degree that a rational basis is obtained to express an opinion on financial statements.

Reporting Standards in Government Auditing

The expression "reporting" embraces both the auditor's opinion and other remarks on a set of financial statements as a result of regularity (financial) audit and the auditor's report on completion of a performance audit. It is not practical to lay down a rule for reporting on every special situation. This standard is to assist and not to supersede the prudent judgment of the auditor in making an opinion or report.

The auditor's opinion on a set of financial statements is generally in a concise, standardized format that reflects the results of a wide range of tests and other audit work. There is often a requirement to report as to the compliance of transactions with laws and regulations and to report on matters such as inadequate systems of control, illegal acts, and fraud. In some countries, constitutional or statutory obligations may require the SAI to report specifically on the execution of budgetary laws, reconciling budgetary estimates, and authorization to the results set out in the financial statements.

In a performance audit, the auditor reports on the economy and efficiency with which resources are acquired and used, and the effectiveness with which objectives are met. Such reports may vary considerably in scope and nature; for example, covering whether resources have been applied in a sound manner, commenting on the impact of policies and programs, and recommending changes designed to result in improvements.

To recognize reasonable user needs, the auditor's report in both regularity and performance auditing may need to consider expanded reporting periods or cycles and relevant and appropriate disclosure requirements.

The reporting standards are:

- At the end of each audit the auditor should prepare a written opinion or report, as appropriate, setting out the findings in an appropriate form; its content should be easy to understand and free from vagueness or ambiguity, include only information which is supported by competent and relevant audit evidence, and be independent, objective, fair, and constructive.
- It is for the SAI to which they belong to decide finally on the action to be taken in relation to fraudulent practices or serious irregularities discovered by the auditors.

With regard to regularity audits, the auditor should prepare a written report, which may either be a part of the report on the financial statements or a separate report, on the tests of compliance with applicable laws and regulations. The report should contain a statement of positive assurance on those items tested for compliance and negative assurance on those items not tested.

With regard to performance audits, the report should include all significant instances of noncompliance that are pertinent to the audit objectives.

INTOSAI's Audit Guidelines (Level 4 of the Framework)

As of January 2012, INTOSAI has issued the following three key sets of audit guidelines:

1. Financial Audit Guidelines (ISSAI 1000-2999).
2. Performance Audit Guidelines (ISSAI 3000-3100).
3. Compliance Audit Guidelines (ISSAI 4000-4200).

In developing the Financial Audit Guidelines, INTOSAI cooperates with the International Federation of Accountants (IFAC) and draws upon IFAC's International Standards on Auditing (ISAs) as a "starting point." (IFAC's International Auditing and Assurance Standards Board [IAASB] and the ISAs issued by the IAASB are discussed in the next section.)

The Financial Audit Guidelines encompass more than 1,000 pages of information and include guidance consistent with and/or very similar to requirements in the IPAC's ISAs and audit standards for financial statement audits of the American Institute of Certified Public Accountants (AICPA). INTOSAI's Financial Audit Guidelines makes numerous specific references to the ISAs. Examples of requirements included in the guidelines include:

- The overall audit objectives.
- Quality control.
- Audit documentation.
- The auditor's responsibilities related to fraud.
- Consideration of laws and regulations.
- Planning an audit of financial statements.
- Materiality in planning and performing an audit.
- Audit evidence.
- Forming an opinion and reporting on financial statements.

The Performance Audit Guidelines encompass approximately 160 pages, including seven appendices totaling approximately 50 pages. The appendices address methodology, criteria, evidence and documentation, information technology (IT), communication and quality assurance, audits with an environmental perspective, and a systems-oriented approach. INTOSAI characterizes performance audits generally as those audits dealing with the economy, efficiency, and effectiveness of government operations. The guidelines address the nature of performance audits in more detail.

The Compliance Audit Guidelines address audits that deal with the responsibility of the SAI to audit whether the activities of public sector entities are in accordance with relevant laws, regulations, and authorities that govern such entities. This involves reporting on the degree to which the audited entity is accountable for its actions and exercises good public governance. More specifically, these elements may involve auditing to what extent the audited entity follows rules, laws and regulation, budgetary resolutions, policy, established codes, or agreed upon terms, such as the terms of a contract or the terms of a funding agreement. Compliance audit tasks performed by SAIs may cover a wide range of subject matters and may vary widely on an international basis.

The Compliance Audit Guidelines are written from two main perspectives:

1. ISSAI 4100 (approximately 70 pages) deals with compliance audit separately from the audit of financial statements; for example, as a separate audit task or related to performance audits.
2. ISSAI 4200 (approximately 70 pages) deals with compliance audit related to the audit of financial statements.

For the second category, the Compliance Audit Guidelines supplement the Financial Audit Guidelines.

In addition to the guidelines for the three "key auditing branches" discussed above, INTOSAI also issues audit guidelines related to specialized issues. The guidelines related to specialized areas are not discussed herein.

As for the other three sets of auditing standards, readers should keep in mind that a full understanding and appreciation of INTOSAI guidance can be fully attained only by reviewing the standards and guidance in their entirety.

Auditing and Assurance Standards Issued Through IFAC's IAASB[5]

The International Federation of Accountants (IFAC) is the worldwide organization for the accountancy profession. Founded in 1977, its mission is to serve the public interest, strengthen the global accountancy profession, and contribute to the development of strong international economies by establishing and promoting adherence to high-quality professional standards, furthering the international convergence of such standards, and speaking out on public interest issues where the profession's expertise is most relevant. IFAC's governing bodies, staff, and volunteers are committed to the values of integrity, transparency, and expertise. As of 2012, IFAC had approximately 160 members and associates in approximately 125 countries.

IFAC's mission, as set out in its constitution, is "the worldwide development and enhancement of an accountancy profession with harmonized standards, able to provide services of consistently high quality in the public interest." In pursuing this mission, IFAC established the International Auditing and Assurance Standards Board (IAASB) to develop and issue, in the public interest and under its own authority, high-quality auditing and assurance standards for use around the world. The IFAC board has determined that designation of the IAASB as the responsible body, under its own authority and within its stated terms of reference, best serves the public interest in achieving this aspect of its mission.

Among six "primary activities" IFAC cites are the following two:

1. Actively encouraging convergence of professional standards, particularly *auditing*, assurance, ethics, education, and public and private sector financial reporting standards (italics added).
2. Seeking continuous improvements in the quality of auditing and financial management.

Major components of IFAC's standard-setting framework of initiatives are:

- Code of Ethics for Professional Standards (discussed briefly later in this chapter).
- International Standards on Auditing (ISAs).
- International Education Standards.
- International Public Sector Accounting Standards (IPSAS).

All four of these initiatives are, of course, valid and worthwhile. However, given objectives of this publication, the primary interest herein will be the International Standards on Auditing (ISAs), and, more specifically, how the ISAs relate to governmental auditing.

IFAC's International Auditing and Assurance Standards Board (IAASB) develops:

- International Standards on Assurance Engagements, which deal with assurance engagements *other than the review or audit of historical statements.*
- ISAs and International Standards on Review Engagements, which deal with audit and review of *historical financial information.*

Per IFAC guidance, an "assurance engagement" means an engagement in which a practitioner expresses a conclusion designed to enhance the degree of confidence the intended user, other than the responsible party, has about the outcome of the evaluation or measurement of a subject matter against criteria. (Some readers may see this as similar to an "attestation engagement" under the GAGAS, although the two types of engagements are not identical.) Two types of assurance engagements are permitted: 1) reasonable assurance (positive form of expression), and 2) limited assurance (negative form of expression). A subject matter, and subject matter information, in an assurance engagement can involve financial or nonfinancial matters, and can take many forms. One example would be an assertion about the effectiveness of internal control using the COSO model (discussed later) as the criteria.

Because the IFAC's ISAs deal only with financial audits, they would not be relevant in certain other audits, such as performance audits, which are commonly performed by many government audit organizations, such as SAIs and government agencies in the United States that adhere to GAGAS.

On the other hand, the objective and general principles in financial audits under the ISAs have many similarities with the financial audits of public sector entities performed under the GAGAS and ISSAI standards. For example, the objective of having a financial auditor express an opinion on the statements common under GAGAS, the ISSAIs, or IFAC is essentially the same. Moreover, all three of these sets of standards use essentially the same four terms to describe the form of opinion the auditor offers — unqualified, qualified, adverse, and disclaimer. Moreover, both the ISAs and GAGAS address similar considerations in planning, establishing materiality levels, considering internal control effectiveness, risk assessment, quality assurance, compliance with laws and regulations, and importance of evidence and its characteristics.

Before turning specifically to how the ISAs may be relevant in financial audits in the public sector, here is a brief summary status on the IAASB's work, since 2004, in updating and clarifying its ISAs. In an August 24, 2011, email,[6] the director of the IAASB stated the following:

> "In 2004, the IAASB began a comprehensive program to further enhance the clarity of its ISAs. This program involved the application of new drafting conventions to all ISAs, either as part of a substantive revision of through a limited redrafting, to reflect the new conventions and matters of general clarity. On February 27, 2009, the Clarity Project reached its completion when the Public Interest Oversight Board approved the due process for the last several clarified ISAs. Auditors worldwide are now using the 36 newly updated ISAs and a clarified International Standard on Quality Control, which became effective for audits of financial statements for periods after December 15, 2009. Further information on the Clarity Project, as well as the individual standards that are currently effective, can be found at http://web.ifac.org/clarity-center/index."

In the past, the IAASB had a Public Sector Committee (PSC), which developed Public Sector Perspectives (PSPs) to be added to ISAs as considered appropriate. This arrangement took into account that financial audits, where required in the public sector by SAIs or others,

can have some added or different requirements than financial audits outside the public sector. For example, the auditors of public sector entities may be required to report on:

- Compliance with legislative or regulatory requirements and related authorities.
- Adequacy of accounting and internal control systems.
- Economy, efficiency, and effectiveness of programs, projects, and activities.

However, the IAASB abolished the PSC, and has a revised approach, as explained in the same August 24, 2011, email cited above. The following two paragraphs from that email are quoted below:

> "While the IAASB no longer has a PSC, it does take public sector input into account in developing the ISAs and strongly believes the ISAs are right for the public sector. Specifically, individual ISAs may include 'Considerations specific to public sector entities' within the application and other explanatory material of an ISA. This additional guidance is aimed to assist in the application of the requirements of the ISA in the audit of public sector entities."
>
> "Also relevant is the IAASB's work with the INTOSAI. For more than six years, the IAASB and the INTOSAI have maintained a mutually beneficial relationship. INTOSAI is represented on the IAASB, and INTOSAI experts serve on IAASB task forces as appropriate to provide public sector input into the development of the ISAs. As part of its Congress in 2010, INTOSAI endorsed a framework comprised of a comprehensive set of ISSAIs to provide guidance to public sector auditors responsible for, among other things, financial audit, calling upon INTOSAI members to use the ISSAI framework as a common frame of reference for public sector auditing by implementing the ISSAIs in accordance with their mandate and national legislation and regulations. This important milestone for the IAASB is particularly relevant to the IAASB, because the ISSAIs for financial audits include the ISAs, as issued by the IAASB, along with supplemental guidance referred to as Practice Notes for each of the 36 clarified ISAs, as developed by the INTOSA's Financial Audit Subcommittee (FAS) of the Professional Standards Committee (PSC). The IAASB has observer status at INTOSAI's PSC meetings and assisted in the development of the Practice Notes by working directly with the FAS over the course of their 5 year project to develop the Practice Notes. Access to the individual ISSAIs is available at http://www.issai.org/composite-344. You will note the numbering scheme is linked to the ISAs (i.e., ISSAI 1200 contains ISA 200, ISSAI 1210 contains ISA 210, etc.)."

I.B Governance

In January 2012, The IIA issued a supplemental guidance document titled *The Audit Role in Public Sector Governance*. This supplemental guidance endorses the importance of auditing in the public sector and identifies key aspects (e.g., independence, competence, standards), but notes that the guidance may not be fully applicable in all jurisdictions. The GAGAS also includes Supplemental Guidance, discussing the role of those charged with governance and the auditor's communication with those charged with governance.

I.B.1 Governance in the Public Sector

The Need for Accountability

Accountability is a foundation of a democratic society. Elected officials are ultimately accountable to the voters; however, all government employees are publicly accountable for their actions. Government employees are answerable for their actions and decisions in a public forum. The public nature of government accountability places an additional burden on government employees.

Accountability in the public-sector context relates to good governance. Good governance in government is defined by The IIA as:

> Governance is the combination of processes and structures implemented by the board to inform, direct, manage and monitor the activities of the organization toward the achievement of objectives.[7]

Stated another way, governance is the exercise of authority, direction, and control over an organization. The following are characteristics of good governance, when governing bodies:

- Involve people with the necessary knowledge, ability, and commitment to fulfill their responsibilities.
- Understand their purpose and whose interests they represent.
- Understand the objectives and strategies of the organizations they govern.
- Understand what constitutes reasonable information for good governance and obtain it.
- Are prepared to ensure that the organization's objectives are met and that performance is satisfactory.
- Fulfill their accountability obligations to those whose interests they represent by reporting on the organization's performance.

Accountability is at the core of a democracy and can be defined as:

> Accountability [is] an obligation on the part of an individual or group to reveal, to explain, and to justify the discharge of responsibilities whose origins may be political, constitutional, statutory, or contractual.

From a government perspective, accountability involves three interrelated groups:

1. The general public and particularly those receiving public services.
2. Political leaders and officials who manage service providers to be accountable for a mixture of public and private interests.
3. Service providers whose objectives differ from the first two.

Aspects of accountability in the public sector may include:

- Performance budgeting and reporting.
- Financial reporting.
- Audits.
- Evaluations.
- Monitoring.
- Open government.

Auditing, because it is done by independent, objective third parties in accordance with standards, is one of the more credible means of accountability. The audit role is discussed below.

Standard Setting

One way to promote accountability and provide assurance to the public that audits are conducted professionally is through the development of government audit standards. In the government sector, there are numerous organizations that set standards and/or provide guidance to management and auditors.

Ethics/Codes of Conduct

Ethical conduct in public administration and, in particular, purchasing is a recurring problem in the public sector. There are four levels of ethics, each of which has its own set of responsibilities:

1. *Personal morality.* The basic sense of right and wrong is a function of social mores, parental influence, religious background, and personal experiences.
2. *Professional ethics.* Professional norms and rules that govern a profession. Some professions, such as auditing, have professional codes of conducts (such as The IIA's Code of Ethics).
3. *Organizational ethics.* The environment or culture of an organization and formal and informal rules of conduct. These can also include specific laws and regulations.
4. *Social ethics.* Rules of conduct that are prescribed by society and include laws and the society's social conscience.

Public Scrutiny

Government accountability and transparency principles (discussed above) have resulted in many governments enacting open government laws. These laws call for public access to government records and/or require meetings of elected officials to be held in public.

As government's role has increased in our lives, so has our necessity to know what it is doing. The public's desire and ability to stay informed about government laws, policies, and procedures has opened the doors to

information surrounding government's day-to-day practices of doing business. This scrutiny has made public agencies and officials more accountable for their actions because there is a greater likelihood that any transactions or duties they perform will be examined.

Policies and procedures for many government entities are increasingly becoming more formalized and documented so that not only their employees, but also the general public, can learn about how decisions are made and subsequently implemented.

The right of the public to protect its own interests by seeking information, and also limiting the manner in which personal records can be used, has affected government practices in the following areas:

- *Agency responsibilities.* Each agency should provide guidance to the public that describes its policies and procedures and steps required to request information. Upon receiving a valid request, a government agency must provide the relevant record(s) in a prompt, nonsolicitous manner.
- *Customer/client privacy.* Some information is exempt from the public, and, conversely, individuals have the opportunity to amend any errant information with regard to themselves.
- *Elected or appointed officials.* Sunshine laws have done away with private "behind closed doors" meetings where decisions, which directly impact citizens, were once made.

Elected or Appointed Officials

Elected officials are placed into office by their constituents to represent their needs and are subject to accountability by a review of their voting records. If a candidate runs for reelection, the public generally reviews the voting records to determine whether the incumbent candidate has voted in accordance with his or her values. If a candidate is reelected, it is generally a sign that he or she represented a majority of the voters when deciding matters of policy.

Freedom of information legislation has set the tone for public officials that all decisions and actions are subject to review. Sunshine laws and open meetings acts require that all official meetings are publicized and the general public is invited so that individuals interested in public affairs might attend. A meeting is generally considered to be a gathering of a majority, or a quorum, of the members of a public council whose main purpose is to confer on matters of the public interest. The outcomes of these meetings are to be documented, usually in the form of minutes, and made available to the public. For example, the Congressional Record is a public document recording the proceedings on floors of the U.S. House and Senate. In fact, many legislative bodies on national and local levels go a step further and now provide Internet access to (or televise) their proceedings on a regular basis.

I.B.2 Role of Audit within the Governance Structure

The audit process within the public sector forms part of the foundation of the public's trust in government. In evaluating whether public agencies are accomplishing their objectives, auditors gather and analyze information and control structures.

Auditing plays an important role in ensuring accountability. Through its various forms (internal and external), auditing provides a method of control to help ensure that objectives are realized appropriately. Some broad areas covered by audits include ensuring:

- The accuracy and completeness of records.
- Compliance with laws, regulations, contract terms, policies, and procedures.
- Accomplishment of objectives.
- Economy and efficiency of operations.
- Safeguarding of assets.

The purpose of auditing in the public sector is to ensure that funds are used as they were intended, act as control over financial management activities, and uncover inappropriate or illegal activities. Audits are a tool available to public agencies and ultimately the public to evaluate the financial and operational performance of public officials. Although audits have a negative connotation, they can be used as a tool for improving agency operations. Audits uncover inaccuracies. They also provide an opportunity to evaluate activities that affect the organization's efficiency and effectiveness.

The relationship of auditing to accountability is discussed in the first paragraph of chapter 1 in the December 2011 version of GAO's GAGAS. Excerpts with specific paragraph references are below:[8]

> (1.01) The concept of accountability for public resources is key in our nation's governing processes.
>
> (1.02) Legislators, other government officials, those charged with governance, and the public need to know whether 1)management and officials manage government resources and use their authority properly and in compliance with laws and regulations, 2) government programs are achieving their objectives and desired outcomes, and 3) government services are being provided effectively, efficiently, economically, ethically, and equitably.
>
> (1.03) Government auditing is essential in providing accountability to legislators, oversight bodies, those charged with governance, and the public.

Audit Committees in the Public Sector

An effective audit committee can provide several important aspects of control, including ensuring the independence of the internal audit function and that appropriate action is taken on audit recommendations. The audit committee serves in a unique capacity as an important communication link among external and internal auditors and operating management, and as a means of reducing the risk of management override of key elements of a public sector entity's internal control structure.

The audit committee should be made up of individuals who are independent of the day-to-day management of the public sector entity and have the necessary program and/or management expertise to perform their review function effectively. One of the primary reasons for this independence is to ensure an unbiased perspective on reports and recommendations brought to the committee.

The responsibilities of the audit committee should be stated in a formal, written charter or equivalent document that is approved by the full board or governing body of the public sector entity, as appropriate. The charter should articulate the authority, responsibilities, and structure of the audit committee. The responsibilities, at a minimum, should address financial and other reporting practices, internal control, and compliance with laws, regulations, and ethics. The charter also should state that the audit committee will meet periodically and may call additional or special meetings as needed. If possible, the authority, responsibilities, and structure of the audit committee should be provided in the governing law of the affected entity.

It should be noted that the use of audit committees in the public sector varies. For example, in the Unites States, while audit committees are extensively used at local levels of government, they are not used as extensively at the national or state levels of government. On the other hand, other forms of review and oversight are sometimes provided by other bodies, such as congressional or legislative entities.

I.C Risk/Control Frameworks

I.C.1 Role of Frameworks

Due to government auditors' responsibilities for assessing or evaluating risk, governance, and control, they can improve their audits by understanding and using risk/control frameworks as criteria for their work. A widely recognized and accepted internal control framework is referred to as the COSO model. Further, there is increasing interest in an extension of the COSO model, known as enterprisewide risk management (ERM). Also, the Canadian Institute of Chartered Accountants (CICA) has undertaken initiatives relating to risk, control, and governance that merit the attention of government auditors.

I.C.2 Elements of Risk/Control Frameworks

The COSO Framework

The COSO project was a private-sector initiative in the United States that started in the 1980s to address the problem of fraudulent financial reporting. In the 1970s, there were a number of scandals that called into question the integrity of corporate financial reporting. Problems continued to persist in the 1980s and the private sector

was wary of additional government intervention, so five organizations banded together to form COSO:

1. American Institute of Certified Public Accountants.
2. American Accounting Association.
3. Financial Executives Institute.
4. The Institute of Internal Auditors.
5. Institute of Management Accountants.

COSO's mission was to improve the quality of financial reporting through a focus on corporate governance, internal controls, and ethical standards.

The initial project was the Treadway Commission Report, issued in October 1987. The Treadway Commission Report called for an adequate system of internal control. The report also recommended a public management report describing management's responsibility for an organization's financial statements and internal controls, and an assessment of the internal control system. The Treadway Commission developed an internal control framework called *Internal Control – Integrated Framework.*[9] The Framework defines internal control broadly and does not limit internal controls to accounting controls over financial reporting. While financial reporting is an important responsibility of the audit committee, there are other very important aspects of the business relating to resource protection, operational efficiency and economy, and compliance with rules, regulations, and policies that are also important. The Framework promotes the concept that effective internal control is management's responsibility and requires the participation of everyone within an organization if it is to be effective.

Two major goals of COSO were to:

1. Establish a common definition of internal control.
2. Provide a standard against which organizations can assess their control systems.

COSO defines internal control, describes its components, and provides criteria against which control systems can be evaluated. It offers guidance for public reporting on internal control and provides materials that management, auditors, and others can use to evaluate an internal control system.

COSO emphasizes that the internal control system is a tool of, but not a substitute for, management and that controls should be built into — rather than onto — operating activities. Although the report defines internal control as a process, it recommends evaluating the effectiveness of internal control as of a point in time.

COSO also addresses the limitations of an internal control system and the roles and responsibilities of the parties that affect a system. Limitations include faulty human judgment, misunderstanding of instructions, errors, management override, collusion, and cost/benefit considerations.

The COSO document, *Internal Control – Integrated Framework*, defines internal control as:

> Internal control is a process, effected by an entity's board of directors, management, and other personnel, designed to provide reasonable assurance regarding the achievement of objectives in the following categories:
> - Effectiveness and efficiency of operations.
> - Reliability of financial reporting.
> - Compliance with applicable laws and regulations.

This definition reflects certain fundamental concepts:

- Internal control is a *process*. It's a means to an end, not an end in itself.
- Internal control is effected by *people*. It's not merely policy manuals and forms, but people at every level of an organization.
- Internal control can be expected to provide only *reasonable assurance*, not absolute assurance, to an entity's management and board.
- Internal control is geared to the achievement of *objectives* in one or more separate but overlapping categories.

As defined under the COSO work, internal controls consist of five interrelated components. (See Figure I.1.) The five components are derived from the way management runs a business and are integrated with the management process. The components are:

- ***Control environment.*** The core of any business is its people — their individual attributes, including integrity, ethical values, and competence — and the environment in which they operate. They are the engine that drives the entity and the foundation on which everything rests.

- *Risk assessment.* The entity must be aware of and deal with the risks it faces. It must set objectives, integrated with the sales, production, marketing, financial, and other activities, so that the organization is operating in concert. It also must establish mechanisms to identify, analyze, and manage the related risks.
- *Control activities.* Control policies and procedures must be established and executed to help ensure that the actions identified by management as necessary to address risks to achievement of the entity's objectives are effectively carried out.
- *Information and communication.* Surrounding these activities are information and communication systems. These enable the entity's people to capture and exchange the information needed to conduct, manage, and control its operations.
- *Monitoring*: The entire process must be monitored and modifications made as necessary. In this way, the system can react dynamically, changing as conditions warrant.

Figure I.1. Five Components of Internal Control

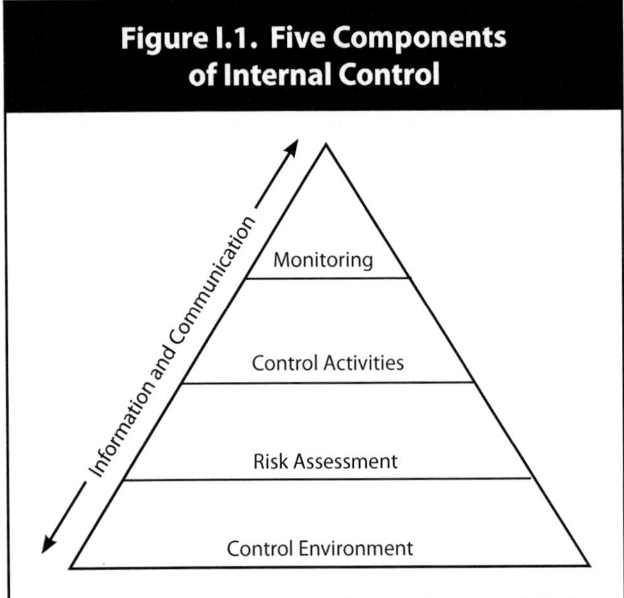

The control environment provides an atmosphere in which people conduct their activities and carry out their control responsibilities. It serves as the foundation for the other components. Within this environment, management assesses risks to the achievement of specified objectives. Control activities are implemented to help ensure that management directives to address risks are carried out. Meanwhile, relevant information is captured and communicated throughout the organization. The entire process is monitored and modified as conditions warrant.

In November 2011, COSO issued an exposure draft to revise and update the COSO framework.[10] Comments were due back to COSO by March 31, 2012. COSO did note that the five interrelated components will remain the same. Both managers and auditors in the government entities should stay abreast of the current status of the COSO "model" as revisions are made in the future.

I.C.3. Application of Frameworks

The COSO Model Is Used in Government Auditing

Internal control is generally of great interest to government auditors and is addressed in the auditing standards that they follow. It is noteworthy that the COSO conceptual framework for internal control is referenced (or generally incorporated) by the four bodies in the auditing standards they issue. For example:

- In Practice Advisory 2130-1: Assessing the Adequacy of Control Processes, The IIA identifies four broad control objectives that are very similar to the three key broad control objectives identified in the COSO model.
- The GAO, which issues GAGAS, also has statutory responsibility for establishing internal control standards for the federal level of the U.S. government. In issuing the 1999 (most current version as of June 2012) internal control standards, GAO referred specifically to taking into account the COSO model. In GAGAS, GAO refers to generally the same three principal internal control objectives (effectiveness and efficiency, relevance and reliability of information, and compliance) as cited in the COSO model.
- INTOSAI has issued a publication titled Guidelines for Internal Control Standards for the Public Sector. INTOSAI specifically implements the COSO guidelines in that publication.
- In ISA 315 (Understanding the Entity and Assessing its Environment and Assessing the Risks of Material Misstatement), IFAC defines internal control similarly to the COSO model and cites the same five components as COSO does.

COSO Enterprise Risk Management – Integrated Framework[11]

An extension of the COSO model that has emerged is called enterprise risk management (ERM), which is briefly discussed below.

The definition of ERM follows:

> Enterprise risk management is a process, effected by an entity's board of directors, management and other personnel, applied in strategy setting and across the enterprise, designed to identify potential events that may affect the entity, and manage risk to be within its risk appetite, to provide reasonable assurance regarding the achievement of entity objectives.

The underlying premise of ERM is that every entity exists to provide value for its stakeholders. The framework describes the essential components, principles, and concepts of ERM for all organizations, regardless of size. All entities face uncertainty. The challenge for management is to determine how much uncertainty the organization is willing to accept as it strives to grow stakeholder value. Uncertainty presents both risk and opportunity, with the potential to erode or enhance value. Enterprise risk management enables management to effectively deal with uncertainty and associated risk and opportunity, enhancing the capacity to build value.

The framework describes the essential components, principles, and concepts of ERM for all organizations, regardless of size.

Value is maximized when management sets strategy and objectives to strike an optimal balance between growth and return goals and related risks, and efficiently and effectively deploys resources in pursuit of the entity's objectives. ERM encompasses:

- *Aligning risk appetite and strategy.* Management considers the entity's risk appetite in evaluating strategic alternatives, setting related objectives, and developing mechanisms to manage related risks.
- *Enhancing risk response decisions.* ERM provides the rigor to identify and select among alternative risk responses — risk avoidance, reduction, sharing, and acceptance.
- *Reducing operational surprises and losses.* Entities gain enhanced capability to identify potential events and establish responses, reducing surprises and associated costs or losses.
- *Identifying and managing multiple and cross-enterprise risks.* Every enterprise faces a myriad of risks affecting different parts of the organization, and ERM facilitates effective response to the interrelated impacts and integrated responses to multiple risks.
- *Seizing opportunities.* By considering a full range of potential events, management is positioned to identify and proactively realize opportunities.
- *Improving deployment of capital.* Obtaining robust risk information allows management to effectively assess overall capital needs and enhance capital allocation.

These capabilities inherent in ERM help management achieve the entity's performance and profitability targets and prevent loss of resources. ERM helps ensure effective reporting and compliance with laws and regulations, and helps avoid damage to the entity's reputation and associated consequences. In sum, it helps an organization get to where it wants to go and avoid pitfalls and surprises along the way.

The framework is set forth in four categories: strategic, operations, reporting, and compliance. It consists of eight interrelated components, which are internal environment, objective setting, event identification, risk assessment, risk response, control activities, information and communication, and monitoring.

To the extent that the ERM concept is applied in the government, government auditors need to understand ERM and identify an appropriate auditor role. In this regard, The IIA issued a Position Paper titled The Role of the Internal Auditor in Enterprise-wide Risk Management, published in September 2004.[12]

The Canadian Institute of Chartered Accountants (CICA) Internal Control Model

In the early 1990s, Criteria of Control (CoCo) was an initiative of the Canadian Institute of Chartered Accountants (CICA) to strengthen control and corporate governance. In any organization of people, the essence of control is the blending of purpose, commitment, capability, and monitoring and learning. Control encompasses all the elements of an organization that, taken together, support people in the achievement of the organization's objectives. The elements include resources, systems, processes, culture, structure, and tasks. Looking at control means looking at all these elements and how they are interrelated and aligned with objectives. At the highest level, the organization's "objective" is its reason for existing, its mission. That mission is lived out through vision, strategic objectives, and plans to realize them. Under CoCo, objectives are in three general categories:

1. Effectiveness and efficiency of operations includes objectives related to an organization's goals, such as customer service, the safeguarding and efficient use of resources, profitability, and meeting social obligations. This includes the safeguarding of the organization's resource from inappropriate use or loss and ensuring that liabilities are identified and managed.
2. Reliability of internal and external reporting includes objectives related to matters such as the maintenance of proper accounting records, the reliability of information used within the organization, and of information published for third parties. This includes the protection of records against two main types of fraud: the concealment of theft and the distortion of results.
3. Compliance with applicable laws and regulations and internal policies includes objectives related to ensuring that the organization's affairs are conducted in accordance with legal and regulatory obligations and internal policies.

> **Note:** See the similarity to the principal categories of objectives under the COSO model.

The CICA's use of the CoCo model has evolved over time, as described in a September 6, 2011, email from the CICA Principal for Risk Oversight and Governance.[13] Following are pertinent excerpts from that CICA email:

> "Under its former title of Criteria of Control, a "control" model (the CoCo Framework) was created, using a systems theory approach to assess organizational control and assist with effective governance. Feedback gathered from market research was viewed as a significant piece of thought leadership and was particularly well received in the Internal Audit population. However, the focus on "control" was limiting and narrow and was difficult to use practically."
>
> "In response to this feedback, the CoCo Board changed its name to Risk Management and Governance Board (RMGB) and revised its vision and mission to reflect a stronger emphasis on risk and governance. CoCo provided a framework that helped organizations to identify and mitigate risks through a systems approach to control. As RMGB, we would broaden the approach to encompass other areas of risk and more broad governance. It was also agreed that materials would use the logical, theoretical soundness of CoCo in a more easily understood and practical manner.
>
> "Over time, RMGB guidance evolved to be more leading edge and it was agreed that leading edge, thought provoking, yet practical guidance be the focus of future materials."
>
> "Approximately two years ago (2009), there was concern that the name Risk and Governance did not reflect the specific activities of the group. While reporting that risk management is an important and logical part of governance, it was suggested that risk "oversight" may more accurately reflect the group's mission. It was also agreed that there is a significant gap in the oversight of risk. To more accurately reflect the activities, the name was changed to Risk Oversight and Governance."

Government auditors may find value in staying current with developments under the risk oversight and governance initiative.

I.D IIA Code of Ethics

All four organizations (The IIA, the U.S. GAO, INTOSAI, and IFAC) that set auditing standards followed by government auditors have also formally established ethical principles.

The IIA

The purpose of The IIA's Code of Ethics is to promote an ethical culture in the profession of internal auditing:[14]

> Internal auditing is an independent, objective assurance and consulting activity designed to add value and improve an organization's operations. It helps an organization accomplish its objectives by bringing a systematic, disciplined approach to evaluate and improve the effectiveness of risk management, control, and governance processes.

A code of ethics is necessary and appropriate for the profession of internal auditing, founded as it is on the trust placed in its objective assurance about risk management, control, and governance. The IIA's Code of Ethics extends beyond the definition of internal auditing to include two essential components:

1. Principles that are relevant to the profession and practice of internal auditing.
2. Rules of conduct that describe behavior norms expected of internal auditors.

These rules are an aid to interpreting the principles into practical applications and are intended to guide the ethical conduct of internal auditors.

The Code of Ethics together with The IIA's International Professional Practices Framework (IPPF) and other relevant IIA pronouncements provide guidance to internal auditors serving others. "Internal auditors" refers to IIA members, recipients of or candidates for IIA professional certifications, and those who provide internal audit services within the definition of internal auditing.

Applicability and Enforcement

This Code of Ethics applies to both individuals and entities that provide internal audit services.

For IIA members and recipients of or candidates for IIA professional certifications, breaches of the Code of Ethics will be evaluated and administered according to The IIA's bylaws and administrative guidelines. The fact that a particular conduct is not mentioned in the Rules of Conduct does not prevent it from being unacceptable or discreditable, and therefore, the member, certification holder, or candidate can be liable for disciplinary action.

Principles

Internal auditors are expected to apply and uphold the following principles:

- ***Integrity.*** The integrity of internal auditors establishes trust and thus provides the basis for reliance on their judgment.
- ***Objectivity.*** Internal auditors exhibit the highest level of professional objectivity in gathering, evaluating, and communicating information about the activity or process being examined. Internal auditors make a balanced assessment of all the relevant circumstances and are not unduly influenced by their own interests or by others in forming judgments.
- ***Confidentiality.*** Internal auditors respect the value and ownership of information they receive and do not disclose information without appropriate authority unless there is a legal or professional obligation to do so.
- ***Competency.*** Internal auditors apply the knowledge, skills, and experience needed in the performance of internal audit services.

Rules of Conduct

Integrity

Internal auditors:

1.1. Shall perform their work with honesty, diligence, and responsibility.

1.2. Shall observe the law and make disclosures expected by the law and the profession.

1.3. Shall not knowingly be a party to any illegal activity, or engage in acts that are discreditable to the profession of internal auditing or to the organization.

1.4. Shall respect and contribute to the legitimate and ethical objectives of the organization.

Objectivity

Internal auditors:

2.1. Shall not participate in any activity or relationship that may impair or be presumed to impair their unbiased assessment. This participation includes those activities or relationships that may be in conflict with the interests of the organization.

2.2. Shall not accept anything that may impair or be presumed to impair their professional judgment.

2.3. Shall disclose all material facts known to them that, if not disclosed, may distort the reporting of activities under review.

Confidentiality

Internal auditors:

3.1. Shall be prudent in the use and protection of information acquired in the course of their duties.

3.2. Shall not use information for any personal gain or in any manner that would be contrary to the law or detrimental to the legitimate and ethical objectives of the organization.

Competency

Internal auditors:

4.1. Shall engage only in those services for which they have the necessary knowledge, skills, and experience.

4.2. Shall perform internal audit services in accordance with the *International Standards for the Professional Practice of Internal Auditing.*

4.3. Shall continually improve their proficiency and the effectiveness and quality of their services.

The IIA's Code of Ethics was adopted by The IIA Board of Directors, June 17, 2000, and remains the same in The IIA's 2011 IPPF.

The U.S. Government Accountability Office (GAO)[15]

GAO's "Yellow Book" addresses ethical principles for auditors. Specifically, chapter 1 in the 2011 version of GAGAS includes ethical principles that provide the foundation, discipline, and structure that influence the application of GAGAS. GAO states that these are fundamental principles rather than specific standards or requirements. The ethical principles are considered a matter of personal and organizational responsibility. GAO further states that auditors also may be subject to other ethical requirements or codes of professional conduct (such as licensed or certifies professionals) and/or relevant laws or regulations.

GAO's five ethical principles, with cryptic explanatory words or phrases, are presented below:

1. The public interest (the collective well-being of people and entities served).
2. Integrity (objective, fact-based, nonpartisan, and non-ideological).
3. Objectivity (independence of mind and spirit).
4. Proper use of government information, resources and positions (not inappropriately used).
5. Professional behavior (compliance with laws, regulations, etc., not discreditable, honest effort).

International Organization of Supreme Audit Institutions (INTOSAI)[16]

INTOSAI has deemed it essential to establish an international code of ethics for auditors in the public sector. INTOSAI defines a Code of Ethics as a "comprehensive statement of the values and principles which should guide the daily work of auditors." The code is directed at the individual auditors, the head of the SAI, and relevant others. INTOSAI recognizes that — due to national differences in culture, language, and legal and social systems — each SAI is responsible for establishing a code that best fits its environment.

Presented below are the key words, with cryptic explanatory words or phrases, included in INTOSAI Code of Ethics, as effective in 2012:

- *Integrity* (honesty, candidness, being right and just).
- *Integrity, objectivity, and impartiality* (in fact and appearance, political neutrality, avoiding conflicts of interest).
- *Professional secrecy* (disclosures only for statutory or other identified responsibilities).
- *Competence* (needed for work performed; knowing standards, procedures, and practices; supervision; high quality audits; continuous obligations to improve skills).

As stated earlier, INTOSAI's General Auditing Standards also include standards with "ethical significance."

International Federation of Accountants (IFAC)[17]

IFAC's Code of Ethics for Professional Accountants, in effect in 2012, has three parts:

1. Part A: General Application of the Code.
2. Part B: Professional Accountants in Public Practice.
3. Part C: Professional Accountants in Business.

Parts B and C present more details on application for the two groups cited. (Collectively, the IFAC Code is more than 100 pages in length.)

For purposes of this publication, only Part A (General Application of the Code) is discussed. Presented below from Part A are IFAC's Fundamental Principles, with cryptic explanatory words or phrases:

- ***Integrity*** (straightforward and honest in all professional and business relationships).
- ***Objectivity*** (not allowing bias, conflict of interest, or undue influence to override professional business judgments).
- ***Professional competence and due care*** (maintaining professional knowledge and skills, following required standards).
- ***Confidentiality*** (using information appropriately, not for personal gain).
- ***Professional behavior*** (compliance with laws and regulations, nothing discreditable).

DOMAIN II
Government Auditing Practice

This section addresses important issues related to the practice of government audits. Three major topic areas in domain II are covered:

1. Management of the audit function.
2. Types of audit services.
3. Processes for delivery of audit services.

II.A Management of the Audit Function

The various sets of audit standards and guidance under which government auditors perform their work address certain aspects of management of the audit function. In addition, other practices required or used for effective management are included in laws, regulations, policies, and/or other authoritative sources.

II.A.1 Need for a Formal Document of Purpose, Authority, and Responsibility

Under The IIA's *Standards*, Attribute Standard 1000 states that the purpose, authority and responsibility of the internal audit activity must be formally defined in a *charter*, and that the chief audit executive (CAE) must periodically review the charter and present it to senior management and the board for approval. Government auditors who perform their work under sets of standards other than the *Standards* generally have other documents (e.g., laws) and mechanisms to achieve a similar purpose.

An audit charter serves as the audit department's statement of purpose, authority, and responsibility. Audit charters should be in writing.

Audit charters are usually brief documents written in general terms. Applicable governing statutes often dictate the specific elements to include in the charter for governmental entities. However, audit charters generally address:

- Definition of the audit unit's responsibilities, goals, and objectives.
- Legislative or other source of audit authority.
- Description of the standards to be followed.
- The scope of work to be undertaken.
- The administrative responsibilities of the audit unit.
- The reporting relationship between the audit unit and management and/or the governing body.
- The process for hiring and dismissing CAEs.
- Access to information and people.

The head of the audit unit is usually responsible for drafting the charter. The chief administrative officer of the governmental unit or agency also should have input into the content of the charter. Further guidance on the charter's content may come from any applicable external governing or reporting bodies, such as a legislative audit committee or a legislative post-audit group.

For governmental entities, the governing body (e.g., legislature, city council, or board) or the head of the unit or agency, such as a director or chief, should approve the charter. (Note: Governmental audit units do not necessarily use the term "charter" but may have their purpose, authority, and responsibility formalized in another manner, e.g., law, regulation, or policy.)

II.A.2 Policies and Procedures

The IIA's Performance Standard 2040 states that the CAE must establish policies and procedures to guide the internal audit activity. The form and content of the policies and procedures are dependent upon the size and complexity of the internal audit activity and the complexity of its work. Sets of audit standards other than The IIA's *Standards* followed by some government auditors are not as explicit in regard to establishment of policies and procedures, but the effective use of policies and procedures is generally consistent with those other standards.

The head of the audit unit is responsible for developing and maintaining written policies and procedures to guide audit staff. The form and content of written policies and procedures should be appropriate to the size and structure of the audit department and the complexity of its work. Formal administrative and technical audit manuals help employees to consistently comply with established performance standards.

Written policies and procedures help ensure consistent performance of audit functions. They also provide guidance that is unique to a single audit office or specific organizational environment. The written policies and procedures should be adequately communicated to all audit staff.

The following items are often contained in written audit policies and procedures:

- Statement of purpose, authority, and responsibility (e.g., audit charter).
- Written code of ethics.
- Description of the steps to be followed during each phase of the audit (e.g., background, survey, fieldwork, reporting).
- Description of audit standards to be followed, plus a description of how the audit unit will achieve compliance with each standard.
- Description of fraud auditing and how detected frauds will be handled.
- Information dealing with personnel and other administrative issues. This should include a list of functions and specific job descriptions for CAEs, managers, supervisors, and staff. This section should address matters such as timekeeping, sick and vacation leaves, travel guidelines and restrictions, confidentiality, and performance evaluations. It is also advisable to include information regarding the annual planning process (e.g., audit plan development, business planning and tracking, and budget development).
- Forms for audit and administrative functions (e.g., audit assignment forms, independence forms, standard workpapers forms, timekeeping forms, etc.).
- Approaches to non-audit (e.g., consulting) engagements.

II.A.3 Quality Assurance

Quality assurance is a topic addressed in some fashion in all sets of audit standards followed by government auditors. For example, IIA Standard 1300 states that the CAE must develop and maintain a quality assurance and improvement program, and Standard 1310 states it must include both internal and external assessments. GAGAS includes a General Standard on Quality Control and Assurance that states the audit organization must develop and maintain a system of quality control (internal) and have an external peer review at least once every three years. Further, The IIA's *Standards* and the IAASB standards include quality control requirements.

Internal Quality Reviews

Quality assurance reviews are designed to determine whether the audit unit's internal quality control system is in place and operating effectively to provide reasonable assurance that established policies and procedures and applicable auditing standards are being followed. Individuals assigned to conduct a quality assurance review make their assessment of the internal quality control system based on a review of selected information, such as:

- A reasonable cross-section of audit reports.
- Audit workpapers (audit documentation).
- Audit planning documents (e.g., methods for assessing auditable activities, assessing risk, and determining the frequency and scope of audits).
- Audit charter (or alternative documentation).
- Code of ethics.
- Policies and procedures.
- Correspondence.
- Continuing education plans and records.
- Staff position descriptions and job requirements.
- Results of interviews or questionnaires completed by audit department staff to determine their understanding of relevant policies and procedures.

Quality reviews can be conducted by internal staff or by a team of qualified and independent external reviewers (sometimes called peer reviews). Internal reviews are periodic assessments of audit quality by members of the audit staff. Many audit units go through internal reviews in preparation for upcoming external reviews.

Independent members of the audit staff conduct internal reviews. The internal review team typically selects a completed audit or group of audits to review. The team reviews the audit report and supporting workpapers to assess overall audit quality and compliance with applicable audit standards. Reviewers also may use the results of interviews and surveys of stakeholders of the audit function, including customer management, customer staff, and governing body officials.

External Quality Reviews

External reviews are conducted periodically by qualified members outside the audit organization. The purpose of an external review is to have an independent assessment of the quality of the audit unit's work. Similar to internal reviews, external reviews focus on assessing the extent to which the audit organization followed applicable standards in conducting its work. The basic methodology of an external review can be summarized as follows:

- An independent team of auditors external to the organization reviews the audit organization's charter, policies and procedures, training records, annual planning processes, personnel expectations, and other records and information related to the management and administration of the audit function.
- The team reviews the audit reports, workpapers, and other documentation associated with the audits selected. Based on these reviews, the team assesses the quality of the audit work in relation to the audit standards used. The assessment is also typically made by analyzing answers provided by audit staff in response to questionnaires given to determine their understanding of their work responsibilities.
- The team prepares a written report for the head of the audit unit.
- External reviews are referred to in the *Government Auditing Standards* (commonly referred to as Generally Accepted Government Auditing Standards or GAGAS) as quality control reviews. Another commonly used name for an external review is peer review.

Review Benefits

The benefits of internal and external reviews include the following:

- The audit unit can learn how well its work meets applicable standards.
- The results of the review process enable audit department management to make necessary changes and improvements in the audit function. These adjustments might include areas such as changes in staffing policies or adjustments in training programs.
- Users of audit information can have greater confidence in the quality of work produced by an audit unit that is subject to quality reviews.

Review Characteristics

The characteristics of internal quality control systems will vary based on the size of the audit unit and the nature of its work. However, in general, reviewers can conclude there is reasonable assurance that an internal quality control system is effective if the audit organization has done the following:

- Followed applicable auditing standards.
- Established and implemented adequate audit policies and procedures.

The frequency of required quality assurance reviews varies based on the type of standards followed. For example, GAGAS requires a review every three years and IIA *Standards* requires a review every five years. The *Standards* requires distribution of the quality assurance review report to the requester of the review and GAGAS recommends distributing the report to available oversight bodies and to the public.

The following guidelines apply to selecting quality review team members:

- Reviewers should be qualified and have current knowledge of the type of work to be reviewed and the applicable auditing standards.
- Reviewers should be independent of the audit organization being reviewed, its staff, and the customers of audits selected for review.

A written report should be prepared communicating the results of the quality control review. The report should express an opinion about the audit unit's compliance with the standards it follows and has been measured against. The report should also contain recommendations for improvement.

The audit department's management is responsible for the quality of the audit function. The methods used to ensure an acceptable level of quality include supervision, internal reviews, and external reviews.

Supervision is an ongoing process. Proper supervision of the audit department includes implementing policies and procedures that address the requirements of audit standards being followed. The head of the audit unit is responsible for ensuring that audits are properly supervised throughout all phases of the audit process. Evidence of proper supervision should be included in audit workpapers. Specific aspects of proper audit supervision include:

- Ensuring that staff auditors are qualified to perform their assignments.
- Providing clear and timely instructions to staff so audit objectives are achieved.
- Approving the audit program and ensuring that it is followed, unless approved changes are made.
- Verifying that audit workpapers adequately support audit findings, conclusions, and recommendations.
- Evaluating staff performance in a fair and timely manner.

II.A.4 Planning

IIA Standard 2010 and 2010.A1 state that the CAE must establish risk-based plans to determine the priorities of the internal audit activity, consistent with the organization's goals. Moreover, a documented risk assessment must be done at least annually, and the input of senior management and the board must be considered. While the *Standards* has a specific focus on *overall planning,* GAGAS and INTOSAI focus on planning for individual audits and engagements. Even so, governmental audit units performing work under GAGAS and INTOSAI typically have a formal overall planning process, typically including preparation of an annual overall audit plan.

There are two types of audit planning. The first type, which is the focus of this section, involves management's role in setting up the audit function, authorizing appropriate resources, and selecting the functional areas to be audited. The second type of audit planning involves the planning associated with specific audits.

Types of Plans

The audit unit's management is responsible for establishing goals and objectives for the audit function, outlining the methods to be used in achieving the goals and objectives, and developing a method to ensure an appropriate level and type of resources are applied to the function. The plans developed for the audit function should be updated as circumstances dictate. Specific types of plans include:

- Goals for the audit unit.
- Criteria to measure progress toward achieving goals.
- Target dates.
- Audit work schedules (e.g., activities to be audited, time frames for audit, resource estimates).
- Staffing plans and financial budgets.
- Recovery plans if audit activities are behind schedule.

Work Schedules

Audits work schedules may generally be based on one or more of the following factors:

- The length of time since the program/subject was last audited.
- The extent and type of findings in the last audit.
- Audits prioritized based on assessment of the degree of risk of potential loss (such as potential loss of dollars, lives, or of public trust) associated with the audit area.
- The occurrence of major recent changes in operations, programs, systems, or controls.
- The availability of audit staff resources.
- Requests by management or policy makers (such as elected officials or governing board members).
- Opportunities to achieve operating benefits.

As stated above, the *Standards* states that the overall plan must be risk based.

Audit department management should develop a plan describing what to audit and when to audit each selected area. In a broad sense, the audit plan describes how the audit department will carry out its responsibilities. The purpose of the plan is to enable projection of items such as work schedules, budgets, resources needs, and training needs. A risk assessment is often used to select audits to include in the audit plan.

Planning for Risk

Risk assessment involves using professional judgment to determine the critical areas for audit attention, based on the potential for adverse effects on the organization. Therefore, risk assessment begins by considering factors that may affect risk and giving the highest audit priority to audit areas that have the highest potential for adverse consequences. The risk assessment model should be updated continuously as additional information becomes available. The potential effects from risk exposures include:

- Loss of assets, errors, fraud.
- Bad decisions.
- Stakeholder or client dissatisfaction.
- Adverse publicity.
- Noncompliance with laws, rules, and regulations.
- Failure to achieve the organization's goals and objectives.

Risk is the probability that an event or action may adversely affect the organization or activity under review. In other words, risk is anything that can prevent an organization from achieving an objective. The three major components of risk are:

1. An event or cause that can interfere with achieving the objective (e.g., what can go wrong?).
2. A probability or likelihood of occurrence.
3. The negative consequences of not achieving the objective.

Inherent risk. Risk is inherent in any activity, regardless of the existence or effectiveness of controls. For example, theft, loss, and an inaccurate recording of cash received are inherent risks in cash-handling operations. Also, inherent risks in a construction program might be noncompliance with building code, failure to meet the customer's facility needs, or excessive cost growth (change orders). Thus, inherent risk is uncertainty or exposure, assuming no controls are in place. Inherent risks are the possible adverse effects based solely on the type of activity, the type of resources, amount of assets, or complexity of transactions.

Control risk. Control risk is the extent of uncertainty remaining after the mitigating effects of the control system are in place. The extent to which an organization has implemented controls to minimize the actual occurrence of the risk determines the vulnerability to the risk actually occurring, or the "control risk."

The risk analysis process involves the following:

- Identify auditable activities (e.g., programs, accounts, contracts, transactions).
- Identify relevant risk factors (e.g., complexity of program, size of program, adequacy of internal control system).
- Estimate the significance of a risk (e.g., magnitude of exposure in dollars or other type of measure, type of threat, duration, etc.).
- Estimate the likelihood that a risk will occur.
- Prioritize risks.
- Determine how to manage the risks.

Determining the numerical degree of risk remains a matter of judgment. Therefore, Lawrence B. Sawyer suggests the following risk assessment method:

> "All audit projects can be given a numerical rating from 1 to 5, based on auditor judgment and experience. An audit project rated 1 has the highest risk and deserves the highest priority. An audit project rated 5 has the lowest risk and would be carried out only when higher rated projects have been completed and time is available. Where budget restrictions require a reduction in audit staff, all or some of the 5-rated and 4-rated projects can be eliminated."[1]

Planning for Statutory Compliance

Some types of audit organizations have less latitude in selecting the audits they perform. Many government audit units are subject to laws that stipulate a time frame in which certain agencies or programs must be audited. For example, many states statutorily require that a legislative post audit unit conduct a financial and compliance audit of each state agency on a set schedule (e.g., every two years). Also, performance audits or other special audits are often done at the request of a governmental authority such as Congress, a state legislature, or a city council.

II.A.5 Staffing

IIA Standard 2030 states that the CAE must ensure that internal audit activities are appropriate, authorized, sufficient, and effectively deployed to achieve the approved plan. *Appropriate* refers to the mix of knowledge, skills, and other competencies needed to perform the plan. *Sufficient* refers to the quantity of resources needed to accomplish the plan. Resources are effectively deployed when they are used in a way that optimizes the achievement of approved plans. Government audit organizations that perform their work under sets of standards other than IIA *Standards* are subject to a wide range of laws, regulations, and policies regarding the management of staffing and resources. Moreover, both GAGAS and the *Standards* have standards relating to aspects of staffing (e.g., competencies for individual audits and engagements and other resource-related matters).

Hiring

The head of the audit unit is responsible for selecting and developing the human resources of the audit department. The following are guidelines for effective personnel management:

- Plan for personnel needs and review hiring results periodically to determine whether personnel needs are being achieved.
- Develop procedures to identify sources of potential hires, methods of contacting and attracting potential hires, and methods of evaluating and selecting potential hires.
- Write specific job descriptions for each level of audit staff.
- Develop specific attributes for jobs and hire individuals who have those attributes.
- Verify applicants' backgrounds, work histories, and references before hiring them.
- Inform new personnel about policies and procedures relevant to them.
- Provide continuing education and training for staff (e.g., external or in-house training courses, professional conferences, or seminars).
- Evaluate each auditor's performance at least annually.
- Provide continuous feedback to staff regarding their performance and professional development.

The audit unit's management should consider staffing as part of the planning process. Specific considerations include:

- Staff assigned to specific jobs should have the necessary skills and knowledge.
- The appropriate number of staff and supervisors should be assigned to each job. Consultants should be used as needed.
- Staff should be given on-the-job training.

It is the responsibility of the audit unit's management to address staffing considerations in the most economical and cost efficient manner possible. Assignments should be made based on the type and complexity of the project, the skills of available staff, and resource limitations. An audit team should collectively possess the skills necessary to perform the particular audit to which they are assigned. In cases where the audit staff does not possess the needed skills, management may temporally contract with a specialist to perform the function. This practice is known as outsourcing.

Audit Staff Skills

Audit staff should be knowledgeable about:

- Auditing skills, including those specific to government auditing.
- Government organizations, programs, activities, and functions.
- Oral and written communication skills.
- Principles of management controls and internal controls.
- Accounting principles, depending on the type of audit work performed.

The audit organization is responsible for establishing and implementing a program to ensure that auditors receive necessary continuing education and training. The organization should keep a record of continuing education received by each audit employee. Continuing education for auditors includes topics such as audit techniques, accounting, internal controls, supervision, sampling, evaluation design, and data analysis. Also, auditors should continue to strengthen their understanding of management principles, as well as those topics related to

the government activity or program under audit, such as corrections, human services, or contracting.

II.A.6 Marketing the Audit Function

> **Note:** "Marketing" the audit function, per se, is not specifically covered in the audit standards followed by government auditors. However, managers of audit organizations can add value to their work by carefully considering and being sensitive to the needs of the users of their audit work. The following discussion addresses marketing.

Government auditing serves a variety of customers. The term *customer* is used somewhat differently here than the way audit organizations often use it; many audit organizations use terms such as *clients, stakeholders,* or *users.* Whatever term is used, there are three categories: primary, secondary, and tertiary.

*1. **Primary customers*** are those individuals or groups that sponsor the audit, such as:

- National governments.
- Regional/state governments.
- Local/city governments.

*2. **Secondary customers*** are those people whose systems or processes are influenced by implementing audit recommendations. Secondary customers also include people who make direct use of the information contained in the audit report. Examples of secondary customers include:

- High-level managers of agencies or bureaus.
- Operating managers of agencies or bureaus.
- University and research groups.
- Special interest groups (e.g., consumer advocacy groups, social service organizations, industry and trade groups, etc.).
- The media.

*3. **Beneficiaries*** are people who may never read the audit report but whose services are improved because the audit was conducted. Examples of beneficiaries include:

- The general public.
- Clients of the audited program.

Auditors can use the following methods to help ensure that the audit function is accepted and valued:

- The audit department should work with customers to help solve problems, rather than simply point out where problems exist. For audits to result in positive change, it is important for customers to accept plans of action described in audit recommendations. Customers will be more willing to implement changes that they agree to and help formulate. Customers are also more likely to support audit recommendations that meet their goals and objectives.
- The audit department should educate its customers about the services available from the audit function. Effective methods of educating customers include presentations and brochures.
- The audit department should ensure that its audit plan is aligned with the needs and expectations of its primary customers.
- The audit department should seek feedback from customers. Customers value audits that help meet their needs and goals. Therefore, it is important to establish lines of communication between the audit department and all customer groups.

II.A.7 Mission/Role/Outcome of the Audit Function within Government

> **Note:** The mission, roles, and outcomes of the audit function within government are not explicitly stated in those terms in the audit standards. However, the standards imply interest and advocacy of approaches as described below.

The audit function within government provides the following benefits:

- The audit function helps keep governments accountable to the public by measuring compliance with established laws and regulations; the effectiveness, economy, efficiency, standards of equity and ethics; and the controls around these matters.
- The audit function provides objective assurance to oversight bodies about the reliability and credibility of financial and performance reports produced by management.

- The audit function can help government management achieve its goals and objectives by improving organizational systems and services.
- The regular presence of auditors can help protect government assets by deterring fraud, waste, and abuse.
- Input from audits can help employees improve their overall job performance and adherence to establish controls.

The following means provide feedback to auditors from clients, stakeholders, and interested parties regarding the quality and effectiveness of the audit function:

- Comments from managers of audited entities on draft audit reports.
- Post-audit surveys.
- Statutory changes resulting from the audit.
- Reduction in repeat findings.
- Prompt implementation of audit recommendations.
- Improvements in program performance.

II.B Types of Audit Services

II.B.1 Audits of Compliance, Risk, and Control

Government auditors have a strong interest in issues of compliance, risk, and control.

Audit Services Related to Governance, Risk Management, and Control[2]

Government auditors generally perform services related to governance, risk management, and control for the organizations and programs they audit.

- IIA Standard 2100 explicitly states that the internal audit activity must evaluate and contribute to the improvement of governance, risk management, and control processes. Other *Standards* expand on this requirement.
- Supplemental guidance to the 2011 version of GAGAS states that — during financial audits, attestation engagements, and performance audits — auditors communicate with those charged with governance. That guidance also recognizes that, in a government structure, it may not always be clearly relevant who is charged with key governance functions, so the organizational structures for achieving objectives are evaluated. GAGAS standards include requirements for evaluating controls, and the supplemental guidance refers to the COSO internal control model (discussed in domain I), which includes "risk assessment" as one of five interrelated components.
- The INTOSAI and the IAASB also have audit standards relating to the evaluation of internal controls. Both have documents that include reference to the COSO model of internal control.

II.B.2 Audits of Financial Statements[3]

GAGAS, INTOSAI, and the IAASB include standards related to financial audits, although the terminology and specific requirements differ somewhat among the three sets of standards. Specific requirements vary, but any government audit organizations are responsible for performing financial statement audits. This work in some instances is performed in part by contracted audit firms. Financial statement audits may be performed for entire entities (organizations) and/or components. The *Standards* does not explicitly incorporate financial statement audits; however, the results of internal audits performed under the *Standards* may be relevant and should be considered.

Purpose of financial statement audits. Whether performed under GAGAS, INTOSAI, or the IAASB, the primary purpose of financial statement audits is to provide an opinion about whether an entity's financial statements are presented fairly in all material respects in conformity with an applicable financial reporting framework (e.g., Generally Accepted Accounting Principles [GAAP] or another comprehensive basis of accounting). Financial statement audits also involve the auditor's consideration of both internal control over financial reporting and compliance with relevant laws, regulations, and/or other requirements.

Two key ideas in financial statement audits are 1) consideration of *material* line items and accounts in deciding the focus of the audit, and 2) limiting or minimizing *audit risk.* The general idea of a material misstatement is one that would affect the decisions of someone who

relied on the information. Auditors consider materiality from both a quantitative and qualitative perspective. Audit risks have three components — inherent risk, control risk, and detection risk. Consideration of audit risk affects how the audits are planned and performed.

Audit Statement Opinions

Financial statement auditors express one of four types of opinions on the audited financial statements:

1. Unqualified, or "clean," no *material* misstatements,
2. Qualified, fairly presented, *except for* identified items,
3. Adverse, the statements *do not fairly present,* or
4. Disclaimer, *no opinion expressed.*

It should be noted that, in a typical financial statement audit, auditors do not express opinions on either 1) the overall effectiveness of internal control over financial reporting, or 2) overall compliance with relevant laws, regulations, or other requirements. However, financial statement auditors can and often do identify, report, and make recommendations on 1) deficiencies in internal control that meet certain characteristics, and 2) instances of noncompliance that meet certain characteristics. Moreover, in some cases, auditors may be required to express such overall opinions; in that case, the engagement would likely be done under other standards, such as the attestation standards in GAGAS.

Internal Control in Financial Statement Audits

Financial auditors in the government consider internal controls over financial reporting in planning and performing financial statement audits. GAGAS (via incorporation of AICPA standards) and IAASB state the following:

> "The auditor must obtain a sufficient understanding of the entity and its environment, *including internal control,* to assess the risk of material misstatement of the financial statements whether due to error or fraud, and to design the nature, timing, and extent of further audit procedures."

ISSAI state that, in a regularity (financial) audit, study and evaluation are made mainly on controls that assist in safeguarding assets and resources, and assure the accuracy and completeness of accounting records. In the Introduction to its Financial Statement Guidelines, INTOSAI points out that public sector auditors who perform financial statements audits may be required to report on the effectiveness of internal control over financial reporting.

In assessing internal controls, financial statement auditors view the financial statements as a set of *assertions* (either explicit or implicit) by management who is responsible for preparation of the financial statements. The five assertions and examples of how they might apply are listed below:

1. Existence or occurrence assertions address whether available information addresses actual transactions, assets, and liabilities. Example: If the balance sheet shows $10 million of long-term assets, management is asserting that those assets actually exist.
2. Completeness assertions address whether all material financial information is included in financial statements. Example: If a multimillion dollar entity shows only $10 in liability on its balance sheet, management is asserting there are no other liabilities.
3. Rights and obligations assertions address whether the entity has material rights to the assets and obligations to the liabilities disclosed on the financial statements. Example: If the audited entity has $100 million in equipment on its balance sheet, management is asserting it has ownership rights to the equipment.
4. Valuation or allocation assertions address whether the financial statements show the correct amounts. Example: A long-term asset's value should be reduced by the amount of accumulated depreciation, and not be shown at the historical cost.
5. Presentation and disclosure assertions address whether elements of the financial statements are properly organized, classified, and disclosed. Example: All items required to be shown on the face of the statements should appear there, and not be buried in the notes.

In reviewing internal controls, financial statement auditors use the above set of five assertions in assessing whether management has not only fairly presented the line items and amounts, but also whether the relevant assertions are supported by the internal controls.

Financial statement auditors use the internal control framework developed by COSO, as criteria against which the auditor assesses control effectiveness. Reference to the COSO model is included in GAGAS, INTOSAI, and IAASB documents, and that model is discussed in domain I.

While typical financial statement audits do not include an over-all opinion on the effectiveness of internal control over financial reporting, financial statement auditors do typically report on weaknesses in internal control if the weaknesses meet certain criteria. In financial statement audits, reporting requirements on internal control over financial reporting varies depending on the audit standards being followed and other factors. For example, under GAGAS, financial statement auditors are to formally report internal control weaknesses in accordance with the definitions from the AICPA:

1. *Significant deficiencies.* Less severe than a material weakness, yet important enough to merit attention by those charged with governance.
2. *Material weakness.* A significant deficiency, or combination of significant deficiencies, that results in more than a remote likelihood that a material misstatement of the financial statements will not be prevented or detected.

Reporting requirements for internal control weaknesses in a financial statement audit under ISSAI are not always required to be labeled or defined as "significant weaknesses" and "material weaknesses," but generally the auditors would include the weaknesses that are considered to be significant or serious.

Consideration of Compliance in Financial Statement Audits

GAGAS, ISSAI, and IAASB all require financial statement auditors to consider compliance matters in planning and performing the audits, although specifics vary. For example, note the following excerpts:

- In addition to incorporating AICPA requirements, GAGAS states, "Auditors should design the audit to provide reasonable assurance of detecting misstatements resulting from violations of provisions of contracts or grant agreements that could have a direct and material effect on the determination of financial statements or other financial data significant to the audit objectives."
- ISSAI states that, in regularity (financial) audits, "tests should be made of applicable laws and regulations. The auditor should design audit steps and procedures to provide reasonable assurance of detecting errors, irregularities, and illegal acts that have a direct and material effect on the financial statements or results of regularity audits."
- IAASB International Standard on Auditing (ISA) 250 includes the following in the Introduction: "When designing and performing audit procedures, and in evaluating and reporting the results thereof, the auditor should recognize that noncompliance by the entity with laws and regulations may materially affect the financial statements."

Compliance Aspect of Financial Statement Audits

Financial statement audit reports are required to include compliance and related matters under GAGAS, ISSAI, and IAASB. For example:

- GAGAS Reporting Standards state auditors "should report…2) all instances of fraud or illegal acts unless inconsequential, and 3) violations of provisions of contracts or grant agreements and abuse that could have a material effect on the financial statements."
- INTOSAI's Reporting Standards state: "There is often a requirement to report as to the compliance with laws and regulations and to report on matters such as inadequate systems of control, illegal acts, and fraud. In some countries, constitutional or statutory obligations may require the SAI to report specifically on the execution of budget laws, reconciling budgetary estimates and authorization to the results set out in the financial statements."
- IAASB's ISA 250 states, in part: "The auditor should, as soon as possible, either communicate with those charged with governance, or obtain audit evidence that they are appropriately informed, regarding noncompliance that comes to the auditor's attention." However, the auditor is not required to communicate matters that are clearly inconsequential or trivial. "If in the auditor's judgment the compliance is believed

to be intentional and material, the auditor should communicate the finding without delay."

II.B.3 Audits of Performance/Value-for-Money/Operations[4]

Many government audit organizations are responsible for a large number of "performance audits." GAGAS and INTOSAI both refer to *performance audits* as a specific category of government audits. While the *Standards* does not refer to performance audits as a specific category, audit work performed under the *Standards* has conceptual similarities to "performance audits" as defined in GAGAS and INTOSAI, and those audits may be relevant. Various other terms used to refer to audits of performance include management audit, value-for-money audit, comprehensive audit, broad-scope audit, operational audit, economy and efficiency audit, and program audit.

Table II.1, Comparison of Performance Audits and Financial Audits, compares key aspects of performance audits with financial audits:[5]

Table II.1. Comparison of Performance Audits and Financial Audits

Aspects	Performance Audits	Financial Audits
Purpose	Assess whether government interventions or measureshave been conducted in accordance with the principles of economy, efficiency, and effectiveness.	Assess whether financial operations have been carried out in accordance with legislation and regulations and whether accounts and financial statements are true and fair, i.e., reliable.
Focus	Policy, programs, organization, activities, and management systems.	Financial transactions, accounting, financial statements, and key control procedures.
Academic Basis and Relevant Experience	Economics, political science, sociology, etc. Experience of professional investigations or evaluations and familiarity with methods applied in social science as well as other relevant methodologies/skills.	Accountancy and law. Professional audit skills.
Methods	Vary from audit to audit.	Standardized format.
Audit Criteria	More open to auditors' judgment. Unique criteria for the individual audit.	Less open to the auditors' judgment. Standardized criteria set by legislation and regulation for all audits.
Reports	Special report published on ad hoc basis. Varying structure and content, depending on objectives.	Annual opinion and/or report. More or less standardized.

Source: INTOSAI.

The nature of performance audits can be very broad or very narrow. GAGAS defines performance audits as those that "provide findings or conclusions based on an evaluation of sufficient, appropriate evidence against criteria." According to GAGAS, they "provide objective analysis to assist management and those with governance and oversight in using the information to improve program performance and operations, reduce costs, facilitate decision-making by parties with responsibility to oversee or initiate corrective, and contribute to public accountability." The word "program" refers to entities, organizations, programs, activities, and functions. GAGAS identifies the following types of performance audits:

- Program effectiveness and economy-efficiency, which may be interrelated.
- Internal control.
- Compliance.
- Prospective analysis.

INTOSAI defines "performance audits" as those concerned with economy, efficiency, and effectiveness.

Economy and efficiency audits include determining:

Economy. Is the entity acquiring the right inputs or resources (e.g., human resources, physical resources, information resources) in the proper amount, at the appropriate time, and at the best cost?

Efficiency. Is the entity getting the maximum quantity of output from related inputs? Efficiency can be described as:

- Unit cost, which is input divided by output.
- Productivity, which is output divided by input.
- The causes of inefficient or uneconomical use of information, personnel, or other resources.
- Whether the entity has complied with laws and regulations on matters related to economy and efficiency.

Economy and efficiency audits may consider whether the entity has:

- Followed sound procurement practices.
- Acquired the appropriate type, quality, and amount of resources at an appropriate cost.
- Properly protected and maintained its resources.
- Avoided duplication of effort by employees.
- Avoided work that serves little or no purpose.
- Avoided idleness and overstaffing.
- Used efficient operating procedures.
- Used the optimum amount of resources (staff, equipment, and facilities) in producing or delivering the appropriate quantity and quality of goods or services in a timely manner.
- Complied with requirements of laws and regulations that could significantly affect the acquisition, protection, and use of the entity's resources.
- Implemented an adequate management control system for measuring, reporting, and monitoring a program's economy and efficiency.
- Reported measures of economy and efficiency that are valid and reliable.

Program (or effectiveness) audits are designed to assess whether a program, activity, or function is achieving the desired results or benefits established by the legislature or other authorizing body. Program audits consider effectiveness issues such as:

- Whether the program is achieving its intended objectives and is making its intended impact on stakeholders.
- Whether the program is achieving output goals.
- Whether the organization has adequate systems for planning, managing, and monitoring to achieve its goals and objectives.
- Whether the program is being administered as directed by law.
- Whether the program duplicates, overlaps, or conflicts with another program.

Program (effectiveness) audits focus on analyzing the outcomes associated with programs, services, activities, and functions. The purposes of program audits are to:

- Assess whether the objectives of a new or ongoing program are proper, suitable, or relevant.
- Determine the extent to which a program achieves a desired level of program results.
- Assess the effectiveness of the program and/or of individual program components.
- Identify factors inhibiting satisfactory performance.
- Determine whether management has considered alternatives for carrying out the program that might yield desired results more effectively or at a lower cost.
- Determine whether the program complements, duplicates, overlaps, or conflicts with other related programs.
- Identify ways of making programs work better.
- Assess compliance with laws and regulations applicable to the program.
- Assess the adequacy of the management control system for measuring, reporting, and monitoring a program's effectiveness.
- Determine whether management has reported measures of program effectiveness that are valid and reliable.

It is important to note that although program audits are concerned with effectiveness or goal achievement issues, simply measuring effectiveness without considering the economy or efficiency of operations may give auditors a limited perspective on the performance of a program. In other words, auditors and stakeholders may wish to know not only whether a program is achieving its goals, but also whether it is achieving them in an efficient, cost-effective manner.

Consideration of Internal Control in Performance Audits

Under both GAGAS and ISSAI, performance auditors are required to assess the effectiveness of internal control in the context of the particular audit objective(s). For example, GAGAS states, in part, "For internal control

that is significant within the context of the audit objectives, auditors should assess whether internal control has been properly designed and implemented and should perform procedures designed to obtain sufficient, appropriate evidence to support their assessment about the effectiveness of those controls." ISSAI Field Standards state that, in performance audits, the study and evaluation of internal control should focus on controls that assist in conducting the business of the audited entity in an economic, efficient, and effective manner, ensuring adherence to management policies and producing timely and reliable financial and management information. Further, INTOSAI states that the extent of study and evaluation depends on the audit objectives and the degree of reliance intended.

Both GAGAS and ISSAI base internal control concepts on the COSO model, discussed in domain I of this manual.

Objectives of internal control include:

- ***Program operations.*** These are controls over operations that convert inputs to outputs. The effectiveness of these controls can indicate how well the program is achieving its objectives.
- ***Validity and reliability of data.*** These are controls over the information that management receives about the operation of its programs.
- ***Compliance with laws and regulations.*** These are controls over the way resources are used. Weak controls in this area suggest a high risk of illegal acts.
- ***Safeguarding of assets.*** These are controls over reducing waste, loss, and misuse of resources.

Testing controls involves interviews, observations, and inspections appropriate to the audit objectives. Auditors often design tests of specific controls based on information gained in previous audits. External auditors also can use the work of internal auditors to assess controls. Weak controls can direct auditors toward areas of unsatisfactory performance, whereas effective management controls will help ensure valid and reliable performance information. An assessment of controls can influence the following elements of the audit program:

- ***Objectives.*** Auditors may focus more attention on poorly controlled aspects of a program, which generally have higher risk of failure.
- ***Scope.*** Auditors may want to increase the extent of testing in reviewing poorly controlled areas.
- ***Methodology.*** Effective controls over collecting, summarizing, and reporting data may enable auditors to rely on management's reports or data without seeking corroborating evidence. On the other hand, if management controls are considered to be weak, auditors may incorporate additional procedures, such as obtaining data from outside the entity, or developing their own data collection methods.

Examples of internal control issues that can be identified as of concern include:

- Poor quality of the organization's control systems.
- Inadequate performance monitoring by high-level management.
- Poor ethical climate within the organization.
- Prolonged understaffing.
- Lack of competence and integrity of management and staff.
- Improper segregation of duties.
- Acceptance of audit findings and corrective action taken.
- Date and results of prior audits.

The following two approaches can be used to evaluate controls in performance audits:

Targeted approach *(also called narrow scope).* This approach is used when the audit objective is to target a specific control weakness that results in a performance deficiency. Auditors identify and test the relevant controls and recommend any necessary changes.

Comprehensive approach. This approach is used when the audit objective is to review how adequately the customer performs a function, service, or activity. The goal of the approach is to identify potential significant control weaknesses for further review. The general steps in the process are as follows:

- Document and evaluate work processes and controls.
- Select a sample of transactions and determine whether processes and controls are functioning as intended.

- If problems are found, select additional transactions for testing.
- Determine or estimate the extent of control weaknesses.
- Determine or estimate the effect of control weakness of program goals and objectives.

How do performance auditors report on internal control issues? Under GAGAS, auditors should include in the report 1) the scope of their work on internal control, and 2) any internal control deficiencies that are *significant* within the context of the audit objectives and based upon the audit work performed. If the deficiencies are not significant in the auditor's judgment, the deficiencies may be included in the report, or communicated in writing unless they are considered inconsequential. Under ISSAI, the required approach for reporting on internal control deficiencies in performance audits varies depending on the nature of the audit and the environment in which the performance audit is completed.

Consideration of Compliance in Performance Audits

As with financial statement audits, performance auditors have responsibilities under audit standards related to *compliance matters.* For example, under GAGAS, in planning a performance audit, the auditors should assess audit risk and significance by understanding — among other factors — the legal and regulatory requirements, contract provisions or contract agreements, and potential fraud or abuse that are significant within the context of the audit objectives. If relevant audit risks are identified, the auditor may need to perform further audit procedures or tests. Under ISSAI, in conducting a performance audit, "an assessment should be made of compliance with applicable laws and regulations when necessary to satisfy the audit objectives."

Compliance matters also may need to be included in the performance audit report. Under GAGAS, when auditors conclude, based on sufficient, appropriate evidence, that fraud, illegal acts, significant violations of provisions of contracts or grant agreements, or significant abuse has occurred or is likely to have occurred, they should report the matter as a finding. If the issues are not significant, the auditors may either include the issue in the report or communicate it in another manner. In some cases, auditors may consult with authorities or legal counsel. Under ISSAI, the report should include all significant instances of noncompliance that are pertinent to the audit objectives.

The Influence of Performance Measurement and Management on Performance Auditing

As discussed in domains III and IV of this manual, the public sectors in the United States and in many other countries have enacted legislation at all levels, and launched various initiatives intended to hold governments accountable by measuring and reporting on performance. This includes developing strategic plans, annual plans, annual performance reporting, and integrating performance management with the budget process (i.e., performance-based budgeting). Some observers see these laws and initiatives as an impetus to have performance auditors become more involved in performance measurement and management, and to develop or refine the audit tools and techniques, especially regarding *effectiveness* audits.

One particular approach to assessing program effectiveness is *evaluation.* This technique is sometimes viewed as a separate discipline, and sometimes viewed as a part or performance auditing, where the focus is on effectiveness. Domain III of his manual expands on the evaluation approach.

There are two broad concepts in conducting performance audits:

1. The *process-based approach* is where the audit determines whether process controls exist and are sufficient to provide reasonable assurance that the desired performance will be achieved. The process-based approach typically uses a narrower range of methodologies than the measurement-based approach (see below). Common methodologies used in the process-based approach include internal control questionnaires or comparisons to typical control systems similar to the one being audited. Auditors identify typical control systems either through research, benchmarking of best practices, reviewing information about similar operations, or applying the fundamental principles of any effective control system.

2. The *measurement-based approach* is where the audit includes methodology for measuring performance either because the audited entity is not measuring its own performance or because its performance measurement efforts are or may be incomplete or unreliable. The measurement-based approach can employ a wide variety of quantitative or qualitative methodologies.

Measuring performance means determining what performance is being achieved. The results of performance measurement activities are then compared to measurement criteria in order to reach conclusions about the economy, efficiency, or effectiveness of the area being audited. Auditors either develop performance measurement criteria or use measurement criteria developed by management. Measurement criteria are considered relevant when they relate directly to the mission, goals, and objectives of the customer. Some possible examples of measurement criteria that could be used in performance audits include:

- Legal or contractual requirements for specific performance (e.g., efficiency standards, quality standards, or goals for outcomes to be achieved by a program).
- Benchmark performance by comparable public or private sector operations.
- Management's established performance objectives.
- Ad hoc criteria asserted by the auditors, such as comparisons to performance for a prior period or comparison of performance among branch offices or similar organizational divisions.

Performance auditors may make observations and review available records, reports, and other documentation to determine whether the customer is meeting relevant measurement criteria. However, if sufficient and relevant performance data does not exist, performance auditors may find it necessary to develop relevant performance measurement data through data collection or other quantitative or qualitative methods. It may be difficult to find relevant criteria in those cases where criteria have not been established by management or policy makers, and must be asserted by the auditors. In such cases, the auditors will find it necessary to obtain concurrence (either from customer management or from the policy makers) for their asserted criteria, or they must find sufficient support for the credibility of their criteria. The credibility of asserted criteria is critical to the success of the rest of the finding and, thus, the audit itself. In the absence of management acceptance of asserted criteria, examples of external sources of credibility include:

- Research.
- Customer input.
- Logical comparisons to similar operations.

Benefits of Performance Audits

Performance auditors provide information to government policymakers in the following ways:

- Providing information for use in the decision-making process.
- Developing conclusions about the economy, efficiency, and effectiveness of government programs and making recommendations for improvement.
- Developing questions for use at legislative hearings.
- Developing methods and approaches to evaluate a new or proposed program.
- Forecasting potential program results.
- Performing investigative work.

Compliance Aspect of Broader Audits[6]

The various sets of audit standards followed by government auditors incorporate requirements to assess compliance matters in broader categories of audits. For example, as stated above, both financial and performance audits include compliance considerations. However, in some government audit organizations, compliance audit is considered a category or subcategory of its own.

The purpose of compliance audits is to test the organization's conformity with some objective standard or criteria, such as one of the following:

- Laws and regulations.
- Contract requirements.
- Grant requirements.
- Organizational policies and procedures.

Some attributes that contribute to an effective compliance system are:

- Requirements are documented and operating procedures are aligned with the requirements to ensure compliance.
- Staff and management are aware of applicable requirements.
- The organization has assigned adequate responsibility for such matters as monitoring organizational goals and objectives, operating functions, and regulatory requirements.
- The organization has a policy regarding acceptable operating practices and codes of conduct.
- Job incumbents are qualified for their positions.

II.B.4 Audits of Financial Systems[7]

Internal controls are the framework that management establishes to ensure that it meets its responsibilities in a variety of areas. Audits of internal accounting controls are designed to determine whether management has in place a good system of accounting and financial reporting that provides required information in a timely manner. The objectives of accounting controls are that all transactions should be authorized, accounted for accurately and completely, and in the correct time frame. All accounting controls are techniques to achieve one of the above objectives.

Internal control questionnaires (ICQs) are used to catalog specific controls in use in a process. Auditors use ICQs to document areas to be covered during the engagement and to indicate control deficiencies. An ICQ for a particular audit area is typically filled out at the beginning of the audit. Any potential deficiencies or weaknesses noted in the questionnaires indicate areas that should be focused on during fieldwork testing. Questions on ICQs are usually written to allow for Yes/No responses, which allows auditors to readily identify exceptions. However, auditors should not rely solely on the absence of a prescribed control (indicated by a "No" on the ICQ) as evidence to support a deficiency finding. Auditors should use the ICQ as a familiarization tool in the early stages of planning the audit, and follow up on exceptions to determine whether the missing control is significant, if its absence is bolstered by compensating controls, or if the identified control is unnecessary or uneconomical in the specific environment.

Methodology

The general methodology for auditing internal accounting controls is as follows:

Identify the functions within the area being audited. Categorize the functions into common groupings or *control cycles*. Commonly used control cycles include:

- ***Revenue cycle.*** Transactions involving the inflow of resources (e.g., tax collections, receivables, or customer receipts).
- ***Expenditure cycle.*** Transactions involving the outflow of resources (e.g., purchases or payroll).
- ***Treasury cycle.*** Resources held (e.g., investments or asset management).
- ***Reporting cycle.*** Accounting data (e.g., preparation of grantor reports).
  - Flowchart the processes and identify controls or control weaknesses based on the flowchart.
  - Perform a walk-through of the process.
  - Perform tests designed to determine the extent to which control weaknesses have allowed the risk (e.g., loss, inaccurate recording) to occur.

An effective internal control system includes a sound control environment, a properly designed and maintained accounting system, and adequate policies and procedures to ensure data integrity and safeguarding of assets.

Control Environment

General questions auditors need to answer when auditing an organization's control environment include:

- Does management provide a favorable control environment in the organization?
- Is management knowledgeable about internal controls?
- Is management committed to establishing and maintaining controls?
- Does management communicate its support for controls throughout the organization?
- Does management continually identify and assess potential risks?
- Does management establish and maintain effective policies and procedures related to control?

- Has management established adequate communication channels within the organization to ensure that the appropriate parties receive key information at the correct time?
- Has management established a system to monitor the effectiveness of the organization's control policies and procedures?
- Has management established a system to resolve potential problems identified by the control system?

Accounting System

Elements of a good internal accounting control system include the following:

- Transactions should be properly authorized. Only specified individuals should have the authority to initiate or change certain transactions. Policies should also require written advance approval for certain transactions.
- Accounting records should be properly designed. For example, the accounting system should be designed to collect useful information, group or classify information in a useful way, and allow for the proper posting or modification of entries.
- There should be adequate safeguards over assets and records. Controls over assets do not protect against losses arising from inefficiency or from poor operating decisions. Instead, controls over assets help prevent or detect other material losses that could result from unauthorized acquisition, use, or disposition of assets. Understanding controls over assets can help auditors assess the risk that financial statements could be materially misstated. For example, an understanding of a customer's control over asset safeguards can help auditors recognize risk factors such as:
    - Failure to adequately monitor decentralized operations.
    - Lack of control over activities, such as lack of documentation for major transactions.
    - Lack of control over access to information system applications that initiate or control the movement of assets.
    - Failure to develop or communicate adequate control activities for security of data or assets, such as allowing unauthorized personnel to have unrestricted access to data or assets.
    - Failure to investigate significant discrepancies found when reconciling control account and subsidiary records.

Safeguards Over Assets and Records

The following are questions auditors may ask when testing controls of safeguards over assets and records:

- Is access allowed only to those individuals who need it as part of their job description?
- Does adequate physical security exist over assets and records? Are storerooms locked? Are equipment and inventories properly recorded? Are there adequate environmental controls over assets (e.g., appropriate temperature)?
- Is confidential or sensitive information kept separate from other records?
- Are there adequate access controls over information systems?
- Does the organization take a regular inventory of assets and compare the results to accounting records?
- Is information available to allow management to continuously monitor the effectiveness of controls over safeguarding of assets and to detect violations of those controls?
- Are incompatible duties properly segregated or separated? For example, one employee should not be responsible for controlling all steps in a cycle, such as receiving cash, depositing receipts, and reconciling bank accounts to accounting records.
- Are accounting systems adequately monitored for accuracy? Accounts should be reconciled to source documents periodically. Edit checks should be used to monitor the accuracy of data entered into the system.
- Are receivables and payables regularly confirmed with customers?
- Are financial statements prepared in a timely manner and in accordance with the relevant comprehensive basis of accounting (e.g., GAAP)?

Attestation and Assurance Engagements[8]

Government auditors are sometimes required to perform 1) attestation engagements in accordance with GAGAS, or 2) assurance engagements in accordance with standards issued by the IAASB. Attestation and assurance engagements are briefly described below. Further explanation is not within the scope of this manual because these engagements are less frequently performed than other engagements.

Under GAGAS, attestation engagements can cover a broad range of financial or nonfinancial objectives and may provide different levels of assurance about the subject matter or assertion, depending on the user's needs. The three types of attestation are:

1. Examination (an opinion on all material respects).
2. Review (essentially negative assurance, i.e., nothing came to the auditor's attention).
3. Agreed-upon procedures (specific procedures on a subject matter).

Examples of subjects of attestation engagements include an entity's internal control over financial reporting, and the accuracy and reliability of performance measures.

Auditors/practitioners performing attestation engagements in accordance with GAGAS should comply with the AICPA's general attestation standard on criteria, the fieldwork and reporting standards, and the corresponding statements of attestation standards (SSAEs), which are incorporated in GAGAS by reference. In addition to the AICPA standards, GAGAS includes additional standards, depending on which of the three types of attestation is being performed.

Under IAASB standards, assurance engagements apply to other than audits or reviews of historical financial statements. The IAASB identifies two categories of assurance:

1. *Reasonable assurance* (a positive form of expression of the practitioner's conclusion).
2. *Limited assurance* (a negative form of assurance).

Evaluations[9]

Evaluations are a specialized type of engagement that may be performed by audit organizations or other offices in the government. The focus of evaluations is generally on whether government programs are *effective*, that is they achieve the intended results. Government auditors are sometimes tasked with audit objectives where the primary focus is on effectiveness. In such engagements, the audit approach can benefit from application of methodologies, tools, and techniques from the evaluation discipline.

In regard to evaluation engagements, GAGAS does not incorporate other standards by reference. However, it does note that auditors may use or be required to use other professional standards, such as:

- Guiding Principles for Evaluators, American Evaluation Association.
- The Program Evaluation Standards, Joint Committee on Standards for Education Evaluation.
- Standards for Educational and Psychological Testing, American Psychological Association.

Due to a significantly increased interest in program effectiveness in recent years, some government audit organizations have chosen to establish separate evaluation units and/or to train some auditors to use evaluation tools. Audits that focus heavily on program effectiveness are sometimes referred to as impact-based audits. Further, limited discussion of evaluation approaches and methodologies are included in domain III of this manual. However, it should be noted that evaluation is a comprehensive topic on its own and is not fully addressed in this manual.

II.B.5 Audits of Information and Related Technology[10]

Like many other professionals, government auditors cannot escape the impact of changing technology. The auditor's involvement takes many forms. In many (if not most) audits, the auditor needs to have some understanding of the impact of IT on internal control. Many audit organizations have specialists to advise the general audit staff in the evaluation of internal control in IT systems. In addition, government auditors may be required to perform a wide range of audits related to various aspects of the entity's acquisition, development, and use of hardware and software. Last, audit organizations may elect to us the computer as a tool to assist in completing the audit work.

While IT is a specialized area, auditors need to continue to gain a basic understanding of the impact and value of IT as audits are performed. Obviously, changing

technology and its impact is complex and far-reaching, and this manual cannot fully address these issues. However, the material presented below is intended to provide an overview of key aspects for the consideration of government auditors.

An Overview of IT's Impact

Organizations depend on computerized information systems to meet organizational objectives and to process, maintain, and report essential information. Auditors need to evaluate the reliability of computerized information that supports financial statements (and performance and other reports) or is used to analyze programs or outcomes. Additionally, auditors may need to evaluate information system controls to help reduce the potential for fraud, errors, security breaches, and disasters that cause a loss or modification of data or that render a system unavailable.

When evaluating whether an organization understands its information needs, auditors should obtain an overview of each computer application that is significant to the financial statements and other reports, or to achieving the mission and objectives. Information that an auditor should be interested in includes:

- Narrative summary of the operating environment and types of computer processing performed (stand-alone, distributed, networked, etc.).
- Overview of the computing environment (hardware, software, configurations, etc.).
- Detailed listing of hardware and software comprising the computer configuration, including:
    - The type, number, and location of central processing units.
    - The role of microcomputers and networks.
- Listing of applications, including a description of the general purpose, impact on the financial statements and other reports, and importance to organizational objectives.
- Listing of significant communication networks.
- Organizational chart.
- Disaster contingency plan.
- Computer security policies.
- Strategic plans for IT.

This information should be reviewed and supplemented with interview information obtained from key staff members. Key personnel should have detailed understanding of the IT infrastructure and how it supports the organization. A progressive organization that relies heavily on information systems should have a detailed disaster contingency plan (DCP). A detailed and thorough DCP outlines the organization's critical applications and provides specific information regarding the impact of technology on the organization. A review of the DCP can give the auditor insight into the degree of management's understanding of its reliance on information systems.

Information is selected, collected, classified, reported, and stored in a variety of ways. An understanding of the elements of information and process integrity can provide the auditor with the foundation to determine the adequacy of controls. Table II.2, Elements of Information and Process Integrity, illustrates this.

Table II.2. Elements of Information and Process Integrity

Element	Definition
Authorized	An element of information, from a transaction to an entire system, is appropriately entered, developed, changed, or used with proper authority.
Accurate	The information and associated processes are correct and may be used as intended.
Complete	No required information is missing. Conversely, information is not duplicated. Rejected transactions are identified, controlled, and reentered as appropriate.
Timely	The work (e.g., transactions, processes) is promptly processed and customer service levels are maintained.
Recorded, Processed, and Reported in the Proper Time Period	Appropriate period and other cutoff dates are followed.
Secure	The information and processes are protected from unauthorized access, update, disclosure, or destruction.

Each of the elements in Table II.2 has a relationship to the selection, collection, classification, reporting, and storage of information.

Selection. With the increased processing power and significant decrease in the cost of storage, the selection of information has become a secondary issue. The emergence of data mining illustrates this point as organizations retain as much information as possible and then analyze it to identify unique relationships between data elements. The computing and storage power presently available provides cost-effective opportunities to obtain, retain, and process huge volumes of data.

Collection. The method of data collection can have an impact on the cost and reliability of information. The integrity of information often depends on the effectiveness of input controls.

Classification. The method of classifying data helps to control risks associated with alteration and disclosure. Data classification schemes can vary from simple to extremely complex. Although a classification should be organizational specific, the following examples of information classes illustrate a reasonable classification approach:

- *Public information* is available to everyone inside and outside the organization (e.g., information on a website).
- *Unclassified information* is generally available to internal staff (e.g., benefit information, organizational policies).
- *Classified information* is only available on a need-to-know basis based on job duties (e.g., payroll lists, audit workpapers [audit documentation], accounting data).
- *Confidential information* is only available to select individuals who have a specific need for the information (e.g., medical records, personnel records).

Some organizations have information protection policies that place the burden of information protection on managers in individual organizational units. An information protection policy may include the following:

- Statements that define information as an asset that must be protected to different degrees based on its sensitivity, criticality, and value, regardless of the media on which it is stored, the manual or automated systems that process it, or the methods by which it is distributed.
- Statements outlining the responsibilities of information owners, custodians, and users.
- Definitions of the organization's data classification categories.
- Provisions stating that each business unit should develop an information protection program to implement these policies.

Access Controls

A sound data classification scheme sets the foundation for the effective implementation of access controls to ensure that data is adequately protected. The elements of a sound data classification scheme are as follows:

- *Reporting.* Reporting methods are needed to control the dissemination of information. There are risks associated with reporting inaccurate information. For example, inaccurate information could corrupt the integrity of database applications, spreadsheets, and external reports.
- *Storing.* An appropriate storage method is needed to securely store information on computer systems and backup media to prevent unauthorized disclosure. The storage controls on the computer system are generally controlled by access control software and should generally correspond to the classification system discussed earlier. Additionally, backup copies of information for recovery purposes must be adequately protected to prevent disclosure.

General Access Controls

General controls set the foundation for effective control over computerized information system assets. General controls apply to the entire computer operation, including:

- *Administration controls* include the procedures necessary to ensure that resources are used efficiently and in accordance with management's intentions. They encompass the overall operation of the computer facility. Administration controls also include functions that maximize organizational efficiency and

productivity. Organizational efficiency can be directed through long-range planning efforts and effective personnel policies. Productivity in the computer facility is enhanced by adherence to standards. Control techniques for administration include:
- o Segregating duties to prevent the performance of incompatible functions.
- o Providing training and direction.
- o Ensuring that information system managers and end-user managers participate in long-range planning.

- *Controls over computer operations* are vital to overall data processing effectiveness. Computer operation's management must ensure that processing meets specifications by requiring the logging of all actions initiated by computer operators and actions performed by computer software. Control techniques for computer operations include:
  - o Maintaining records of operator actions, system actions, and operating problems.
  - o Establishing procedures for restart and recovery.
  - o Controlling and monitoring system changes.
  - o Controlling job schedules and magnetic tape/cartridge usage.
  - o Using available error correction techniques.

- *Security controls* reduce or prevent disruption of service, loss of assets, and unauthorized access to equipment. An effective physical security program is necessary to protect the system and data. Control techniques for security include:
  - o Establishing control over access to and within the facility.
  - o Developing an adequate equipment-servicing program.
  - o Ensuring that there are adequate backup power sources, alarms, and prevention equipment.
  - o Implementing a written and tested disaster contingency plan.

- *Security administration* is responsible for security over the computer facility, including all aspects of physical and data security. Control techniques for security administration include:
  - o Ensuring that the computer security administration function is independent of computer operations.
  - o Providing reports and performing reviews of attempted security violations.
  - o Ensuring that users and employees are counseled on security considerations.

- *System programmers* control the operation of the computer system and are responsible for the efficient use of computer resources. Systems programming must develop a method of evaluating the performance of computer hardware and software. Criteria for measuring performance must be formalized and deviations from the performance criteria must be corrected. Control techniques for systems programming include:
  - o Implementing standards, policies, and procedures for administering the systems programming function.
  - o Implementing standards, policies, and procedures for measuring system performance.
  - o Implementing procedures for testing and approving system software changes.

- *Telecommunication systems* control the transmission of messages between users and the computer. Through the telecommunication network, users at remote sites can access data and applications at the computer facility. The majority of devices interface with the computer facility by a telecommunication device. Control over the telecommunication network is necessary to ensure that only authorized users have access to the computer facilities. Telecommunication network controls should encompass the network's operating performance and security. Control techniques for telecommunication include:
  - o Implementing procedures for testing and approving telecommunication software changes.
  - o Securing dialup lines for access to computer resources.
  - o Analyzing response time, detecting problems, and documenting problem resolutions.
  - o Selecting available security options built into the telecommunications software (i.e., data encryption).

- *Systems software* consists of computer programs and related routines that control computer processing. The operating system is the prime component of system software because it controls the execution of user application programs. System software products can be tailored to meet user needs. System tailoring is accomplished by setting optional system parameters and, therefore, has an impact on system performance and security. Control techniques for systems software include:

- Setting appropriate system parameters and security options for operating systems.
- Controlling procurement and maintenance of software licenses.
- Using the security features of security software effectively.

Application Access Controls

Application controls apply to a specific application or system, such as payroll. Application controls are specific to the flow of transactions for a system and are designed to ensure accurate, authorized, and complete processing of transactions (e.g., input, processing, output). Application controls are designed to prevent, detect, and correct errors and irregularities as transactions flow through the application. Unlike general controls that apply to the entire computer operation, application controls for each application must be reviewed individually. Application controls are classified into the following categories:

- ***Input controls*** are concerned with the accuracy and completeness of data entered into an application. Two common input controls are edit and transaction logs. Edit controls are programmed routines that check the validity and accuracy of input. With real-time systems (i.e., where information is input directly into the system without the benefit of a hard copy source document) becoming increasingly prevalent, edit routines are critical to maintaining the integrity of data. Examples of edit controls include:
    - Field tests that ensure that only numeric data are entered into numeric fields and only alphabetic data are entered alphabetic fields.
    - Validity tests that check against an existing table to ensure that a match exists (e.g., an employee number or product code number).
    - Reasonableness tests to reject any data of an abnormal amount (e.g., a check for a weekly salary over $10,000).
    - Completeness tests ensure that all required fields contain data (e.g., name, address, phone number, and Social Security number may be required fields in an employee record).
    - Check digit tests are computed using a formula to calculate an amount or digit. When data are entered into the field, the digit is recalculated and compared to the original value. If the digit differs from the original value, then an apparent error in input has occurred.
    - Transaction logs are computerized records of input activities that become an audit trail to verify the accuracy and timing of input activities. Transaction logs maintain the history of input activities and are used to recreate transactions and determine when and who entered a transaction.

- ***Processing controls*** are concerned with the proper processing of data entered into an application. Processing controls include:
    - Header and trailer label information to help ensure that the proper data was processed.
    - Record counts that compare input record counts to output records to ensure that all records were processed.
    - Echo checks are the sending of automated verification messages between computer systems to verify the receipt of data.

- ***Output controls*** are concerned with the verification and proper distribution of computer output. Output controls include:
    - Ensuring that output is only distributed to authorized parties (this includes hard copy and electronic distributions).
    - Verifying the accuracy of output through manual or automated reconciliation activities.

Systems Development Processes

Controls over systems development help ensure system reliability, quality, predictability, and user satisfaction. The acceptance of a structured systems development methodology helps ensure that system designers meet the requirements of system users. A structured approach includes the use of standards for systems design, documentation, testing, and post-implementation review. It

also ensures that new and enhanced computer systems meet organizational requirements. Control techniques for application systems development include:

- Appropriate standards, policies, and procedures to control systems and programming functions.
- Standards to ensure that system development activities are properly authorized, tested, reviewed, documented, implemented, and approved.
- Active user and management participation in defining, developing, testing, and reviewing systems and programming activities.

A systems development methodology should include standards on:

- Feasibility studies and cost benefits analysis.
- Approval process for initiating system development and implementation of systems developed.
- Change control procedures for new system developments and modifications to existing systems to ensure that only authorized changes are moved to production.
- Appropriate documentation required for each phase of the development life cycle, including the development of systems, operations, and user manuals.
- User training.
- Software and hardware specifications.
- General and detail design specifications.
- Testing requirements, including requirements for user and programmer testing.
- Project reviews, including periodic milestone reviews and post-implementation reviews.
- Contracting procedures that include the requirements for describing expected project deliverables, such as system components and source codes, project time frames, estimated hours, and the maximum allowable expense for each phase.

An audit of systems development activities may include a review of the:

- Adequacy of systems development standards and methodology.
- Method to update and distribute the methodology.
- Adequacy and use of project management tools and techniques.
- Adherence to the methodology for systems development projects.
- Formal approval process for new and modified application systems.
- Adequacy of system, operations, program, and user documentation.
- Testing requirements for new systems and major modifications to existing systems.
- Post-implementation review activities.
- Controls associated with placing authorized programs into production.
- Adequacy of the quality assurance function.

Useful IT References for Auditors

Standards related to information technology are not as well-developed or universally accepted as standards in some other audit areas. The lack of generally accepted information systems standards has prompted many organizations to develop their own standards. However, there have been efforts to develop uniform standards for processing and audit activities. The following are three examples of information systems audit and assurance standards that may be helpful to auditors.

Federal Information System Control Audit Manual (FISCAM), U.S. GAO, and Federal OIG's[11]

The *Federal Information System Controls Audit Manual* is issued by the U.S. Government Accountability Office (GAO). It is not an audit standard but provides detailed audit guidance for assessing controls information systems. FISCAM is applied by GAO, the U.S. Federal Offices of Inspectors General (OIG) community, and other government auditors, primarily in support of financial statement audits. FISCAM is available for use by other government auditors. (See GAO-09-232G, Feb. 2, 2009 or latest version at www.gao.gov.)

The purposes of the FISCAM are to:

- Inform financial auditors about computer-related controls and related audit issues so that they can better plan their work and integrate the work of information systems (IS) auditors with other aspects of the financial audit.

- Provide guidance to IS auditors on the scope of issues that generally should be considered in any review of computer-related controls over the integrity, confidentiality, and availability of computerized data associated with federal agency systems.

The FISCAM describes a three-step general methodology to use in assessing computer-related controls:

- Evaluate general controls at the entity or installation level.
- Evaluate general controls as they are applied to the application(s) being examined, such as a payroll system or a loan accounting system.
- Evaluate application controls, which are the controls over input, processing, and output of data associated with individual applications.

The manual also describes the major steps in assessing information systems in financial statement audits:

Planning phase. During the planning phase, the auditor gains an understanding of the entity's computer-related operations and controls and related risks. If the controls are not likely to be effective, the auditor should obtain a sufficient understanding of related controls risks:

- ***Internal control phase.*** During the internal control phase, auditors obtain detailed information on control policies, procedures, and objectives and perform tests of control activities. The objectives of these tests are to determine whether controls are operating effectively.
- ***Testing phase.*** The testing phase focuses primarily on substantive tests. These tests generally involve examining source documents that support transactions to determine whether they were recorded, processed, and reported properly and completely. An IS auditor may assist financial auditors in identifying and selecting computer-processed transactions for testing, possibly using computer audit software.
- ***Reporting phase.*** During the reporting phase, the financial auditor draws conclusions and reports on the financial statements, management's assertions about internal controls, and compliance with laws and regulations.

IT Standards, Guidelines, and Tools and Techniques for Audit and Assurance and Control Professionals, ISACA[12]

GAGAS identifies these ISACA references as one of other professional standards that auditors may use or be required to use in conjunction with GAGAS. ISACA got its start in 1967 by a small group of individuals with similar jobs who believed there was a need for a centralized source of information and guidance in the field. Over the years, the organization that emerged evolved through several name changes. Previously known as the Information Systems Audit and Control Association, ISACA now goes by the acronym to reflect the broad range of IT governance professionals it serves. (See www.isaca.org for more information.)

One well-known framework issued by ISACA is the Control Objectives for Information and related Technology (COBIT). COBIT was initially released in 1996 and has been updated several times, with Version 5.0 scheduled for release in 2012. The ISACA website describes COBIT as a "globally accepted IT governance framework," which is intended to "minimize IT-related risks and maximize the benefits of...the only framework that comprehensively addresses the complete life cycle of IT-related investments and services." The COBIT framework includes four high-level domains: 1) planning and organization, 2) acquisition and implementation, 3) delivery and support, and 4) monitoring and evaluation.

In addition to the COBIT framework, ISACA issues an extensive amount of guidance, which is beyond the scope of this manual. However, readers of this manual should be aware of the following ISACA issuances:

- Information Technology (IT) Audit and Assurance Standards.
- Standards for Information System (IS) Control Professionals, and the IT Assurance Framework.

The components of the IT Audit and Assurance Standards are as follows:

- The standards themselves, which are mandatory.
- Guidelines, which provide guidance on how to comply with the standards.
- Tools and techniques, which do not set requirements but provide additional information.

IASACA's Standards for IS Control Professionals also has the same three levels as the IT Audit and Assurance Standards.

The IIA's Global Technology Audit Guide (GTAG)[13]

Another useful source of guidance for government auditors in the area of the impact of technology are the collective body of knowledge in The IIA's GTAGs and the Guide to the Assessment of IT Risk (GAIT).

A listing of relevant GTAG titles as of early 2012 is presented below:

1. Information technology controls
2. Change and patch management controls: critical organization success
3. Continuous auditing: implications for assurance, monitoring and risk assessment
4. Managing of IT auditing
5. Managing and auditing privacy risks
6. Managing and auditing IT vulnerabilities
7. Information technology outsourcing
8. Auditing applications controls
9. Identity and access management
10. Business community management
11. Developing the IT audit plan
12. Auditing IT projects
13. Fraud prevention and detection in an automated world
14. Auditing user-developed acquisitions
15. Information security governance

The IIA's GAIT includes four parts — the methodology, general control deficiency assessment, business and IT risk, and case studies.

In conclusion, the impact of technology is an area where specialized knowledge and experience is of great value. Auditors should be alert to the potential need for specialized assistance. The additional references above are not intended to be all-inclusive and additional guidance is frequently issued form the above and other sources. Thus, auditors should stay abreast of the latest available guidance.

II.B. 6 Consulting/Assistance Services

Government auditors can assist management by providing information about a wide assortment of topics such as proposed projects, new systems, strategic planning, or even staffing. Auditors may be asked to advice on such matters of system design or re-design, or various problem-solving matters. These services can be of significant assistance to management in assessing and improving an organization's governance, risk management, and internal control. It should be noted that, in general, these services will usually not be the primary types of services provided, but can still be of great value to management. In providing such services, government auditors need to assure that their independence is not unduly impaired, and audit standards address this concern.

II.B.7 Integrity Services[14]

The term *integrity services* is used in this manual to refer to the auditor's role in addressing issues of fraud, waste, abuse, and related issues. The audit standards followed by government auditors include requirements and guidance in determining the auditor's roles and responsibilities. For example:

- The IIA's IPPF and *Standards* address auditors' consideration of fraud and illegal acts. For example, under the Attribute Standard, Due Professional Care, Implementation Standard 1210.A2 states the following: "Internal auditors must have sufficient knowledge to evaluate the risk of fraud and the manner in which it is managed by the organization, *but are not expected to have the expertise of a person whose primary responsibility in detecting and investigating fraud*" (italics added). Another example is Performance Standard 2060 which states that the chief audit executive must report to senior management and the Board on "...significant risk exposures and controls, including fraud risks..." The IIA has also issued a Practice Guide titled Internal Auditing and Fraud.
- GAGAS includes requirements for auditors to consider fraud, noncompliance with provisions of laws, regulations, contracts, and grant agreements, and abuse in performing financial and performance audits, and attestation engagements. For financial audits and attestation engagements, GAGAS incorporates AICPA

requirements concerning fraud, and also adds fieldwork and reporting requirements. For performance audits, GAGAS includes fieldwork and reporting requirements. GAGAS defines abuse as involving deficient or improper actions when compared with behavior that a prudent person would consider reasonable and necessary; because determinations regarding abuse are subject, auditors are not required to detect abuse, but should be alert to the possibility. GAGAS's supplemental guidance further addresses these issues; for example, providing examples of significant deficiencies in internal control, fraud indicators and abuse, and guidance for assessing noncompliance issues. Note: GAGAS recognizes that it may be appropriate for auditors to work with investigators or legal authorities.

INTOSAI's ISSAI includes the following requirements:

- In regularity (financial) audit, tests should be made of compliance with applicable laws and regulations.
- In performance audits, tests should be made of applicable laws and regulations *when necessary to satisfy audit objectives.*

ISSAI also requires the audit reports to include, as appropriate, information on compliance and fraud.

IAASB's International Standard on Auditing (ISA) 240 addresses "The Auditor's Responsibility to Consider Fraud in an Audit of Financial Statements."

Table II.3. Differences Between Internal Audits and Fraud Investigations

Characteristic	Internal Audit	Fraud Investigations
Time.	Based on risk.	Based on allegation or suspicion.
Objective.	Opinion on governance, risk management, controls.	Information for judicial or quasi-judicial proceedings.
Scope.	Broad management issues.	Specific concern with wrongdoing.
Level of evidence.	Audit.	Legal.
Typical relationship.	Cordial.	May be adversarial.
Assumption.	Probable propriety.	Possible impropriety.

Source: Treasury Board of Canada.

General Discussion of Auditor's Role in Integrity

Table II.3, Differences Between Internal Audits and Fraud Investigations, shows the ways in which fraud investigations differ from other internal audit work. Auditors play a key role in responding to integrity violations, which include fraud, waste, abuse, irregularities, illegal acts, and acts of noncompliance. The possibility of integrity violations should be considered when planning audits and developing audit tasks so there is reasonable assurance of detection. However, because determining abuse involves considerable subjectivity (see definition below), auditors are not generally required to provide reasonable assurance of detecting abuse. The significance of an integrity violation relates to how an act affects the organization financially or in terms of negative public perception.

Additional audit tasks may be performed when auditors become aware of the possibility or likelihood that a specific and significant integrity violation occurred.

Integrity violations can have an effect on an organization's performance and reports of performance, as well as on the financial statements. Specific categories of integrity violations include:

- Illegal acts are violations of laws and regulations.
- Fraud is a type of illegal act that involves obtaining something of value through willful misrepresentation.
- Noncompliance includes illegal acts, as well as violations of provisions of contract or grant agreements.
- Abuse is distinct from illegal acts and noncompliance. Abuse occurs when conduct falls short of societal expectations for prudent behavior. Because

determining abuse is subjective, auditors are not expected to provide reasonable assurance of detecting it.

- Irregularities are intentional misstatements or omissions of amounts or disclosures in financial statements.
- Waste is the uneconomical or inefficient use of resources.

If specific integrity violations are suspected or detected, auditors may find it necessary to seek guidance from legal counsel, investigative staff, or law enforcement officials to:

- Identify applicable laws and regulations.
- Design specific tests of compliance with applicable laws and regulations.
- Assist with areas of the audit or investigation requiring special expertise.
- Evaluate the results of the audit or investigation.

In some cases, auditors may be required by law, regulation, or policy to report indications of certain types of integrity violations to law enforcement or investigative authorities. Auditors also may be required to temporarily suspend work on the audit or withdraw from the audit completely to avoid interfering with the work of law enforcement officials. Auditors and other investigators should coordinate their reporting to ensure that the audit report does not compromise legal proceedings.

Auditors should focus on obtaining sufficient, competent, and relevant evidence related to possible integrity violations. Before reporting to management, auditors should attempt to determine the extent of management's knowledge of or involvement in the violation (i.e., collusion). It is especially important to follow proper techniques for obtaining, documenting, and securing information related to an investigation.

Areas where auditors can assist in fraud prevention activities include:

- Reviewing the adequacy of the organization's integrity violations policy.
- Reviewing the organization's ethics policy or written code of conduct.
- Confirming that related policies include specific references to prohibited activities and that the policies are properly distributed and effectively communicated to all employees (employees should be required to confirm their understanding of their responsibilities in writing annually).
- Encouraging whistle-blowing and integrity violations hotlines.
- Performing tests to identify likely fraudulent activities.

Auditors can assist management by reviewing the program to promote internal and external whistle-blowing activities. The auditor may determine:

- Whether a mechanism exists for employees to notify management of inappropriate activities without the fear of retribution (e.g., an independent ethics officer).
- Whether a mechanism exists for external organizations or individuals to notify management or auditors of inappropriate activities (e.g., integrity violations hotline).

A written policy should describe specific responsibilities of management, staff, and auditors in preventing, detecting, and reporting integrity violations. The integrity violations policy should be developed based on input from the CEO and the heads of the following departments: fiscal, information processing, legal, and security. Integrity violations policies should do the following:

- ***State management's position against integrity violations.*** The organization should make it clear that integrity violations will not be tolerated and that perpetrators will be prosecuted.
- ***Make all employees responsible for reporting integrity violations.*** This will help alleviate any fear employees may have about retaliatory actions against whistleblowers.
- ***Establish reporting channels.*** The policy should specify how employees should report integrity violations (e.g., direct notification of legal counsel).
- ***Describe the investigation process.*** The policy should describe how due process will be served, including the specific rights of accused employees.
- ***Establish consistent penalties.*** The policy should specify what types of action will result in reprimand, termination, or other consequences.

Nonaudit Services[16]

Auditors often have exposure to a broad range of organizational systems and functions. For this reason, stakeholders may call upon auditors to assist them in a variety of ways. Some of the assistance services auditors may be called on to perform include:

Consulting. Auditors can assist management by providing relevant information about a wide assortment of topics such as proposed projects, new systems, strategic planning, or staffing. Auditors are useful sources of information in these areas because of their broad knowledge of the organization and technical expertise. Auditors also are asked to provide advisory assistance during program and system design or redesign. Auditors' understanding of management and internal transaction controls can be useful in ensuring that appropriate controls are included during the design phase. Organizational problem-solving teams often request participation by auditors because they are trained in methods of evaluating problems and possible solutions. Auditors also are frequently requested to comment on development or revision of policies, procedures, or organizational plans.

The audit standards followed by government auditors address the auditor's role in nonaudit work in differing ways. For example:

- The ISPPIA defines internal audit as including both assurance and *consulting* work.
- In contrast, GAGAS addresses nonaudit work in the context of the impact on the auditor's independence.
- ISSAI recognizes that some work performed does not qualify by strict definition as "audits," but do contribute to "better government."

The IIA's *Standards* glossary defines consulting services as advisory and related client service activities, the nature and scope of which are agreed upon with the client and which are intended to add value and improve an organization's governance, risk management, and control processes without the internal auditor assuming management responsibility. Examples include counsel, advice, facilitation, and training.

Regarding independence, Implementation Standard 1130.C2 states the following:

> "If internal auditors have potential impairments to independence to independence or objectivity relating to proposed consulting services, disclosures must be made to the engagement client prior to accepting the engagement."

Under GAGAS, if nonaudit services are performed, GAGAS includes extensive discussion about concerns of auditor independence. GAGAS notes that providing services may create threats to an auditor's independence. GAGAS points out that, if providing nonaudit services results in assuming "management responsibility," the threats would be so significant that that no safeguard could reduce them to an acceptable level. GAGAS includes examples of activities that are considered "management responsibility" and would therefore impair independence. On the other hand, GAGAS notes that certain "routine activities" (e.g., providing certain forms of advice) are not considered nonaudit services and would generally not impair independence. Readers are encouraged to carefully review the relevant discussion (13 pages) under the General Standard of Independence in GAGAS.

ISSAI provides the following examples of nonaudit work:

- Gathering data without providing substantial analysis.
- Legal work.
- An information mission of the elected Assembly as regards the examination of draft budgets.
- An assistance mission for members of the elected Assembly as regards investigations and consultations of SAI's files.
- Administrative activities.
- Computer processing functions.

ISSAI states that nonaudit work must follow appropriate standards and be of high quality.

Control self-assessment. To ensure that internal controls exist and are operating properly, organizations should conduct a self-assessment of the control system. This process places responsibility on the organization and individuals in charge of key areas to develop procedures to adequately control their functions. Control self-assessments help identify internal control weaknesses and solutions. Auditors can assist in this process by providing direct assistance or specific information related to such

areas as establishing and monitoring effective internal controls, risk assessments, and sampling.

Training. Because of their training and experience, auditors are often asked to provide training to staff and management on subjects such as management control theory and techniques, performance measurement, and other management principles.

II.C Processes for Delivery of Audit Services

II.C.1 Management of Individual Projects

Staff must be properly guided and supervised throughout the audit process. Supervision is the process by which the objectives of quality control and individual responsibility are balanced. Goals of supervision are to:

- Provide sufficient direction to staff.
- Provide sufficient oversight of work to provide reasonable assurance that the work meets quality standards.
- Keep staff motivated by giving them a level of responsibility commensurate with their experience and performance.

Some important elements of supervision include:

- Instructing staff members.
- Developing staff performance expectations.
- Planning audit work.
- Reviewing work performed.
- Providing effective on-the-job training.
- Providing informal feedback to staff regarding work issues.
- Conducting regular performance appraisals of staff.

Managers are responsible for ensuring that staff understand the following:

- What is expected of them (e.g., scope of work, specific details).
- Why their work is important (e.g., how it relates to the goals of a particular task, project, or entire organization).

Project management involves the considerations and activities audit managers undertake when conducting an audit. A project is defined as an endeavor in which resources are organized to undertake a unique scope of work, of a given specification, within the constraints of cost and time, so as to achieve a change defined by quantitative and qualitative objectives. The distinguishing features of a project are:

- It has a beginning and an end.
- It is defined by a specific objective.
- It is characterized by phases or milestones (e.g., needs analysis/feasibility assessment of options, project plan, project implementation, completion/post-project evaluation).

The major considerations in project management can be modified to fit specific projects, but generally include the following:

Clarify understanding about the audit mandate. Some types of government audits are performed on a regular cycle and require little clarification (e.g., mandated financial audits). However, some types of audits (e.g., performance audits) that are requested by a governing body (e.g., Congress, state legislatures, city councils) may require additional explanation. Assigned audit managers and staff may find it useful to meet with sponsors of specially requested audits to obtain additional background information about potential audit issues and concerns.

Develop budgets. Managers should develop budgets for time and dollars. Variables to consider when preparing budgets include:

- Goals of the project.
- Availability of data.
- Cooperation level of customer management.
- Experience level of assigned staff.
- Projected travel (e.g., whether customer information is centralized or decentralized).
- Staff constraints (e.g., vacations, holidays).
- Time schedules/phase milestones.

Assign staff to the project. The manager's goal is to select appropriate staff for the job. This involves determining the number of staff needed and the collective mix of qualifications and skills that assigned staff should possess.

The manager should also determine and communicate the appropriate reporting relationships for assigned staff during the project.

Develop and assign specific tasks. Tasks should be assigned to maximize staff productivity. The manager should consider the skills, abilities, and goals of individual staff members when assigning specific tasks. When possible, assignments should be made in writing, such as in a formal audit program.

- ***Monitor progress.*** The manager is responsible for ensuring that the audit does not exceed its budgets and meets its objectives. Therefore, the manager should monitor the work being performed to identify problems or opportunities as they arise.
- ***Develop a written report.*** The written report should describe the objectives, scope, and methodology, of the audit. The report should also be complete, concise, and unbiased. The various sets of audit standards offer additional comments on the form and quality of audit reports.
- ***Assess project success and lessons learned.*** Project completion should be marked to provide closure to participants.

II.C.2 Planning

As discussed in domain I, the audit standards followed by government audit organizations include requirements to carefully plan individual engagements.

Planning is important to help ensure the efficient use of audit resources and the fulfillment of audit objectives. Auditors should understand the area to be audited, including regulations, goals, operations, efforts, outputs, and outcomes. Specifically, the role of laws, regulations, rules, and ordinances should be considered in the planning process. While audit planning is described as the first phase of the audit process, planning activities should be performed continuously throughout the entire audit.

The major areas to consider in the audit planning process include:

- Identify what is to be audited.
- Collect and analyze background information on the area to be audited.
- Assess risk and vulnerability.
- Establish audit objectives, scope, and methodology.
- Develop specific issues and questions for the audit.
- Develop audit criteria (criteria should be reasonable, attainable, and relevant).
- Design data collection and measurement procedures.
- Determine resources available and needed to conduct audit.
- Communicate with management about the audit.
- Establish an audit timeline and a completion date.
- Develop a written audit program that incorporates the above information.
- Assign specific tasks to audit staff.
- Determine staff independence.
- Determine the need for external assistance or outsourcing.
- Estimate travel costs and other expenses.

The following sections discuss some of the major aspects of the planning process in greater detail.

Collect and analyze background information on the area to be audited. Generally, auditors should obtain background information before determining and finalizing the audit objectives. An exception to this guideline is when the audit objective is known at the start of the audit. The following is a list of background items auditors should review to determine their impact on audit objectives:

The purpose and goals for a specific program or the entire organization: Purpose is defined as the result or effect that is intended or desired. The purpose of a program may be implicitly or explicitly stated in laws and regulations. On the other hand, management is responsible for defining a program's goals, which are defined as the level of desired performance. Auditors may use the purpose and goals as criteria for assessing program performance.

- The relevant history of the program or entire organization.
- Organizational data (e.g., organizational charts, job descriptions, policy and procedure manuals, information system manuals).
- Financial data (e.g., budgets, management reports).
- Results of prior audits and their workpapers.
- Applicable laws, rules, and regulations: Specific items usually set forth in laws and regulations include:

- o What the program is supposed to do.
- o Who is supposed to do it.
- o What population is to be served.
- o How much can be spent on what.
- o Work of external audits in process.
- o Correspondence files to determine potential significant audit issues.
- o Authoritative technical literature related to the audit activity.

Auditors can use background information to define and modify the scope of the audit. An assessment of background information may result in the need to modify projected audit completion dates, the level or type of testing, or staffing plans.

Auditors may decide to conduct a survey to become familiar with the activities, risks, and controls associated with an audit area. A survey is a process for gathering information — without detailed verification — on the activity being examined. The main purposes are to assist with the following goals and tasks:

- Understand significant audit issues.
- Identify significant areas warranting special emphasis.
- Obtain information for use in performing the audit.
- Determine whether further auditing is necessary.
- Define audit objectives, audit procedures, and special approaches such as computer-assisted audit techniques.
- Identify potential critical control points, control deficiencies, or excessive controls.
- Identify important aspects of program operations: Program operations are the strategies, processes, and activities the customer uses to convert efforts into outputs.
- Identify inputs or efforts (e.g., the amount of resources such as money, material, and personnel) that are put into a program.
- Identify output measures: Outputs are the quantity of goods and services provided. Examples of output measures are tons of solid waste processed, number of students graduated, and number of students graduated who have met a specified standard of achievement.
- Identify outcome measures: Outcomes are accomplishments or results that occur (at least partially) because of services provided. Outcomes may be intentional or unintentional, immediate (e.g., number of graduates placed in jobs) or ultimate (e.g., whether program graduates are more likely to remain employed than similar persons who are not in the program).
- Develop preliminary estimates of time and resource requirements.

A survey may involve:

- Discussions with the customer.
- Interviews of users of the activity's outputs.
- Onsite observations.
- Review of management reports and studies.
- Analytical auditing procedures.
- Flowcharting.
- Document key control activities.

Auditors performing government audits need to have an understanding of applicable laws, regulations, and relevant judicial interpretations. Additionally, government auditors need to understand the process of establishing laws, regulations, rules, and ordinances to fulfill the entity's responsibilities. The process of establishing laws, regulations, rules, and ordinances is complex and varies depending upon the unit of government.

A competent review of compliance with laws and regulations must encompass all aspects of law, including the overall legislative process, regulations and rules, and judicial interpretations. The appendix to domain IV of this manual presents one example of an overall legislative process. Government auditors need to be aware of the overall process, as opposed to only the narrower view of being aware of the current law alone.

Define audit objectives. Audit objectives broadly define the intended accomplishments of the audit. More specifically, audit objectives are questions that need to be answered during the audit. Auditors define audit objectives based on information gained either from knowledge they already have or from inquiries and observations. Auditors should use risk assessments to identify audit objectives. Risk is defined as the probability that an event or action may adversely affect the activity under audit.

The following is a list of principles for formulating well-stated audit objectives:

- Phrase objectives either as precisely worded questions or as items to determine (e.g., "To determine whether…").
- Eliminate ambiguous, abstract, or unfocused terms.
- Clearly identify the customer.
- Clearly identify the type of performance to be audited and separate objectives if more than one element of performance is to be reviewed.
- Identify the specific elements of finding needed to meet the objective.
- Frame objectives that consider a realistic scope and methodology.
- Review the audit objectives with management or others requesting the audit.
- Answer the audit objectives in the report.

Carefully crafted audit objectives are important for the following reasons:

- Objectives provide direction.
- Limit collection of unneeded information.
- Control scope, methodology, timing, and nature of the audit work.
- Increase probability that questions will be answered.
- Determine how audit findings should be formulated.

Define audit scope. The scope defines the boundaries of the audit by addressing such items as the audit period or number of locations to be reviewed. Some important considerations when defining the scope of an audit include:

- Type of audit (financial, compliance, performance, etc.).
- Program or management objectives (e.g., the audit may be limited to a specific program within an organization).
- Needs of the potential users of the audit report.
- Time period to be audited.
- Specific audit requirements.
- Type and extent of problems found in prior years' audit reports.
- Preliminary judgment about materiality levels.
- Availability of staff and other resources.
- Statutory mandates.
- Risks identified (inherent and control risks); also called level of risks and extent of vulnerability to the risk/strength of control activities.

The following is a list of elements that should be documented in the audit scope:

- Time period to be covered by audit tests.
- Description of the audit universe.
- Time allotted to conduct audit.
    - Staff time.
    - Reporting deadline.
- Available data.
    - Number of records.
    - Locations.
    - Need to create data.
    - Form.
    - Reliability.
- Site selection rationale.
- Sample size rationale.
- Customer officials, customers/requesters for audit results.
- Expert advice.
- Scope limitations encountered or anticipated.

Determine resources needed to conduct the audit. Some considerations for determining required audit resources include:

- The time frame for the release of the audit.
- The audit objectives and scope.
- The number of audit staff needed to meet the audit objectives based on resource or time constraints.
- The experience level (e.g., knowledge and skills) needed by assigned staff.
- Training needed by audit staff to meet the audit objectives.
- Contractual assistance needed to meet the audit objectives.

Communicate with management about the audit. Customer management often has a negative perception of the audit process; therefore, communication throughout the audit process is essential to alleviate some of the concerns of management. Some basic steps to communicate with the customer include:

Formal notification of the audit. The typical first step in the process is to formally notify the audited organization in writing. The notification letter may include information that describes:

- The assigned audit manager.
- The entity to be audited.
- The audit period.
- The type of audit.
- The preliminary audit scope and objectives.
- The assigned staff.
- A request for a formal entrance conference.

Entrance conference. The entrance conference may be the auditor's first face-to-face contact with the officials of the audited entity. The objectives of the entrance conference are to:

- Explain audit processes.
- Explain preliminary audit scope and objectives.
- Establish mutually agreeable working relationships.
- Present projected audit milestone dates and completion dates.
- Introduce assigned audit staff.
- Identify key contacts and desired communication protocols.
- Obtain an overview of the program or activity being audited, including a description of recent changes in management or major systems.
- Solicit and address any customer questions or concerns.
- Discuss auditor space requirements.
- Give the customer an initial written request for information and data.
- Take a tour of facilities.
- Discuss any types of data or information that the customer may consider sensitive or confidential.
- Request management to identify programs or activities most susceptible to fraud.

The information obtained from meetings with management of the audited entity should be recorded in writing, distributed to appropriate individuals, and retained in audit documentation.

Determine appropriate audit methods and strategies. Proper planning allows audit management to make decisions about the future conduct of the audit. Audit management must determine which methodology is appropriate for which audit objective and customer conditions. For example, audit management must decide whether to sample (judgment or statistical) or use the entire universe, and which specific quantitative and qualitative methodologies will provide sufficient, competent, and relevant evidence to answer the questions posed in the audit objectives.

Develop an audit program with appropriate procedures and tasks to achieve audit objectives. The form and content of the written audit program will vary depending on the size and complexity of the area audited. However, examples of information that may be included in an audit program include:

- Background information about the audit area.
- Procedures for collecting, analyzing, interpreting, and documenting information during the audit.
- Audit objectives and requirements.
- Audit scope and degree of testing required to achieve the audit objectives.
- Technical issues, risks, processes, and transactions to be considered or examined.
- Discussion of relevant legal issues.
- Specific tasks assigned to staff.
- Timeline for completing the various audit phases and the final report.

The audit program should be updated as necessary to reflect any significant changes made during the audit.

II.C.3 Risk and Control Assessment Practices

Risk assessment allows organizations to identify potential effects and their significance. Management should continually monitor and assess potential risks that could keep the organization from achieving its goals in the following key areas:

- *Effectiveness.* Whether the organization is meeting its objectives.
- *Efficiency.* Whether the organization is making optimal use of its resources in achieving its objectives.
- *Compliance.* Whether the organization is meeting laws and regulations or not exceeding appropriated budgets.

- ***Safeguarding of assets.*** Whether the organization is protecting its assets against integrity violations.
- ***Reliability of financial reporting.***
- ***Reliability of operational information.***

Generally, risks become more difficult to manage the longer they remain undetected. Therefore, early detection of potential internal and external risks will give management more opportunity to take required preventative or corrective actions.

The questions addressed in assessing risk are:

- How likely is it to go wrong?
- What will happen if it goes wrong (e.g., assets lost, clients not served, noncompliance with law, etc.)?

Risk assessment can be used in individual audits to prioritize the use of audit resources. The process involves:

List potential audit subjects. An audit subject can be an entity, program, function, or activity. Auditors may identify audit subject by organizing the organization's operations, activities, and processes into major categories such as:

- Function (e.g., purchasing, disbursement, inventory, or payroll).
- Location.

Identify relevant risk factors. Risk factors are the criteria used to identify the *relative significance* of conditions and/or events that could adversely affect the organization or audit unit. For example: the relative pervasiveness or complexity of a specific activity might cause it to have a larger impact on the audit unit as a whole compared to other activities. The number of risk factors used should be sufficient to provide confidence that the risk assessment is comprehensive. Risk factors may include:

- Changes in the external operating environment (e.g., new laws or regulations, increased public scrutiny).
- Pressure on management and staff to meet difficult or ambiguous objectives.
- Size of unit.
- Complexity of activities, laws, or regulations.
- Degree that operations are decentralized.
- Presence of cash receipts or cash-like payments (e.g., food stamps or electronic benefit transaction [EBT] cards).
- Rapid growth.
- New programs and services.
- Recent changes in operational, technological, or accounting systems.
- Reliance on obsolete technology.
- Recent changes in key personnel.
- Numerous changes of staff in high-level or sensitive positions.
- Functions controlled by one person.
- Potential for public embarrassment of the organization (loss of public trust).
- Impact from failure to accomplish objectives.
- Amount of funding (expenditures or budget).

Assess the relative significance of the risk. The head of the audit unit may obtain information from the following sources to assess the significance of risk factors:

- Various members of management.
- Audit unit staff.
- External auditors.
- Applicable laws and regulations.
- Financial and operating data.
- Prior audits.

Auditors must use professional judgment to determine the impact a risk factor may have on the use of audit resources. Generally, higher risk areas are assigned higher audit priorities. However, changing conditions can affect the significance of risk factors and require that the results of the risk assessment be updated.

Assess the likelihood that a given risk will occur. The organization will generally want to focus on implementing corrective and preventative actions in areas that have the highest significance along with the highest likelihood of occurrence.

Auditors should obtain sufficient knowledge about how the organization's management addresses risks. Management may choose from three broad alternative courses of action to address a specific risk:

- ***Control the risk.*** Risk can be controlled by various preventative measures, such as adding personnel to

a function, installing burglar alarms, increasing the frequency and level of management review, or implementing tighter standards.
- *Transfer the risk.* Risk can be transferred by purchasing insurance policies to cover losses of several types, such as cash, property, or facilities.
- *Accept the risk.* It is actually quite difficult to control or transfer all risk associated with an area of operation. Therefore, organizations often must decide how much loss they are willing to accept. For example, an organization might decide that the risk of fire is high so it will pay a high premium on its fire insurance policy to transfer as much risk as possible; however, the organization will still have to pay the deductible amount on the policy if a fire occurs.

The organization's control environment influences the level of risk. The control environment sets the tone of an organization and influences the control consciousness of its employees. An unfavorable control environment increases the risk of fraud, abuse, or illegal acts. The characteristics of an effective control environment include:

- Management communicates the importance of internal controls to all employees.
- Employees have clearly defined responsibilities.
- Employees are held accountable for their performance.
- A system is in place to monitor controls on a regular basis.

The following factors influence the state of an organization's control environment:

- Organizational history of control weaknesses or violations.
- Whether management emphasizes and values competence, integrity, and ethical behavior.
- Whether the organization has a strong code of conduct.
- Whether the organization has a strong ethics policy.
- Whether the code of conduct and ethics policy are communicated to employees and enforced by management soundly and consistently.
- An inconsistent or unfair employee performance evaluation, compensation, and promotion system.

The controls that follow are categorized based on when they occur in the control process:

- *Preventative controls* are designed to deter undesirable events from occurring.
- *Detective controls* are designed to identify and correct undesirable events that have occurred.
- *Corrective controls* help bring performance back into compliance, or address problems that have been identified — such as the employee grievance system, employee performance appraisals, or an administrative appeals process.

Control activities are policies and procedures used by the organization to address identified risks. Some examples of control activities include:

- Internal accounting controls (e.g., segregation of duties, monitoring, reconciliation).
- Management controls (e.g., the plan, methods, and procedures adopted by management to ensure its goals are met, including systems for measuring, reporting, and monitoring program performance).
- Physical controls (e.g., security).
- IT controls (e.g., access security controls, data center operation controls).

There is no universal formula or mix of control activities that can be applied to all organizations. Rather, each organization should design the type and degree of control activities it needs to mitigate its own specific identified risks.

The internal and external environments of all organizations are subject to constant change. Therefore, it is necessary for organizations to monitor and reevaluate the effectiveness of their control systems. Examples of ongoing monitoring functions include:

- Management's review of performance reports and comparing them to budgets and other benchmarks.
- Feedback obtained from external parties (e.g., complaints from stakeholders).
- Direct supervision and review of work by functional-level managers.
- Internal and external audits.
- Physical inventories of assets.

II.C.4 Performing the Engagement

The purpose of performing the engagement is to gather audit evidence for use in supporting the facts, conclusions, and findings that will be contained in the audit report. The categories below describe evidence in a *legal* sense, and may be particularly important if issues of fraud or illegal acts are being evaluated:

- ***Primary or direct evidence*** supports a finding with the greatest degree of certainty. This type of evidence provides direct proof of a fact without requiring additional inference or presumption. For example, a signed contract is generally considered direct evidence of the terms of a contract. However, if the authenticity of the signatures is questionable, auditors should reexamine the evidence or obtain additional supporting evidence.
- ***Secondary evidence*** provides less certainty than direct evidence. This type of evidence generally requires the use of additional evidence to develop and support conclusions. Examples of secondary evidence include information obtained from interviews and internally prepared documents. The way secondary evidence is used and the importance of the finding determine whether such evidence is considered primary or secondary.
- ***Corroborative evidence*** is additional evidence in support of primary or secondary evidence. Therefore, this type of evidence provides indirect support for a conclusion. Corroborative evidence does not have power to support a finding or conclusion by itself.

Auditors also classify evidence in the following ways:

- ***Documentary evidence*** includes internally or externally prepared documents such as letters, contracts, records, external reports, bank statements, and invoices. Auditors should exercise a healthy degree of professional skepticism when reviewing internally generated information. It is always possible that the evidence may have been manipulated or altered. If there is any doubt about the validity of evidence, corroborative evidence (e.g., through independent tests of the data) should be obtained.
- ***Analytical evidence*** is compiled from other types of evidence. It includes calculations, comparisons, and interpretations made by the auditor. If the customer prepared the analysis, it is considered documentary evidence.
- ***Testimonial evidence*** is information obtained from individuals through oral or written statements such as interviews, surveys, and questionnaires. Important interview information should be corroborated by examining records and performing tests.
- ***Physical evidence*** is obtained through auditors' direct inspection or observation of people, property, or events. Physical evidence may be in the form of memos summarizing items or events observed, photographs, drawings, charts, maps, or physical samples. Findings and conclusions based on physical evidence require a substantial number of unbiased observations using a predetermined sample design and plan. Inspection and observation may be used for:
    - Documenting work flows, processes, and control.
    - Counting inventory or estimating transaction volumes.
    - Testing compliance with statutes, rules, policies, and procedures.

Each of the above four categories of evidence has strengths and weaknesses, so the auditor should determine whether collaborative forms of evidence are needed.

Auditors should base findings and conclusions on solid evidence. The evidence should be retained in the audit documentation (workpapers). The following adjectives are used in audit standards to define the qualities of audit evidence:

- The *Standards* states that evidence should be *sufficient, reliable, relevant,* and *useful.*
- GAGAS states that evidence should be *sufficient* (a quantity characteristic) and *appropriate* (a quality characteristic).
- ISSAI states that evidence should be *competent, relevant, and reasonable.*
- IAASB states that the evidence should be *sufficient* and *appropriate.*

Sufficiency refers to whether there is enough evidence (e.g., different sources, large sample, statistical support, number of examples) to justify a finding. Individual items of evidence that, when standing alone, would be insufficient may be combined to be sufficient to support conclusions.

Relevancy is the determination that evidence has a logical relationship to its intended use, such as in the audit findings. The relevancy of evidence should be considered in the context of the specific audit, issue, and finding.

Appropriateness encompasses the relevance, validity, and reliability of evidence.

Reasonableness and usefulness are terms that necessitate auditor judgment.

Audit documentation (workpapers) needs to be prepared, organized, and summarized in sufficient detail and with sufficient care to enable the work to be reviewed, judged, and understood by persons independent of the audit. Workpapers:

- Assist the audit manager in monitoring and controlling audits.
- Assist auditors in conducting their work.
- Provide evidence to support audit findings and conclusions.
- Provide evidence to show how work was planned and performed.
- Provide evidence that audit work was performed in compliance with standards.
- Identify who performed and reviewed the work.
- Provide information for audit evaluations, including internal quality assurance reviews and external peer reviews.

Laws and regulations for some audit entities require that workpapers become open to public inspection after the audit report is issued. In these cases, it is important that all confidential information (e.g., Social Security numbers) be removed from the workpapers before they are made public.

The *traditional* elements in an audit finding are listed below:

- *Condition* is the situation or practices found during the review. The condition can be summarized as "what is." The statement of condition should be accurate, clear, and precise, in addition to being supported by sufficient, competent, and relevant evidence. The finding statement also may indicate whether the condition is isolated or widespread.
- *Criteria* is defined as "what should be." Noting a difference between the condition and criteria is the first step in developing an audit finding. Criteria should be based on authoritative sources such as laws, rules, or policy guidelines. When auditors rely on their professional judgment as criteria, they are obligated to convince the report reader that the criteria are valid.
- *Cause* is the reason why things went wrong (or right). Identifying the cause is important in making constructive recommendations. It is also important to identify the primary or root cause of the deficiency (or improvement), instead of merely identifying contributing causes or symptoms.
- *Effect* demonstrates the importance or significance of the deficiency. Measures of effect are frequently stated in quantitative terms such as dollars, time, or number of transactions. Effects also can describe how a program or operation has resulted in changes in actual physical, social, or economic conditions. If past effects cannot be identified, potential effects may be presented.

Recommendations are not an element of a finding, but are part of the report if problems are found. Recommendations are suggestions to improve significant problems. Recommendations are most constructive when they are specific, feasible, action oriented, and cost effective.

> **Note:** GAGAS, IIA *Standards*, and INTOSAI all make reference to the elements above. While the above four elements are traditional, GAGAS states that the number of elements required for completeness is dependent on the audit objective.

II.C.5 Communicating Results

Obtaining feedback from management throughout the audit is encouraged to ensure that appropriate information is being obtained and to alleviate problems at the conclusion of the audit. Some specific components of continual communication to consider include:

- Keep management of the audited organization informed of audit issues and concerns as they arise.
- Submit a draft audit report to ensure that accurate and appropriate information has been reported.
- Advise management of the audited organization of projected audit timelines and any delays.

An exit conference should be held with the customer to eliminate any factual errors in the audit report, to add clarity to findings and recommendations, and to obtain customer responses. Specific objectives of an exit conference include:

- Provide the management of the audited organization (management) with findings and recommendations identified during the audit.
- Allow management to state concerns and objections to the findings and recommendations.
- Give the management and the audit team the opportunity to identify and correct any errors or misinterpretations that may appear in the draft report.
- Provide the audit team with the formal opportunity to explain the remaining steps in the audit process the final report is released.

The format and content of audit reports will vary by organization and type of audit. Therefore, the following elements should be included in audit reports as appropriate:

Audit reports should state the audit objectives, scope, and methodology. If appropriate, the report should describe any performance aspects examined (e.g., outputs, outcomes). The audit scope should describe, as necessary:

- Organizations audited.
- Geographic locations of customers.
- Period covered.
- Audit standards followed.
- Management controls assessed.
- Criteria used.
- The question(s) they attempt to answer.
- Assumptions made.
- Sampling plans used.
- The kinds and sources of evidence used.
- The depth and coverage of work performed to accomplish the audit objectives, including a description of specific controls tested.
- As applicable, the relationship between the universe and what was audited.
- Significant scope impairments or data limitations.
- Confidential information omitted from the report.

Audit reports may include background information about the customer and the programs or functions reviewed. The report also may include information about the status of prior findings and recommendations.

Audit reports should include findings, conclusions, and recommendations for corrective actions, as well as the audited organization's response to those recommendations. Recommendations are most constructive when they:

- Are directed toward resolving the cause of the problems.
- Are action-oriented and address specific organizational objectives.
- Are addressed to parties that have the authority to take corrective action.

Audits reports should include all significant integrity violations. In some cases, illegal acts should be reported directly to responsible external parties. Insignificant noncompliance should be communicated to the audited organization, preferably in a management letter that is documented in the workpapers and mentioned in the report.

Audit reports should include a description of significant noteworthy accomplishments and issues that need further work. If significant issues warrant further work but are not directly related to the audit objectives or there is not enough time or resources, auditors should refer the issues to those responsible for planning future audits.

Subject to any legal restrictions, written audit reports should be distributed to those responsible for acting on the findings, legislators, and other interested legal officials. Also, unless restricted by law or regulation, copies of audit reports should be made available for public inspection.

II.C.6 Monitoring Results

Auditors should monitor the results from previous audit findings and recommendations to ensure that the audited organization has taken corrective action or consciously accepted the risk of not implementing corrective measures. The corrective action taken should be timely, appropriate, and sufficient enough to achieve desired objectives.

Auditors should determine that implemented actions have corrected the underlying causes and conditions of deficiencies, not just the symptoms of the problem.

The level of appropriate follow-up on prior findings is determined by:

- The amount of risk and exposure involved if corrective actions fail to correct the problem.
- The amount of time management has had to correct the problem.
- The complexity of management's corrective action plan.
- The amount and quality of interim feedback the auditor has received from the audited entity regarding the status of correcting the finding since the prior audit.

DOMAIN III
Government Auditing Skills and Techniques

This section addresses common methods, tools, and techniques used by government auditors. Methods selected for each audit depend on the type of audit being conducted, the objectives selected to direct the audit (sometimes known as "questions to be answered"), and the evidence needed to support findings, conclusions, and recommendations. Tools and techniques used by government auditors vary because the nature of auditing is interdisciplinary. Sources of methods, tools, and techniques are derived from various academic disciplines — including accounting, general business, public administration — and various specialty areas — including IT, statistics, human resources, and engineering.

Methods, tools, and techniques covered in this section include management concepts and techniques, performance measurement within the context of management and auditing, research and data collection techniques, quantitative methods, including methods for applying "total quality management" tools to auditing, qualitative methods, program evaluation, and methods for identifying and investigating integrity violations. Finally, we provide an overview of analytical and conceptual skills needed to apply the methods, tools, and techniques previously described.

While other methods, tools, and techniques could be included in this section, these are some of the most common. For more in-depth background on methods, tools, and techniques, government auditors are encouraged to review methodologies found in management and auditing publications from a wide variety of sources, including professional associations, academic institutions, and research organizations. Furthermore, individual audit offices, especially national audit offices or very large offices, have developed methodology manuals and audit programs associated with various types of audits and objectives. These can usually be accessed through websites or direct contact with those offices.

III.A Management Concepts and Techniques

Governmental auditors should be familiar with basic managerial principles and practices to understand how organizations function and how decisions are made.

Organizational Theory and Techniques

The two broad classifications of management styles are *autocratic management* and *participative management.* Autocratic managers make decisions themselves and issue orders to subordinates without seeking their input and without regard to their feelings. Participative managers use a more democratic approach to leadership. Practitioners of participative management seek out and incorporate input from subordinates when making decisions. Workers under a participative system also may help set goals and design new systems or procedures. There is generally a favorable response to participative management among workers and managers, but the process can be time-consuming. There are environments, such as military, law enforcement, or public safety organizations, in which autocratic decision-making is appropriate.

Auditors should be aware of basic variations within each of these styles. For example, both participative and autocratic managers can vary in how exacting they are in directing the details of subordinates' work. Managers who pay great attention to detail ("micro managers") can hinder the creativity of staff, while those who pay little attention to detail can make an operation susceptible to errors. Either extreme could lead to inefficient or ineffective operations. The best approach is often situational. For example, in a research lab it is often best to allow scientists to decide on the details of their own experiments. But a hospital may need to standardize many of its processes down to very specific details that employees must follow.

Strategic planning in government is the process of making decisions about how to achieve an entity's mandates and goals and determining the resources required to accomplish those goals. In the United States, appointed officials (such as agency heads) are most frequently responsible for developing the entity's strategic plans, although staff working in key functional areas and the internal audit department should be consulted with during the process. In some U.S. governments, elected officials participate at the start to determine a "vision" or broad long-range goals and later may approve a strategic plan submitted by management to achieve those goals. In a parliamentary system, the elected officials appointed as ministers over a specific governmental function will set the policy and direct the strategic planning process.

Often, a core planning team of managers or staff representing different parts of an organization is formed at the start. Then there are four major steps in the strategic planning process:

- *Step 1.* Develop one or more general statements that address what the entity aims to achieve, in the form of mission, goals, and objectives. Organizations use a variety of processes to develop or reassess their mission, goals, and objectives. Some common elements of these processes are:
  - Review of the current baseline of performance and legislative mandates.
  - Environmental assessment, including analysis of customers, stakeholders, competitors, and issues and trends.
  - Evaluation of organizational strengths, weaknesses, external opportunities, and threats (SWOT).
  - Scenario planning.
  - Identification and prioritization of critical performance gaps.
- *Step 2.* Develop specific plans, a method for achieving those plans, and resource allocations. The plans should contain measurable objectives and implementation or achievement time frames.
- *Step 3.* Communicate the plan to affected staff. Consider sharing early drafts of the plan with staff to obtain their input and to ensure their support of the plan. Members of a planning team may solicit feedback from their parts of the organization at various points in the process, both to get insights from others and to build support for the final plan.
- *Step 4.* Monitor the plan and its effectiveness. Strategic plans are dynamic tools, not static documents. Management should continuously monitor the effect of changes in the entity's external environment and modify the strategic initiatives as necessary.

Strategic plans are long-term in nature (three-year and five-year strategic plans are common) and should be updated regularly (e.g., annually).

Auditors may need to examine the entity's decision-making processes during consulting or management assistance engagements. This might involve reviewing whether the problems identified are linked to flaws in management's decision-making processes. Therefore, auditors should know the basic steps in any decision-making process. These are:

- *Step 1.* Define the issue about which a decision must be made. Many decisions treat symptoms instead of causes because the issue is not clearly defined. It is important to identify the issue clearly so the decision will be effective.
- *Step 2.* Identify the interests and values of individuals and groups affected by the decision.
- *Step 3.* Identify possible alternatives. Consider how each will influence affected groups.
- *Step 4.* Gather information relevant to each proposed alternative. Methods of obtaining this information include interviewing experts, reviewing available research, and conducting feasibility studies or cost/benefit analyses.
- *Step 5.* Consider the benefits of each proposed alternative as well as the potential risks, costs, or constraints.
- *Step 6.* Make the decision.
- *Step 7.* Communicate the decision to affected parties and implement it.
- *Step 8.* Monitor the effectiveness of the decision in resolving the issue.

German sociologist Max Weber coined the term *bureaucracy*. While many people consider "bureaucracy" to be a pejorative term synonymous with waste and inefficiency, bureaucracies have some positive functions:

- Bureaucracies create a division of labor that allows each employee to have specific functions and duties.
- Bureaucracies create levels of authority that enable decisions to be made.
- Bureaucracies create a framework of rules that give employees direction about what they are supposed to do.

In the public sector, bureaucratic structures are seen as a means of buffering the governmental functions and expert staff from the effects of the political processes that surround them. For example, the public interest can be better served when bureaucrats' conduct is subject to systemic control rather than political pressures. Among the controls that help to buffer government activities from purely political motivations include personnel systems in which:

- Appointments to office are based on technical qualifications, not political contacts.
- The functions of each position are clearly specified in writing.
- Rates of pay and benefits are based on a systematic structure. The existence of a documented career system provides opportunities for reward based on experience, merit, or performance rather than political involvement or sponsorship.

However, the control systems that protect the public interest in bureaucracies can also breed inefficiencies. For example, government can become less effective when its organizations create excessive layers of management, usually evidenced by narrow spans of control. Another pitfall for bureaucratic effectiveness is overemphasis on control; for example, requiring 11 signatures for a small-dollar purchase or collecting and maintaining large quantities of unused data.

Teamwork and Group Dynamics

The quality of decisions and work products is often enhanced by input from more than one person. Teams or groups can benefit from the expertise of all associated members. Individuals are also generally more willing to accept decisions that they helped formulate.

Groups may be informal (e.g., peer groups) or formal (e.g., work groups defined by management). Members of the group can have either assigned or adopted roles. Groups also develop a set of norms or accepted standards of behavior that group members are expected to follow.

The goals of a well-functioning group include:

- The group should make decisions based on sound logic and evidence. Input from all group members, regardless of rank or experience level, should be heard and evaluated fairly.
- The group should recognize that individuals have different strengths and weaknesses. Roles and assignments of group members should take these strengths and weaknesses into account.
- Time should be spent on solving major problems instead of petty personal conflicts and concerns. Given enough time, personal issues will inevitably have an effect on a group. But a well-functioning group will surface personal issues early and find a way to resolve them, or quickly move them to an alternative process so the group can get back to focusing on its goals.
- Achieving the overall goals of the group should be the priority of all group members. It is important that members believe that the goals of the group are valid and achievable. The group should strive to answer and resolve the doubts or concerns of members in an acceptable manner.

Centralized Versus Decentralized Management

Auditors need to be aware of the differences between a centralized or decentralized approach to management and take into consideration which one exists in order to appropriately address the associated risks. More importantly, government auditors must be aware of both the discretionary policies and requirements of the operating entity, as well as those imposed externally by a central management function. The purpose of this section is to outline the basic components of centralization of management and discuss the inherent advantages and disadvantages. This knowledge will help auditors understand where the operating entity's flexibility to revise procedures might be limited. It also will help auditors meet audit standards' requirements for evaluating compliance relevant to the audit objective.

Some of the objectives of a centralized management function are:

- Setting standards: Establishing and defining standards and guidelines to perform a specific function.
- Establishing reporting requirements to ensure that common budget and financial reports have similar characteristics and can be used for comparative analysis.
- Collecting and analyzing reports in order to provide summary reports to the oversight body.
- Overseeing compliance with standards and requirements.
- Reducing the need for the development of guidelines by each component agency.
- Reducing the need for independent oversight activities.

As indicated above, a centralized approach has benefits; however, there are also some pitfalls associated with the approach.

- Additional layers of bureaucracy are created.
- Processing delays may occur.
- The emphasis is on the process, rather than the result.
- Centralization may not be the best alternative in all cases.

A centralized function creates an additional layer of bureaucracy and potentially creates a new base of political power that can impede progress. Centralized agencies can become extremely powerful, as they have the ability to influence the speed and delivery of services through requirements and enforcement actions. One of the most common pitfalls is the increased time needed to complete a transaction. As a result, delays may impede the agency's ability to meet its actual mission or objective and may have a negative impact on public service. In other words, compliance with the process is emphasized rather than the end result. The common name for this phenomenon is "government red tape." The inherent bureaucracy of the centralized approach may create a conflict as agency staff attempt to deliver timely services to constituents. As a result, centralization may not always be the best approach to provide efficient government services.

The following illustration shows the basic conflict between centralization (bureaucracy) and a customer-driven (individual agency) approach.[1]

Bureaucratic Agency	Customer-driven Agency
Focuses on own needs.	Focuses on customers' needs.
Defined by resources it controls.	Defined by results it achieves for customers.
Controls costs.	Creates value.
Sticks to routine.	Responds to changing customer demands.
Fights for turf.	Competes for business.
Follows standard procedures.	Builds choices into operating systems.
Separates thinking from doing.	Empowers all frontline employees.

The customer-driven approach operates under the business model in which all efforts are geared toward developing and retaining the customer base. This approach promotes the ability to react and adapt to customer needs and to provide services in an efficient and effective manner. Not all public services want to "retain" customers (e.g., those that help people solve economic or social problems) and some services view people they interact with less as customers than other kinds of stakeholders (e.g., people arrested or incarcerated). But the idea of people-focused service that empowers employees to respond to individual or small group needs still applies and can improve the quality of service to each person or community. However, this approach can create problems as staff try to react quickly and forgo adherence to standards and guidelines. Also, increased discretion affords a higher potential for conflicting interests to influence use of resources. For example, a decision to select a preferred vendor to implement a program may assist in meeting the program goals; however, the decision may be subject to criticism for a lack of impartial vendor selection and compliance with purchasing rules.

Centralized management agencies have been developed to promote an effective and consistent approach to activities such as purchasing, budgeting, and personnel management. Although there are many types of centralized activities (fleet management, construction management, IT management, etc.), we provide examples of three functions:

- Purchasing.
- Budgeting.
- Personnel.

1. Purchasing. A centralized purchasing agency organizes purchasing efforts and procurement decisions. It has proven to be particularly effective in the purchase of commonly used commodity items such as office supplies. A central purchasing authority has the ability to receive volume discounts and can reduce the administrative burden of small agency purchases.

Some advantages of central purchasing are:

- Increasing control over purchases, because all purchases are made through a single source.
- Reducing improper purchasing activities.
- Receiving better price and payment terms.
- Reducing the administrative burden of individual agencies, departments, or units.

Some disadvantages are:

- Delays in purchasing decisions.
- Difficulties in receiving products to meet specific needs.

2. Budgeting. The budgeting cycle incorporates:

- Executive preparation.
- Legislative consideration.
- Execution.
- Audit and evaluation.

In this section, we focus on executive preparation using a centralized approach.

Most governments have some form of a centralized budgeting agency. In the United States, the federal government's budgeting agency is the Office of Management and Budget (OMB). States and many local governments have a body similar to OMB those forecasts and controls budget activities. Like the OMB in the federal government, the state budget office is generally under the chief executive for the state. Some of the areas addressed by budget offices are:

- Assessing financial performance: Reviewing and analyzing revenues, expenditures, and cash balances at various times throughout the year.
- Assessing the national economy and the impact it will have on finances.
- Assessing economic forecasts in areas such as:
  - Business activities.
  - Labor market.
  - Personal income.
- Developing a budget document that incorporates all agency requests into a government-wide request or plan.

The primary purpose of budgeting is to allocate resources among government activities. The basic framework for budgeting includes:

- Control.
- Accountability.
- Evaluation.

A centralized approach enhances the control and accountability of the budget process by centralizing the control and accountability to the executive branch.

Some disadvantages are:

- Difficulties or delays in shifting funds from one program or service to another or in changing the mix of resources used by agencies as needs, demands, or opportunities change during the budget year or other budget period.
- Disincentives to staff to make operations more efficient or economical if they cannot use the savings they achieve in their own program but will "lose" savings to a central control system.

3. Personnel. Government personnel systems have been developed to address historical concerns regarding government employment selection and compensation. Abuses of patronage systems in which the victor of political elections hired political allies led to the introduction of merit systems.

The personnel function is critical in a public organization. Government has been a leader in attempting to ensure that personnel decisions are made in a fair and equitable manner. Personnel systems and central personnel offices typically provide the following services:[2]

- *Recruitment.* The process of advertising job openings and encouraging candidates to apply. The primary objective is to provide an adequate number of qualified candidates from which a selection can be made.

- *Selection.* For non-patronage positions, a process that focuses on the merits of individual candidates is used to determine the final selection.
- *Training to ensure that employees possess the necessary skills to perform job duties.* Unfortunately, training is often viewed as an unproductive endeavor (similar to an insurance policy that has never been used) and is often neglected. Centralizing functions that promote, encourage, and even mandate training activities is an accepted approach to ensure that adequate training is provided.
- *Position classification and compensation plans.* A centralized system often standardizes position classification and associated pay plans. The purpose is to organize jobs based on job duties and responsibilities and to provide equitable compensation for similar jobs.

In addition, central personnel offices often set standards to assist supervisors with:

- *Evaluation.* The formal method by which an employee's work product is appraised. A centralized approach promotes a consistent and fair method of evaluation The purpose of an evaluation is to:
  - o Change or modify unacceptable behavior.
  - o Communicate management's perception of work quality.
  - o Assess the future potential of the employee and document developmental needs.
  - o Assess the adequacy of the employee's compensation level.
  - o Provide a documented record for disciplinary and termination actions.
- *Discipline.* There should be formal guidelines that promote fair and equitable discipline and help ensure that employees are made aware of behavioral problems and have the option to modify their behavior. There is often a step approach to discipline that has harsher penalties for continued violations of rules of conduct.
- *Termination.* The ultimate penalty is generally termination, and formal guidelines are developed to ensure that the termination is warranted and that the employee has been adequately apprised of his or her behavioral problem.

Some disadvantages of a centralized personnel system are:

- Long time periods for hiring, especially for new types of personnel for whom new classifications must be created.
- Long time periods and a great deal of management effort to fire personnel "for cause" (e.g., due to poor performance or insubordination).

Change Management

Change is a basic fact of life. Managers must be able to respond to change in several categories quickly and effectively.

- Changes in the built or natural environment can create the need for new policies or for a different quantity or mix of services (e.g., more parks or roads can create a need for more maintenance efforts; more buildings can create a need for more fire safety inspections).
- Changes in the economic or social environment (e.g., in income levels or in the size, age, ethnic, or racial makeup of the population) can alter the need or demand for some services or create a need for different policies, procedures, or level or type of resources used.
- Changes in technology can result in a need to alter policies, procedures, staffing levels, or goals.
- Changes in the political environment (e.g., a new administration or new legislation) can result in a need to refocus or increase emphasis.
- Changes in the moral environment (e.g., increased emphasis of ethics in government) can result in the need for tighter controls and performance measures.
- Changes related to personnel within the organization (e.g., new staff in key positions) may require modification of training policies or personnel rules.

Managers are responsible for ensuring that the staff undergoing organizational changes understand the reasons for the change, the timetable, and the planned phases. If the anticipated changes are incongruent with the personal or professional goals of some staff members, managers need to plan the appropriate transitions for these individuals.

Many authoritative sources suggest that organizations should plan for change to the extent possible. The report

advises organizations to try to anticipate changes and their effects on the organization. Planning for change involves the constant monitoring of the organization's internal and external environment. Specific elements related to planning for change include:

- Looking toward the future when developing missions and goals.
- Continuously assessing the effectiveness of programs.
- Maintaining effective management controls.
- Benchmarking best practices.
- Developing strong communication channels within the organization.

An effective risk assessment process also helps organizations anticipate and prepare for change.

Specific audit approaches. Specific approaches, methodologies, tools, and techniques are dictated by the types of government audit, as well as the audit objectives. The remainder of this section discusses audits related to performance management, the program evaluation discipline, a variety of quantitative and qualitative techniques, audit roles in "integrity violations," and the auditor's use of logic. While a significant component of government auditing relates to financial auditing, the approaches followed are specialized and are not included in this manual. Government auditors responsible for financial audits need to gain familiarity with those specialized methodologies.

III.B Performance Measurement[3]

Principles of Performance Measurement and Management in Government

Performance measurement is defined as *the ongoing monitoring and reporting of program accomplishments,* particularly progress toward established outcome goals. There are four major categories of performance measures associated with the four components of all government programs: input, process, output, and outcome:

- ***Input measures*** quantify the resources used or planned for a specific service or program. Inputs can be financial or other, such as personnel, equipment, or physical plant. Examples of input measures include the total cost of road maintenance, the maintenance cost per mile of roads in the jurisdiction, and the number of police officers assigned to a crime investigation team.
- ***Process measures*** provide a means for evaluating the use of inputs to achieve outputs. The most common process measures are efficiency measures such as productivity (output divided by input) and unit cost (input divided by output). Process measures can be, for example, counts of operational activities (e.g., number of library books re-shelved, as opposed to finished products or services) or internal process or cycle times (e.g., time for an application to move from being checked in to being worked on by a reviewer).
- ***Output measures*** report quantities of products or services delivered by a program or agency. Examples of output measures include the number of lane-miles of road repaired and the number of library items circulated. An output is distinguished by being a quantity of "finished products" or "completed services," not of a step along the way to completing the service, which would be a process measure (above). Some organizations consider a complete response time (e.g., to a fire or crime) or the timeliness to complete a service (e.g., percent of applications reviewed within two weeks of submission) as outputs.
- ***Outcome measures*** report the results associated with the products or services delivered by a program or agency, both qualitative and quantitative. Therefore, outcome measurement is the assessment of the results of a program activity compared to its intended purpose. Examples of outcome measures include the percentage of lane-miles of road in excellent condition and the percentage of residents rating their neighborhood as safe. For many programs, especially in health and human services, there are short-term outcomes (trainees get jobs), intermediate outcomes (trainees stay employed for at least six months), and long-term outcomes (trainees' families' savings increase, debts reduced, or living standards measurably improved).

In addition to the major categories described above, organizations also track measures of demand (such as eligible clients in a specific population), as well as explanatory data that report information about nondiscretionary conditions that have an impact on performance.

Also, when the concept of efficiency is expanded to include outcomes, it can be defined and reported separately from "process efficiency." In this expanded definition, *efficiency measures* not only establish the cost to complete a unit of service (input/output) but also to achieve an outcome (input/outcome). Efficiency measures are important because they enable cost and performance comparisons across work units or organizations that spend different amounts of resources or produce different amounts of services. And when cost or performance levels change over time for the same program, it is useful to know whether a program achieved proportionally more or fewer outputs or outcomes compared with changes in cost. Finally, efficiency measures provide a way to forecast how much more or less a program can be expected to achieve if its budget is increased or decreased.

Performance Management Systems

A complete performance management system incorporates performance measurement and includes performance expectations (such as standards, goals, objectives, and targets) against which actual performance is reported, monitored, and compared. If significant differences are identified between the objective and the actual performance, managers should determine the causes of the differences and either develop solutions to bring performance into line with the objective, or adjust the objective to make it more realistic and achievable. Consequently, management should consider performance measurement to be an ongoing process. An effective performance measurement system can serve to improve public management and increase public confidence in government programs.

Complete performance management systems can be viewed as containing four major components or subsystems:

- *Strategic and annual planning.* Performance plans are developed for all organizational levels, including performance expectations for individuals. The plans contain performance expectations in the form of missions, goals, objectives, and targets that are linked and aligned.
- *Performance budgeting.* Annual plans drive budget requests, and accountability is established by linking budget approval to expected accomplishments that will be monitored through subsequent performance reports.
- *Performance measurement and reporting.* This constitutes the "checking" phase when performance of government programs is assessed. Measurements of program inputs, processes, outputs, and outcomes are reported internally and externally.
- *Performance-based decision-making.* Performance information and reports should be used at every decision-making level, including employees, supervisors, managers, and elected officials. Ultimately, citizens use performance information and reports to hold government accountable for delivering services at a reasonable or sustainable cost.

Performance Measurement and Management in the Government Environment

Government auditors work in environments with increasing use and emphasis on performance measurement and management. This is so in both the United States and many other countries. Domain IV discusses more details of the laws, regulations, and initiatives in this regard. However, a few examples are briefly cited below:

- At the federal level of government in the United States, two major statutes include requirements: the Government Performance and Results Act (GPRA) of 1993 and the GPRA Modernization Act of 2010.
- In the United States, many state and local governments have enacted laws or ordinances (or have other initiatives) requiring performance measurement and management.
- Many other countries have established performance initiatives.

Government auditors need to keep abreast of the extensive government performance measurement and management systems and initiatives, and devise appropriate audit approaches and methodologies. The specific audit requirements vary and, in some cases, may be established by law or regulation or requested by oversight

bodies. Measurement-based auditing, a corollary to management's performance measurement, is discussed below.

Measurement-based Auditing

The four key steps in conducting a measurement-based performance audit are:

- Determining what program or activity is to be audited.
- Determining what the expectations or goals of the program or activity are.
- Determining whether management is accomplishing the expectations or goals.
- If not, determining what needs to be done to accomplish (or exceed) the expectations or goals.

To accomplish these steps, the auditor applies the following methodology, consisting of iterative and interrelated steps:

- Identify or map the program or activity's inputs, processes, outputs, and outcomes.
- Identify the relevant performance expectations and actual conditions.
- Develop and prioritize performance audit objectives based on risk and vulnerability assessment and client request.
- Assess the existing performance measurement system, including relevance and reliability of existing performance measures (to the extent the system contains relevant and reliable measures, and the auditor can rely on existing measures to accomplish audit objectives focused on determining actual performance levels).
- Develop and implement ad hoc performance a measurement system, if necessary, to accomplish the audit objectives (due to time and resource constraints within the context of performance audits to determine actual performance levels, the auditor is usually limited to developing measures to address specific aspects of performance, such as cost, timeliness, quality, or efficiency).
- Analyze program or activity performance using selected performance expectations as criteria and performance aspects or measures as conditions.
- Quantify effects of variances, identify causes of variances, and develop recommendations to reduce or eliminate variances.

To specifically implement these steps requires a wide variety of methodologies, tools, and techniques for measuring the various aspects of performance, including economy; unit cost; productivity; and output timeliness, quantity, quality, and price; and short- and long-term outcomes, including accomplishing performance-based goals, objectives, and targets. For example, timeliness can be assessed using a variety of formulas or approaches, including aging schedule analysis, queuing theory analysis, and backlog analysis.

The methods for measuring the many aspects of performance are discussed in this chapter and in the book *Performance Auditing: A Measurement Approach, 2009.*

Methods for Evaluating Reliability of Performance Measures and Data

Data obtained from direct observation to evaluate performance (e.g., interviews or surveys) should be supplemented with data from agency records or related secondary sources. Both Government Auditing Standards (Yellow Book) and IIA *Standards* call for auditors to assess the reliability and usefulness of secondary data to ensure that conclusions reached from the data are valid.

The following process should be followed to evaluate the reliability of performance data in cases where a performance measurement system exists:

- Document (map) the component's existing performance measurement system.
- Compare the existing system to the:
  - Performance accountability requirements (input economy, process efficiency, output effectiveness, crosscutting performance requirements).
  - Standards for effective performance measures. The models serve as benchmarks or audit criteria.
- Assess reliability, accuracy, and validity of data supporting the existing systems.
- Determine whether the reports produced by the existing system are adequate.
- Identify causes for tolerating an inadequate system.
- Develop recommendations for improving the existing system and issue the audit report.

The following process should be followed to evaluate the reliability of performance data in cases where a performance measurement system does not exist:

- Select appropriate performance criteria and measures.
- Test availability, reliability, and validity of existing data to support measures.
- If existing data are inadequate, design and implement a data collection instrument.
- Collect, present, and interpret data to describe conditions based on measures.
- Compare measures to performance criteria and identify variances.
- If performance does not meet expectations or exceeds expectations, determine why (causes).
- Quantify effect (difference between condition and criteria).
- Based on cause, develop recommendations for improving performance.

Measuring and Collecting Performance Information

Auditors and managers are both concerned with performance measurement. Managers must measure and track performance because citizens and legislative bodies are increasingly demanding evidence of the appropriate use of public resources and the achievement of public goals. Auditors must understand performance measurement because their audit objectives may call for independent measurement of organizational performance. Or the auditors may be called upon to assess the adequacy of the performance measurement system in place.

Performance measures help management monitor progress toward achieving the goals and objectives of the organization. The first consideration in measuring performance is to identify the specific performance that might be measured. The following areas should be considered when identifying specific performance to measure:

- *Identify stakeholder needs.* Stakeholders are the people who use or rely on the program to meet a need, who are otherwise affected by the program, or who have policy or advocacy interests related to the program. Citizens in general, as well as specific subgroups such as customers and clients, may be considered stakeholders for a particular program. Legislators, government agencies, and public interest groups are other examples of potential stakeholders. Sometimes locally affected people are stakeholders, such as residents or property owners near a public facility or proposed site for a new land use. The performance measurement system must identify stakeholder needs and ensure that the goals of the program match those needs. The organization also must identify specific outcomes or outputs by which to measure the effectiveness of the program.
- *Document major processes.* This step allows management to identify redundancy, inappropriate steps, inappropriate sequences of steps, omissions, or other indicators of inefficiency or waste.
- *Assess performance through benchmarking or best practice reviews.* These practices involve comparing the program's performance with other similar programs that are effective. This step allows management to ensure that the entity's processes relate directly to the desired outcomes and outputs and operate at appropriate levels of efficiency (though efficiency comparisons can be problematic unless management knows whether cost accounting is comparable across programs or organizations). Management should also ensure that there is a method for capturing relevant performance information.
- *Determine whether recommendations for improvement or change are warranted.*

Methods of collecting performance information include:

- *Manual tracking and summarizing of activity.* For example, class attendance records may be tracked manually, or numbers of clinic visits may be manually counted from appointment logs for routine reporting.
- *Routine collection of data either through entry or upload into automated systems.* For example, standardized results for tests that are machine-scored can be preserved electronically and aggregated for performance reports on school success.
- *Periodic sampling, such as through citizen surveys, random time studies, or random sampling of agency data.*
- *Trained observers or machine tests.* Examples are New York City's routine use of trained observers to rate street cleanliness, and the use of machines that

measure road bumpiness. Other automated means for collecting performance data include turnstiles in subway stations and emergency call center logs for tracking usage trends.

- *Calculations based on historical trends.* For instance, Texas's state juvenile corrections agency, the Texas Youth Commission, periodically reports "offenses prevented" due to the incarceration of offenders by projecting expected arrest rates of currently committed juveniles based on their documented arrest histories.
- *Photographic rating scales.* For example, the cleanliness of various areas in a community can be ranked based on photographs taken of litter conditions on streets and alleys.
- *Technical tests.* For example, chemical tests can be used to detect the effects of landfill runoff on groundwater and surface water quality.
- *Physical inspection.* For example, fire hydrants can be regularly inspected to determine their water pressure in relation to established guidelines.

According to Harry Hatry, criteria to use for selection of performance measures and data collection procedures include:

- *Appropriateness and validity.* Does the measure relate to the government objectives for that service and does it really measure the degree to which a citizen's need or desire is being met, including minimizing detrimental effects?
- *Uniqueness.* Does it measure some effectiveness or other performance characteristic that no other measure encompasses?
- *Completeness.* Does the list of measures cover all or at least most objectives?
- *Comprehensibility.* Is the measure understandable?
- *Controllability.* Is the condition that is measured at least partially the government's responsibility? Does the government have some control over it?
- *Cost.* Are cost and staffing requirements for data collection reasonable? The answer to this will depend partly on the government's funding situation and its interest in a particular measure.
- *Timeliness of feedback.* If the information is needed for specific decisions — possible launching of new programs, setting budget levels for the coming year, and the like — will the data and analysis become available before the decision makers reach their deadline?
- *Accuracy and reliability.* Can sufficiently accurate and reliable information be obtained? This is a problem not only with procedures that use samples, such as citizen surveys, but also with many government statistics, such as crime rates.

Evaluation of the Adequacy or Relevance of Performance Measures

It is often difficult to determine appropriate performance measures for government programs. People have different values and thus often have different ideas about what constitutes adequate performance for a given program. The following are guidelines for developing adequate performance measures.

- Use a family of measures to capture multiple dimensions of performance. For example, a program may be operating at peak efficiency, but if the program is not effective, all the resources allocated to it are being wasted. At a minimum, performance measures should address the program's economy, efficiency, and effectiveness, as well as the program's compliance with laws and regulations. A common mistake is to rely on only one or a few selected performance measures relevant to the program. This approach gives a limited view of the program's overall performance.
- Measures used should focus on quantifiable aspects of performance that lend themselves to practical data collection periodically (e.g., monthly, quarterly, annually). Use periodic performance measurement to monitor and improve service operations. Use program evaluation to assess accomplishment of characteristics that are not measurable or not practical to measure frequently. Program evaluations may draw upon performance measurement data, but will almost always involve additional data collection. For example, analysis of performance data alone would not be appropriate to determine the impact of correctional therapy and self-esteem programs on recidivism of juvenile offenders. A program evaluation would be needed that uses recidivism rates from a performance measurement system but would also involve other

quantitative and qualitative data collection about the therapies and programs.

- Performance measures should be comprehensive enough to reach valid conclusions about the program.
- The level of measurement should be appropriate for the program. That is, the costs and potential benefits associated with the measurement should be congruent.
- Performance measures should be updated as necessary. Updates should reflect changes in social, economic, environmental, and political situations. However, updating the measures used should be balanced with the need to have consistency over time to use the performance measurement system to track and manage performance. This suggests the need for "change controls" on measures — specific rules for when and how measures can be changed, and transparent documentation of each change and the reason for the change.

Quality Standards for Performance Measures

Relevance: Measures should provide data that are useful and complete enough for assessing accountability and making decisions. Measures are genuine representations of the entity's performance. Measures for specific programs should be directly related to those programs' objectives.

Reliability: Performance data reported are accurate and error free.

Comparability: Performance data can be tracked over time, compared to other organizations or other units (branch operations), or to externally established norms or standards.

Understandability: Performance measures as reported should be free of jargon, with key terms defined as necessary, and be readily understood by stakeholders.

Consistency: Measures should be defined and data collected and reported in a similar manner from period to period to enable users to have a basis for comparing performance over time.

Timeliness: The most up-to-date information should be used. Data should be reported in the time frame specified for reporting and received by stakeholders in time for them to use it for decision-making or accountability.

Evaluation of Performance Reports

As stated above, a performance measurement system should provide sufficient, relevant, accurate, timely, and useable data to management. Management should then be able to effectively analyze and interpret the performance measurement information.

The following are guidelines for using performance data to evaluate performance.

- Note deviations from normal or expected values. Note any patterns. Consider creating graphs or summary tables to assist in this process.
- Try to determine the reasons for deviations from expected values. Look for relationships between variables such as customer or stakeholder satisfaction and processing time. Consider other factors such as equipment changes or disruptions caused by weather during the reporting period.
- Note positive indicators in the data as well as problem areas.
- Compare performance reports with those used by other divisions or similar operations outside the entity. Benchmark with best practices as appropriate.
- Discuss performance data with responsible individuals in the entity.
- Concentrate on developing ideas to improve performance in areas that are most important to the entity's goals and objectives.

The following are guidelines for evaluating performance reports.

- Do the reports reflect the most significant aspects of operations?
- Are the reports usable by their intended audience?
- Are the reports available in a timely manner for decision-making?
- Are the reports accurate (i.e., do they contain reliable data)?
- Was the reported performance reported aggregated or disaggregated at a meaningful level?
- Was the performance information collected in a cost-effective manner (i.e., do the benefits of a performance report justify its cost)?

III.C Program Evaluation[4]

Retrieving Data from a Variety of Systems

Auditors must master a variety of techniques for gathering information. These techniques, which involve both manual and electronic means, include:

- *Interviews.* It is important to meet with personnel involved in the processes being audited to discuss key issues. Interviews are especially useful at the beginning of an audit to help the auditor understand the process being studied. Auditors also use interviews as the audit progresses to clarify their understanding.
- *Direct observation.* Auditors can obtain valuable information and evidence by directly observing the client's operations and work processes. Direct observation can help the auditor verify items such as inventories, equipment usage and downtime, operating inefficiencies, and personnel issues.
- *Reviewing management reports.* A variety of internal reports is often available for review. Much internal data is now kept electronically on an organization's internal network, known as a local area network (LAN) or a wide area network (WAN) depending on its size and coverage. Depending on how the information will be used, auditors should do adequate testing to verify the validity of the information. Methods to evaluate the validity of internal data include sampling and verifying a portion of the data, reviewing controls over data input and security, and checking the accuracy and appropriateness of data programs and formulas.
- *Data extraction software.* Auditors can use software to extract data from a variety of database structures and import it into a PC environment for analysis. Two examples of data extraction software are Interactive Data Extraction Analysis (IDEA) and ACL. IDEA allows auditors to analyze large amounts of data (e.g., all of a state's general ledger revenue and expenditure transactions) and convert it into usable information. ACL is another powerful data analysis tool that allows auditors to read, analyze, summarize, and report on data.
- *External information and data sources.* Books, articles, industry reports, and existing audit reports are among the external sources of information available. In addition, other similar government organizations, nonprofit research entities, and institutions of higher education may share data collected for performance tracking or research purposes.

  Yellow Book standards address the issue of reliance on externally supplied data. GAGAS outlines procedures that provide a sufficient basis for relying on the work of others.

  Auditors should focus on information from reputable and reliable sources. Information on websites, for example, can range from very useful and timely to inaccurate and misleading. The following guidelines apply to the review and use of external data:
  - Make sure the entity or individual who created the analysis is clearly identified. It is often possible to identify authors' possible biases by understanding their background and current affiliations.
  - Make sure all methodologies (e.g., scope definition, sampling plan) are clearly and completely described. Review and evaluate the adequacy of the methodologies. Note any limitations or biases.
  - Make sure the information used is reliable and unbiased.
  - Make sure the tone of the report is balanced and fair. Any report that takes a completely positive or completely negative position should be viewed with a degree of skepticism. This is because there are usually good points and bad points associated with any program, and the best researchers will present all sides of the story.
  - Make sure the author of the report properly cites all external sources of data used.
- *Surveys.* Auditors use surveys to obtain information from individuals about items such as the effects of services or how service delivery could be improved. The subjects of surveys might include clients, service users, suppliers, or other stakeholders.
- *Expert judgment.* Some complex audits might require assistance from experts. For example, the opinion of a civil engineer might be needed to evaluate the adequacy of construction materials and designs used to build a bridge. Auditors should take steps to ensure that the chosen expert is independent of the client and free from biases that could impair judgment. Moreover, experts or consultants must meet auditing standards for competence and their work should comply with standards for due professional care.

The following basic rules apply to gathering information.

- Information obtained should relate to the objectives and scope of the audit.
- Sufficient and appropriate information should be collected to support audit findings and recommendations.
- Data collection methods should be described in the audit program.
- The results of data collected should be documented in workpapers.

These general guidelines apply to auditors requesting secondary data.

- Request the original data and any required modifications from the person in the organization directly responsible for maintaining it.
- Develop an understanding of how the agency obtains, creates, modifies, presents, and controls the data.
- Make data requests in writing.
- Consider requesting and reviewing a sample of the data before requesting the complete data set.

Problems may occur with the use of secondary data. Some potential problems and suggested methods to correct for them are:

- ***Incomplete data.*** It is important to determine how much information is missing and how those gaps affect the quality of the data. Next, the auditor should determine whether the missing information is obtainable. Based on the results of these steps, the auditor has the following options:
  - Try to obtain as much missing data as possible.
  - Omit the missing data from the analysis.
  - Estimate values for the missing data (e.g., based on the mean value of available data).
  - Change the objectives of the evaluation to focus on available data.
- ***Irrelevant data.*** Clients may provide auditors with summary information that is not relevant or useful for a specific audit objective. Options for handling this problem include:
  - Request new summary information from the client.
  - Obtain the raw data directly from client records.
  - Identify surrogate measures from existing data that can substitute for the measures the auditor would like to collect.
- ***Noncomparable data.*** Data obtained from different sources or from different years may not be comparable. For example, data obtained from a variety of sources may contain duplicate records. Another possibility is that data elements (e.g., overhead costs) might be calculated using different methods or criteria. If noncomparable information is found, auditors have the following options:
  - Exclude the noncomparable data.
  - Modify the data as appropriate (e.g., recalculate all costs using the same criteria).
  - Add clarifying footnotes that indicate the limitations of the data being used or compared.

Tools or Instruments for Use in Collecting Data

Data collection tools or instruments are used to help ensure that information is collected consistently. Regardless of what type of data collection is undertaken (e.g., surveying stakeholders, reviewing records and files), a properly designed data collection instrument will help improve the quality and reliability of the information obtained.

The following guidelines apply to designing data collection tools or instruments.

- Have clearly defined reasons for collecting the data. This will provide assurance that only essential information is collected.
- Develop a list of individuals to be surveyed or items to be reviewed. Carefully document any sampling plans used.
- Scrutinize the sampling plan to ensure representation by target populations.
- Determine whether data will be collected by direct observations, interviews, mail or phone surveys, or some other method.
- Develop the data collection instrument(s).
- Pretest data collection procedures before use. The use of a pilot will provide the team members with an opportunity to review the data collection instrument's relevance to actual conditions and revise as

needed. The pretest, along with decision guidelines for responding consistently to ambiguous conditions, will help strengthen reliability.

- Thoroughly train all data collection personnel.
- Collect the data. Take necessary steps to ensure that the information is kept confidential, if warranted.
- Attempt to triangulate field findings with confirmatory responses from multiple sources.

III.D Quantitative Methods

Statistical Methods

The term *descriptive statistics* refers to methods designed to describe or summarize the characteristics of a data set. The following analysis procedures are associated with descriptive statistics:

- Collection and organization of raw data. Existing data may be used, or new data may be created through collection techniques such as interviews or questionnaires. Data are often classified in an array, which is the arrangement of data in either ascending (from lowest to highest value) or descending (from highest to lowest value) order.
- Classification and graphic presentation of the data in a *frequency distribution* format. A frequency distribution is a method of grouping data items into a relatively small number of classes. Below is an example of a frequency distribution.

Frequency Distribution
Timeliness of Police Responses in July

Response Time	Number of Responses (Frequencies)
Up to 5 Minutes	14
Over 5 and up to 10 Minutes	27
Over 10 and up to 15 Minutes	10
Over 15 and up to 20 Minutes	4
Over 20 Minutes	2

- The following guidelines apply to the construction of a frequency distribution:
  - Divide classes to ensure that the smallest and largest values in the array are shown.
  - Assign each item in the array to only one class.
  - Keep the size of each interval the same. For example, in the chart above, each of the first four intervals represents a five-minute time frame.
- Computation of the *central tendency* of the data. The following are measures of central tendency:
  - The *arithmetic mean* is the sum of the values of a group of items divided by the count of those items. Arithmetic mean is most commonly considered as the "average" but can be misleading if there are outlier data points (a small number of very high or low values) that skew the average in one direction or another. Remedies include not including outliers in the calculation or using the median instead of the mean.
  - The *median* is the middle position in an array of values. The median value can be misleading in small data sets, so it is usually used to characterize a large number of values.
  - The *mode* is the most frequently occurring value in an array. The mode is a less frequently used measure of central tendency because a mode may not exist in some data sets, or there may be more than one mode in the data.

Measures of central tendency are not sufficient to describe and summarize a set of data. It is also necessary to measure the dispersion of those values. Standard deviation is a widely used measure of dispersion. The standard deviation represents the distance of individual data points from the mean. As individual data points become more widely scattered about their mean, the standard deviation will become larger. The standard deviation may be distorted by a few extreme values in the population (outliers).

The term *inferential statistics* refers to methods designed to allow estimates (inferences) to be made about the characteristics of a data set. In cases where it is not possible to make a decision based on complete knowledge about the data, it becomes necessary to make inferences based on sample data gathered and analyzed objectively. However, results from the application of statistical techniques are not certain; they merely reduce and define the level of doubt about a data set. Statistical sampling techniques are discussed later.

Sample results may be used to test a hypothesis about a parameter value. For example, an agency might state that it believes the average number of overtime hours for each employee in a particular classification is 30 each month; that is the hypothesis. The auditor might take a sample to test that hypothesis. The results will indicate whether a hypothesis should be accepted or rejected. However, the sample mean most likely will not equal the assumed parameter value. Therefore, the auditor must determine how large a difference between the sample mean and the assumed value should be in order to provide sufficient basis for rejecting the agency's claim.

These are the general steps to follow when testing a hypothesis:

- ***Step 1.*** State the null and alternative hypotheses. The *null hypothesis* is the assumed value of the parameter prior to sampling. For example, a null hypothesis might be that the average number of overtime hours for each employee in a particular classification is equal to 30 each month. A conclusion reached based on the rejection of the null hypothesis is known as the *alternative hypothesis*. In this example, alternative hypotheses would be that the average number of overtime hours for each employee in a particular classification is greater than 30 each month or that is less than 30 each month.
- ***Step 2.*** Establish the criteria for rejecting or accepting the null hypothesis. Theoretically, a test never proves that a hypothesis is true. When a hypothesis is accepted, it means that there is no statistical evidence for rejecting the assumption.
- ***Step 3.*** Analyze the data. Data analysis involves collecting sampled items, estimating the parameter, and calculating the value of the sample mean.
- ***Step 4.*** Accept or reject the null hypothesis.

Sampling occurs when less than the entire data set is examined to reach conclusions about the entire population. Therefore, a sample is any portion of the population selected for study. The purpose of sampling is to provide sufficient information to allow inferences to be made about the characteristics of the population. The goal of sampling is to select a portion of the population that maximally represents the characteristics of the population. The following basic definitions apply:

- The *population* is the total number of units being studied.
- A *parameter* is a characteristic of the population. For example, an age-related parameter might be the number of people in a given population over or under 65 years old.
- A *statistic* is a characteristic of the sample. For example, possible statistics for the above example include the average age of the population or the percentages of the population over and under 65 years old.
- Sampling can be done in one of two general approaches — non-statistical or statistical. In *judgment (or non-statistical) samples,* specific items are selected based on the auditor's knowledge about the population. *Statistical sampling* allows the auditor to limit sampling risk to an acceptable level.

Major classifications of statistical sampling are discussed below:

- ***Statistical (probability) samples.*** The probability of selecting each item in the population is known before the sample is chosen. Two types of samples commonly used by auditors include:
  - ***Simple random sample.*** Each item in the total population has an equal chance of being selected. The sample can be selected by using a random number generator or a systematic method (e.g., every *n*th after a random start); or
  - ***Stratified sample.*** The population is divided into relatively homogenous groups and the sample is selected from the various groups.
- Samples can be made more efficient by using either of the following methods:
  - ***Sequential or stop-or-go sampling.*** The sample is selected in stages. If the first stage results in no deviations, the auditor may choose to stop testing and conclude that the controls are strong. However, if deviations are found, an additional sample will probably be drawn.
  - ***Discovery sampling.*** When the auditor expects no deviations in the area being tested due to strong controls, a sample may be drawn to validate that assumption. However, if deviations are found in the discovery sample, the auditor should conduct additional testing.

In using sampling, auditors need to consider two types of risk:

- ***Sampling risk,*** that is, the risk that the auditor's conclusion based on sample testing may be different than the conclusion reached if the audit procedures were applied to all items in the population.
- ***Non-sampling risk,*** which occurs when an auditor fails to perform his or her work properly.

Generally, sample size needs to be increased under the following circumstances:

- As the population increases. However, the variability of the population influences required sample sizes. Because it is assumed that adults are not generally taller in one area of the country than another, a same-sized sample could be used to calculate the average height of adults in the United States and the average height of adults in the city of Houston. The U.S. sample would be drawn from a larger population and area, but the sample sizes would not vary because the two populations have generally the same height characteristics. Also, sample size does not increase proportionally as the population increases, because there is no discernible effect on the results from increased sample size when the population exceeds 5,000 units.
- As variability within the population increases. For example, if the target sample was a group of children aged 14 to 18, a smaller sample would be needed at a high school where most members of the population fall within the desired range, as opposed to a sample taken in an airport where the variability of ages is greater.
- As the expected error rate increases. *Attributes sampling* focuses on the existence of an attribute on a two-way scale (e.g., yes or no). Error rates are relevant only to attributes samples. The auditor would calculate the population error rate based on the number of "No" answers in the sample. A higher expected population error rate requires a larger sample size. A smaller sample is allowable in cases where few errors are expected in the population.
- As the confidence level increases. *Confidence level* is the likelihood that sampled items represent the true values of the population. For example, a 90 percent confidence level allows for 10 percent sampling risk (i.e., the chance that the sampled items do not represent the true values of the population), and a 95 percent confidence level allows for 5 percent sampling risk.

However, fewer sampled items are required as the tolerable error level increases. *Tolerable error* is the maximum rate of deviation that auditors would accept and still assess controls as effective. Therefore, the more error the auditor is willing to tolerate, the fewer number of items need to be sampled.

Properly conducted samples can be used to make inferences or generalizations about the entire population. The accuracy of inferences drawn from a sample to a population is critically affected by the sampling procedures used. The following four principles should guide sampling design.

- The population of interest must be reasonably known and identifiable.
- A sampling technique should be used in which the probability for selecting any unit in the population can be calculated.
- A sample should be drawn that is of appropriate size relative to the size of the population about which generalization is desired.
- Always test samples to ensure that they are truly representative of the population to which the evaluators hope to generalize on variables of critical interest.

Auditors should be able to distinguish between attributes sampling and variables sampling. The two techniques are described below:

- ***Attributes sampling.*** As described in the discussion of error rates, attributes sampling calls for an answer on a two-way scale (e.g., yes or no; right or wrong). Attributes sampling is usually applied to testing systems of internal control and is concerned with estimating the number of errors in the population.
- ***Variables sampling.*** Variables sampling can be used for values such as dollar values, time periods, or weights. Estimates are based on a sample of items such as the value of inventories, the value of disallowances of travel vouchers, or the value of accounts receivable.

Auditors can now take statistical analysis to a more comprehensive level using more advanced techniques in the field of "data mining." Because of the large amounts of data available to auditors, which sometimes includes the entire "universe" of relevant transactions, analyzing the entire population of items rather than sampling may be cost/beneficial. When auditors have access to the entire population and have or can be supported with the appropriate level of expertise, they can deploy advanced data mining tools, which include statistical exploration of large amounts of data, model building to identify patterns or systematic relationships between variables, and further analysis and prediction to validate potential audit findings.

One example of a "data mining" approach pertinent to auditors is to attempt to detect potential fraud using statistical tools based on Benford's Law, also called the first-digit law, which states that in lists of numbers from many real-life sources of data, the leading digit is distributed in a specific, non-uniform way. According to this law, the first digit is 1 about 30 percent of the time, and larger digits occur as the leading digit with lower and lower frequency, to the point where 9 as a first digit occurs less than 5 percent of the time. By applying statistical tools based on Benford's law, auditors are about to identify numbers or patterns of numbers not conforming to the law and therefore potentially reflecting some form of human intervention. Through additional analysis and follow-up, the auditor can determine whether some type of situation exists which indicates noncompliance or fraud.

Analytical Review and Analytics

Analytical reviews are audit tests that involve a comparison of some type. Analytical reviews can be used during the early planning phase of the audit, using both financial and nonfinancial information to help identify the audit's focus. In this use, the auditor may focus on the logical relationships between financial and nonfinancial information to identify potential risks and vulnerabilities, which then become the basis for developing and focusing on selected audit objectives. In the later planning stage, the auditor may employ risk-based data analytics to determine the nature, extent, and timing of further data procedures that the auditor will apply during fieldwork. As the audit progresses into fieldwork, analytical procedures become part of the methodology to assess the strength of various types of audit evidence, which in turn support findings and conclusions.

There are many different types of quantitative and qualitative analytical reviews, including:

Ratio analysis allows comparisons of proportionality by showing the relationship of one type of unit to a different type of unit. This is useful for comparing activities over time (such as number of complaints per 100 employees each year) or across organizations (e.g., number of complaints per 100 employees at each facility). Ratios are used because they allow comparisons among units that might otherwise be difficult to compare. For example, 200 employee complaints during FY 2010 appears to be significant growth when compared to 100 the previous year. However, when rationalized by their proportion to the total number of employees in the organization, this comparison may in fact show little change if the number of employees also doubled.

Cost/benefit analysis involves the comparison of projected costs and projected dollar value of benefits associated with a project or decision. Cost and benefits can also be compared after the project is implemented or a decision is made. The methodology of a cost/benefit analysis involves identifying the benefits and assigning dollar values. The total costs are then calculated and compared with the value of the benefits. It is important to include all relevant costs and benefits to ensure that a valid comparison is made. Benefits can include cost savings, time savings, increased productivity, increased value, or increased service delivery. Examples of costs include items such as personnel, supplies, equipment, buildings, research and development, training, and overhead.

Cost-effectiveness analysis, in contrast to cost/benefit, compares the cost of a program or activity to a measurable unit of output or outcome (rather than to the estimated or actual dollar benefits). For example, a cost-effectiveness analysis compares the cost of a highway safety program per life saved, or the cost of a fire inspection program per structural fire prevented.

Regression analysis is a method of measuring the statistical relationship that exists between two or more variables. Auditors might use regression to estimate the effects of a particular program on its target population. For example, regression could be used to study the effects of prison work programs on recidivism rates. Regression analysis is conducted by developing an estimating equation that describes the relationship between the *dependent variable* (the variable to be estimated) and the *independent variable* (the variable that creates differences in the dependent variable). Available data where there is a value for the dependent and independent variable are plotted on a scatter diagram to determine the relationship between the two variables.

Time series is the classification of data values over a period of time. This technique allows for the study of past and current patterns, and (under certain circumstances) can be used to project future patterns. Thus, time series is closely associated with *trend analysis*. A *secular trend* is the regular long-term growth of a series and can be caused by changes in population or technology. Weather changes or holidays can cause a *seasonal trend*.

Interrupted time series is a form of quasi-experimental design that allows auditors or evaluators to compare observations (such as behavioral indicators, outcomes, or other observations) from before a specific intervention to observations from after the intervention. It is used in program evaluation and auditing as one means of determining the impact of an intervention or activity. For example, researchers might compare the number or percent of traffic fatalities before speed limits are changed in a state to those after the new speed limits go into effect.

Benchmarking is the process of identifying best practices and comparing them to one's own organization. Benchmarking allows organizations to apply state-of-the-art practices to establish goals and improve operations. Organizations also can use the results of benchmarking to update performance measures, modify information systems, or change strategic plans. Challenges in benchmarking include access to relevant data and comparability of measures as reported. For a fair comparison of performance data, an auditor needs to know if the different organizations define measures the same way and if all use data from reliable sources. If an auditor can get measure definitions and complete enough data sets from benchmarking organizations, the auditor may be able to recalculate measurement values to adjust for different definitions and still make valid comparisons. However, even if performance measures cannot be made comparable enough for benchmarking performance data, benchmarking practices can still be a valuable exercise. For example, an auditor may be able to analyze the work flow of the audited entity as if it were using practices of the benchmark organization to see if the change would offer opportunities to improve efficiency (e.g., by reducing steps) or effectiveness (e.g., by reducing response time, increasing customer contact, or improving quality assurance).

Additional Analytic Tools and Techniques

The following are nine additional analytic techniques auditors can use to identify and analyze problems, their causes, and possible solutions. Over the years, auditors have experimented with a number of ways to analyze data to better evaluate management claims relative to performance, or to better plan and more efficiently conduct audits. In addition, analysts have developed methods for evaluating data and problem solving, which are of benefit to auditors.

The techniques below are derived from both of these sources.

Run Chart Analysis

The run chart is used to identify a potential problem and its extent. It does this by tracking and displaying changes in the aspect of performance being measured over a selected period of time (trend analysis). It creates a picture of what is happening in the situation the auditor is analyzing. The performance being tracked could be cycle time to complete a specific product or service, level of errors, efficiency, etc.

A run chart analysis can be used to identify a potential problem by showing whether performance is increasing or decreasing, extremes in process variation, how far performance is from a goal (e.g., criteria), and the extent of change in "before" and "after" performance due to installation of a new process or some other intervention.

Control Chart Analysis

The control chart is a special type of line graph that can be used to identify and define a problem and show the extent. Specifically, you can use a control chart analysis to interpret data about a process by creating a picture of the boundaries of acceptable variation, and objectively determining whether a process is "in control" or "out of control."

A control chart is a useful tool for determining the normal or acceptable variation within a process. It can be used to measure whether defects are within tolerance, time is within acceptable parameters, volume meets specifications, etc. Plotting the data on variation from an established norm will show you when these boundaries are exceeded. You can then look for clues to the causes.

Radar Chart Analysis

A radar chart can be used to identify and portray an imbalance between two situations. These charts — combination circle and line graphs — are particularly useful in showing: 1) imbalances between two variables, such as workload and staffing for a selected time period, and 2) changes from one period to another in particular attributes of performance, such as the attributes of service quality.

The data can be presented in numeric form, but the graph (also called a spider graph) convincingly presents the information in a single chart that shows immediately and visually what the situation is.

Histogram Analysis

A histogram is used to analyze a problem. Further investigation can verify the source or causes of the problem. The primary uses of a histogram are to analyze information about variations in a process and make decisions on where to focus improvement efforts.

The histogram provides information on the variation in performance for the dimension being studied. It is usually presented as a bar chart. The width of each bar represents an interval of observations within a range while the height represents the number of observations falling within a given interval. It can represent such observations as weight, size, frequency, error rates, efficiency levels, etc. The clues on performance given by the histogram lie in its shape. Normal or expected performance is indicated by a "bell curve." The "bell curve" indicates a process wherein variation is under control. The greater the deviation from the "bell curve" the greater the need to examine what is causing the differences in performance.

Pareto Analysis

A Pareto analysis separates the "vital few" from the "trivial many." It is designed to point out inequalities. The familiar "80-20 rule" "Eighty percent of our business comes from twenty percent of our customers," is an example of Pareto analysis.

A Pareto analysis involves the ranking of data. The results are usually presented in a chart — a special type of bar graph. It draws attention to problems systematically. It shows which are the greatest problems or causes. Auditors can use it to determine the relative frequency or importance of different problems or causes, and identify vital issues for audit by ranking them in terms of significance.

Cause and Effect Diagram

The cause and effect diagram (hereafter referred to as fishbone analysis) is an analysis that can be used to:

- Categorize many potential causes of a problem in an orderly way.
- Analyze what is really happening in a process.
- Teach teams and individuals about current or new processes and procedures.

The problem is stated on the right side of the chart (fish head) and the major causes are stated on the left (fishbone). The major causes are summarized under categories, such as people, machines, methods, and materials.

Scatter Diagram

The scatter diagram is a tool used to interpret data to determine the strength of the relationship between two variables (i.e., money spent on a drug education program and reduction in drug use); the validity of a "hunch" about a cause-and-effect relationship between types of variables; and the type of relationship that exists (positive, negative, etc.).

Scatter diagrams are easy to use and the results are easy to understand. This technique can be adapted for use in many situations where the relationship of two variables is important to decisions about investment in procedures or choice between procedures. Auditors use this tool to identify the cause of a problem.

Sequence Flow Chart Analysis

The sequence flow chart is an analysis tool used to:

- Produce a visual "picture" of a process, making it easy for people to understand and discuss how work is being done.
- Analyze the flow of work in a process. In many government applications, the "work" would be a document (claim, report, etc.) flowing through the process.
- Identify opportunities to improve the process — identify problem areas (e.g., where delays and repeat steps occur) and the causes (e.g., of delays, inefficiency, errors, security faults).
- Identify the necessary controls within a process.

Usually a sequence flow chart should include all of the processing tasks or steps from the beginning to the end. In so doing, it will typically transverse an organization's boundaries.

Force Field Analysis

The force field analysis is a problem-solving model. The concept behind the model is that any situation is the result of opposing forces, some of which push for positive problem resolutions and others that push against positive resolution. It identifies those forces that both help and hinder an organization from closing the gap between what is and what is required, desired, or possible.

The force field model comes from the idea that there are always opposing forces in motion that constantly push against each other. The forces for change are called driving forces and the forces against are called restraining forces. When they exert the same force, status quo is the result. Change happens when the driving forces exceed the restraining forces. To produce a change in status quo, an unfreezing of the balance must take place. This is done by strengthening the driving forces or weakening the restraining forces. When this happens, the problem of stagnation or a status quo will be replaced by a solution, a refreezing will take place, and a new situation will become the relative balance.

Auditors can use a force field analysis to:

- Create a picture of the situation.
- Identify those forces that both help and hinder one from reaching a goal.
- Identify manageable pieces of a problem.
- Move from defining the problem to deciding on actions (recommendations for auditors) for problem solving.
- Develop a plan to implement the actions (management's responsibility).

Analytics. Many of the specific techniques discussed above have been in use for years; in recent years, a term that has come into increasing use is analytics. Analytics refers to a broad set of tools (using software as a powerful aid) that can be used by both auditors and management. This topic in all its ramifications is beyond the scope of this manual, but government auditors should stay abreast of these developments to identify how to use analytics to isolate information that will be helpful in finding opportunities for improved economy, efficiency, and effectiveness.

> **Note:** The IIA has issued two Practice Advisories, 2320-1: Analytical Procedures, and 2320-2: Root Cause Analysis, that may be relevant in the auditor's consideration of analytical tools. The first one addresses comparisons of information with expectations, potential identification of fraud or error, and considerations such as internal control effectiveness. The second one focuses on the importance of properly identifying the cause and how tools such as fishbone, Pareto, and statistical correlations might assist the auditor to find the true cause.

III.E Qualitative Methods/ Research/Data Collection

Qualitative methods are techniques that enable systematic identification of non-quantifiable or hard to quantify attributes of inputs, processes, and outcomes. The contrast between qualitative methods and quantitative approaches is most strongly seen in how the data collection process is conducted. First, in qualitative evaluation, the evaluator literally becomes the primary measurement instrument, in contrast to quantitative analysis, where the analyst is removed from the process of measurement. Second, qualitative data collection and data analysis are mutually interdependent, interacting with one another as the data collection process proceeds, unlike the distinct phases that characterize collection and analysis in quantitative analysis.

Survey Questionnaires

Auditors and evaluators develop survey questionnaires to obtain information from service customers, program staff, or other stakeholders that is not readily available in the organization's data sources. Surveys can often be used to quantify qualitative information, such as people's perceptions of community conditions or satisfaction with a service. Questionnaires can be administered by mail, telephone, or in person. Each form of administration carries unique issues related to ensuring that responses are representative and relevant.

The following are key elements in the development of effective survey questionnaires.

Administration Issues

- Clearly define the purpose of the survey; every question must be relevant to that purpose.
- Select an administration method (e.g., mail, telephone, in person) based on:
  - Time and other resources.
  - Complexity of questions.
  - Necessity for anonymity/confidentiality.
  - Desired coverage/target populations.
  - Desired sampling precision.
- It is advisable to pretest a questionnaire on a small group before administering it to the entire survey population.
- Administer the survey in a way that enables follow-up on non-respondents. For example, in mail surveys, one way to enable follow-up is to tag each survey with a code indicating the individual or household the survey is to be sent to. When all responses have been received, select a random or representative sample of non-respondents and conduct the survey by telephone or in person. Then compare the distribution of response types of non-respondents to that of the initial respondents to determine if there are any biases in the results from those who responded. If biases are found (e.g., more negative opinions expressed in the initial group of respondents), they can be adjusted for by use of weighting.
- Use the order of the questions to help encourage response. In other words, place the simpler, less sensitive or less threatening questions first, with the more personal or politically charged issues later in the survey. Also, use logical groupings to keep related subjects together.
- Security. While in most cases auditors cannot fully guarantee the confidentiality of survey responses unless they are collected anonymously, respondents should be advised of the extent to which their responses will be reported in a manner that is identifiable, and of the efforts the audit organization will employ to maintain confidentiality of the responses.

Construction Issues

- The questions should be as simple, direct, and unambiguous as possible.
- Any unique or seldom-used terms should be clearly defined.
- Response choices should be consistent (e.g., avoid having the most positive choice first in one question, followed by a question for which the most negative response choice is first).
- Each question should address only one issue. A common mistake is to ask "double-barreled" questions, such as asking for a yes-or-no response to the question "Was the program helpful and timely?" It would be more effective to ask about the helpfulness and timeliness of the program in two separate questions.
- Pay attention to the brevity or complexity of questions; shorter questions will be easier to answer.

Fairness of the Survey Questions

- Option symmetry. Provide response choices that allow the respondents a full range of opinions. For example, in the typical choice of "Excellent, Good, Fair, Poor" only one of the options is truly bad, while the other three are all generally positive. Better symmetry would be found in "Excellent, Good, Poor, Unacceptable."
- Do not use terms that exclude potential respondents. For example, asking the question "Do you think bus service to work is adequate?" could confuse retired persons, unemployed persons, students, or other groups of possible nonworkers who might receive the survey.
- Avoid asking leading questions, such as "Do you believe that minority quotas are an unfair means of allocating political favors to specific voter groups?"

Additional elements related to survey questions are discussed in the next section on interviews.

Interviews

Interviews allow auditors to obtain testimonial evidence regarding a client's operations, activities, concerns, and initiatives. Both Yellow Book Standards and IIA *Standards* indicate that wherever possible, testimonial evidence should be further corroborated by other types of evidence, such as documentary or physical. Information obtained through interviews also can help auditors uncover and document instances of fraud and abuse. Interviewers should ensure that questions are unbiased and responses are recorded accurately.

The following guidelines are key features in conducting interviews:

- Set clear objectives for the interview.
- Be prepared. Before the interview, develop a point sheet that will remind the interviewer(s) of key questions to be asked.
- Ask questions in a low-key, professional style.
- It is advisable to have two audit team members conduct the interview, allowing one to focus on documenting the interviewee's remarks while the other asks the questions and follows up on answers requiring more explanation. This method also provides for greater accuracy when the interview is documented; one auditor prepares the write-up and the other reviews it to identify missing information or areas where the interviewers disagree on interpretation.
- Maintain a separate list of documents or other information sources described by the interviewee. The list also should include notations indicating those documents that were requested during the interview.
- Write up the interview promptly to avoid memory lapse.
- If the subject matter of an interview is complex or controversial, it is advisable that auditors request the interviewee to review and sign the final write-up.

Interviews can serve a variety of purposes during an audit. During the planning phase of the audit, open-ended questions can be used to obtain information on risks, environmental or political constraints, and issues of concern to the client. Open-ended questions ask the interviewee to provide narrative responses, such as "What are the key constraints that affect your operations?"

Closed-ended questions (those that provide for response within a limited range of choices) are often used during later stages of audit work to obtain specific details required by the auditors. An example of a closed-ended question is, "When you receive a purchase request that is unsigned, do you return it to the manager or do you process it without the signature?

Flowcharting

A flowchart is a visual representation of how a process works. The following commonly used symbols serve to diagram the flow of events or data through a system.

Symbol	Name	Function
	Process	Any type of operation that executes a defined function.
	Input/Output	Identifies general inputs and outputs.
	Decision	Used to ask a question that can be answered in a binary format (Yes/No, True/False).
	Flow Lines	Flow lines link symbols; crossed flow lines indicate no logical interconnection; and incoming flow lines may join an outgoing line at a junction point
	Arrowheads	Arrowheads indicate a path that is not left to right or top to bottom.
	Off-page Connector	Allows the flowchart to be carried forward to another page, while preserving a link back to an original point of reference.
	On-page Connector	Allows for the continuous flow of logic to be described on the same page without intersecting lines or a reverse flow.
	Predefined Process	Used to invoke a subroutine or an interrupt program.
	Terminal	Indicates the start or end of the program, process, or interrupt program.

The following general rules apply to flowcharting:

- Flowcharts generally flow from top to bottom and from left to right.
- All boxes of the flowchart should be connected with lines or arrows.
- The exit point for all flowchart symbols should be at the bottom, except for the decision symbol. The decision symbol should have two or more exit points; these can be on the sides or on the bottom and one side.
- Connectors should be used to connect breaks in the flowchart (e.g., from one page to another).
- All flowcharts should start with a terminal or predefined process symbol.
- All flowcharts should end with a terminal or a continuous loop.

Conducting Best Practice Reviews

Benchmarking is the process of identifying best practices and comparing them to one's own organization to improve quality. The process of identifying best practices begins with an initial organization selecting programs to benchmark and finding similar programs in other organizations for comparison. It is then necessary to identify specific processes where programs chosen for comparison

are most successful and the specific practices that enable them to excel. The initial organization then assesses its practices against best practices found in other programs and establishes goals and plans to implement quality improvement changes.

Program Evaluation

Program evaluation is well suited to government programs that provide direct services to people, such as health care, education, food stamps, job training, or correctional programs. Program evaluation typically addresses the effectiveness of programs. Economy and efficiency issues are generally the focus of performance audits. The purpose of a program evaluation is to assess program effectiveness. Program evaluations assess the overall effect of a program and its outcomes/results, and are typically conducted on a periodic or as-needed basis, in contrast to performance measurement, which is ongoing. Government officials use the results of program evaluations to assist in making major policy and budgetary decisions. The two major types of program evaluations are *summative evaluations* and *formative evaluations*.

Techniques of Summative Program Evaluation

Summative program evaluations focus on the results of the program to determine the program's effect. The net effect of a program can be analyzed by studying its outputs and outcomes in relation to the program's objectives. The program's effect also can be estimated by considering what would have occurred if the program did not exist. Summative evaluations also may analyze the cost of the program in relation to its outputs and outcomes, and unintended consequences of the program.

Typical methodologies used to conduct summative evaluations include:

- Case studies. This technique is useful in identifying best practices. For example, organizations for study may be identified based on their reputation in a given field. Evaluators then collect data, document, and evaluate the best practices of these organizations.
- Experimental and quasi-experimental, and interrupted time-series measurements.

Data collection techniques for summative evaluations include:

- Observation.
- Examination of documents or data analysis.
- Interviews.

Two methods of analyzing data that are used in summative evaluations are:

Content analysis is an analytic method that investigates the *meaning* of data. It is primarily a coding operation in which any form of communication is coded or classified in line with some conceptual framework. Important considerations for a content analysis effort are dealing with interpretations of meaning, the unit of analysis, coding categories, and the actual coding techniques. For example, content analysis could be used to determine the number and percent of contracts that include any type of language giving the contracting entity the right to audit the vendor. For this study, coding procedures could be refined to allow the reviewer to determine the number of right-to-audit clauses that included specific characteristics, such as record retention time standards, accessibility to staff and suppliers, timeliness of response to audit engagement announcements, availability of space for auditors on site, or other features. Content analysis also can be used to analyze answers to open-ended questions from surveys and interviews.

Contact summary form is a single sheet that contains a series of focusing or summarizing questions about a field contact. Evaluators can create matrices, graphs, or charts to supplement the text on the form.

Techniques of Formative Program Evaluation

Formative program evaluation considers the processes associated with the program, or factors in the program environment, to determine which components adversely affect effectiveness or do not add value to the program's goals, and which components have a positive influence on effectiveness and can be building blocks for increasing program value. Also called *process evaluations*, formative evaluations typically assess factors such as appropriateness of program design, involvement of stakeholders in the development and implementation of the program, congruence of program implementation to the original program design, and appropriateness of any modifications in design or delivery during the implementation.

Some techniques used in conducting formative evaluations are:

- ***Program modeling.*** Specify all activities/interventions and link the program activities to their expected intermediate and ultimate results.
- ***Focus groups.*** Small groups of stakeholders (e.g., staff, recipients) discuss their experiences with (and proposed changes to) an activity.
- ***Direct observation by evaluators.*** Unobtrusive evaluator observations are most effective (i.e., when the object of observation does not know it is being observed).
- ***Open-ended interviews.*** Open-ended questions have no preset response categories so interviewees must formulate their own answers.
- ***Ethnographic analysis.*** Observations and interviews are used to study, for example, how people learn, interact with others, or make decisions.
- ***Expert judgment.*** Individuals with extensive experience provide opinions related to proposed program components.
- ***Message or forms analysis.*** Evaluators determine reactions to or understanding of written or verbal communications.
- ***Equipment trials.*** Program equipment is tested to determine whether it serves its intended purpose.

III.F Methods for the Identification and Investigation of Integrity Violations[5]

Identifying and Evaluating Controls to Prevent and Detect Integrity Violations

Due professional care requires auditors to be alert for:

- The possibility of wrongdoing.
- Errors and omissions.
- Inefficiency.
- Waste.
- Ineffectiveness.
- Conflicts of interest.
- The possibility of material irregularities or noncompliance.

An effective system of controls is the most important deterrent an organization can have against integrity violations. Auditors are responsible for testing and evaluating internal control systems to ensure they adequately discourage undesirable employee behavior and actions. Areas auditors can consider when evaluating controls to prevent and detect integrity violations include:

- Management of the entity should have a positive attitude toward internal controls. In addition to establishing a system of internal controls, management is responsible for communicating what the controls are and the importance of following them. The likelihood that integrity violations will occur increases when employees perceive that management does not take controls seriously.
- The entity should have written policies (e.g., code of ethics, fraud policy) that describe codes of conduct and prohibited activities. These policies also should describe how integrity violations will be handled if detected.
- The entity should establish and maintain policies to ensure that transactions are properly authorized.
- The entity's policies and procedures should include adequate controls over information, activities, and assets. There should be special emphasis to ensure that controls are adequate over high-risk areas or sensitive information.
- Managers of information mechanisms (e.g., computers and telecommunications) should ensure that the information supplied to users is adequate and reliable by, for example, building adequate security into systems concerning who is allowed to enter, change, or approve data.
- Management should require reasonable productivity by its employees so they do not have to resort to unscrupulous practices to meet goals or quotas.
- The entity should have proper screening policies for employees, vendors, and contractors.

In testing the controls established by management, auditors should be able to identify if there are high-risk areas for integrity violations. Auditor responsibilities in detecting integrity violations include:

- Auditors must have the knowledge and skills to adequately identify when violations have occurred.
- When significant control weaknesses are found, the auditor should conduct sufficient tests to determine if these weaknesses resulted in integrity violations. The level of testing should increase as the number or significance of control weaknesses increases.
- Auditors should evaluate the evidence and determine the appropriate course of action. An investigation may be warranted if indicators strongly suggest that integrity violations have occurred.
- Auditors should notify the proper legal authorities, if warranted.

Auditors should communicate to management any recommendations for establishing additional controls or enhancing existing controls. Cost-effectiveness should be a primary consideration to ensure that the recommended level of control is appropriate for the importance of the function being reviewed. A greater level of control should be associated with areas where integrity violations have a high risk of occurring.

Appropriate Steps When Integrity Violations Are First Suspected

If the fraud indicators (e.g., "red flags") suggest that integrity violations have occurred, a formal investigation may be warranted. Based on the nature of the potential violation, auditors, lawyers, investigators, security personnel, or other specialists from inside or outside the organization may be assigned to the investigation.

The general goals of an integrity investigation include:

- Establishing that a loss occurred or that the organization was at risk of loss.
- Identifying who committed the violation. The investigation can also clear innocent people.
- Proving who committed the violation and that the violator acted with malicious intent.
- Recovering lost assets.
- Preventing repeat violations.

The basic steps in conducting an integrity investigation include:

- Determining the knowledge and skills needed by the investigative team. The investigative team should collectively possess the technical expertise necessary to conduct an effective investigation. All members of the team must be independent of all persons being investigated to avoid an actual conflict of interest or the appearance of impairment.
- Designing adequate investigative procedures. The investigation should be designed to determine who committed or assisted in the violation and why/how it was committed, its extent, and what control weaknesses allowed the violation to occur.
- Coordinating investigative activities. A wide variety of individuals may be involved in the investigation. The roles of management personnel, legal staff, and other specialists should be coordinated as necessary.
- Determining the extent of the violation and who is involved. Individuals who allowed the violation to occur by acts of omission or commission are also guilty of wrongdoing. Therefore, before questioning employees, it is important to understand not only how the violation occurred and who committed it but also which employees could have been in a position to abet the violation by failing to recognize or report it. The quality of information will be more reliable if, before beginning the questioning, investigators understand each individual's role in the organization and his or her possible role in the violation.
- Maintaining professionalism. Alleged perpetrators have the right to expect an objective investigation and that allegations against them will be kept as confidential as possible until they are substantiated. Any unprofessional conduct by investigators or breach of confidentiality could cause the party under investigation to file a lawsuit against the organization or an individual investigator.

After the investigation is concluded, auditors should take the steps necessary to prevent similar violations from occurring again. This can be achieved by determining whether additional controls are needed or if existing controls should be strengthened. Appropriate audit tests should be included in future audit programs to test for similar violations.

Designing Audit Procedures to Detect Integrity Violations

Although auditing standards require due professional care in designing audit procedures to detect fraud, auditors also should know about and be cognizant of typical red flags that can be the first indication that an integrity violation is occurring. Some examples follow.

Employee Red Flags

- Employee lifestyle changes: expensive cars, jewelry, homes, clothes.
- Significant personal debt and credit problems.
- Behavioral changes; these may be indications of drug, alcohol, or gambling problems.
- High employee turnover, especially in areas that are more vulnerable to fraud.
- Refusal to take vacation or sick leave.
- Lack of segregation of duties in a vulnerable area.

Management Red Flags

- Reluctance to provide information to auditors.
- Excessive number of checking accounts.
- Frequent banking changes.
- Excessive number of year-end transactions (particularly if backed out in the next period).
- Unexpected overdrafts or declines in cash balance.

Cash/Accounts Receivable Red Flags

- Customer complaints that they are not receiving notices for nonpayment on account.
- Excessive amounts of supplies held by employee or abnormal number of expense items.
- Presence of employee checks in petty cash.
- Bank accounts not reconciled timely.

Payroll Red Flags

- Inconsistent overtime hours for a cost center.
- Overtime charged for exempt employees.
- Overtime charged during a slack period.

Purchasing/Inventory Red Flags

- Increase in purchasing inventory, but no increase in productivity.
- Abnormal inventory shrinkage.
- Lack of physical security over assets/inventory.
- Payments to vendors not on approved vendor list.
- Vendors without physical addresses.

Investigators should focus on gaining:

- Physical evidence.
- Documentary evidence.
- Testimonial evidence of witnesses and/or the accused person.

The investigation should be kept confidential to avoid alerting the violators. Discussion information and internal memoranda should be shared only with those people who have a genuine need to know.

The following guidelines apply to handling records that have a bearing on the investigation to ensure their admissibility in court:

- All original documents should be secured and logged at the earliest possible stage of an investigation.
- Original documents should be kept separate from working copies.
- Important single documents should be put in transparent plastic bags.

Documents may be altered as part of the integrity violation. Therefore, investigators should look for indicators of integrity violations when examining documents. These include:

- Erased or crossed out figures.
- Inconsistent inks and typefaces.
- Unusual dates, amounts, notes, phone numbers, and calculations.
- Records missing (from sequential checks).
- Unexplained adjusted figures after authorization and posting.
- Excessive voids or refunds.
- Excessive uncollectible accounts or numerous write-offs.
- Checks payable to individuals in large, even-sum amounts.
- Invoices printed on other than prepared forms.
- Vendor address is the same as an employee address.
- Unusual number of payments to one payee or address.
- Unusual endorsements on canceled checks.
- Unusual patterns in deposits.
- Unusual delays in providing information.

According to authoritative sources, experience in both the public and private sector indicates that the most common means of detection of integrity violations is through passive means. These passive means take the form of tips received from the violator's fellow employees or from alert citizens or service customers. However, short of implementing a fraud hotline in an organization, there are other methods that auditors can use to identify potential integrity violations.

The following list includes some of the common audit procedures that may be used to detect integrity violations:

- Conduct unannounced cash counts.
- Review the composition of deposits.
- Reconcile sequentially pre-numbered documents.
- Review procedures for voiding checks.
- Compare actual warrants to register entries.
- Review controls over warrant authorization.
- Review bank reconciliations.
- Search for duplicate payments.
- Match vendor addresses against employee addresses.
- Analyze and confirm overtime.
- Take a sample of credit customers and confirm their account balances.
- Take a test count of sample inventory items.

Interrogatory Interviews

Investigations of integrity violations may require interviews of witnesses, informants, or suspects. The objective of interrogatory interviews is to obtain formal evidence in writing. Guidelines for conducting effective interrogatory interviews include:

- Setting clear objectives for the interview.
- Listening to subjects and watching their reactions.
- Holding the interview in a private setting, but not in the suspect's own office or home.
- Being persistent.
- Not allowing biases to impair judgment and independence.
- Minimizing interruptions and distractions (e.g., disconnecting telephones, removing clocks from the wall).
- Arranging furniture so the suspect and interviewer are close together and not separated by desks or tables.
- Enlarging and pinning to the walls any pieces of particularly incriminating evidence (e.g., forged documents, altered accounts).
- Asking questions in a low-key, professional style.
- Keeping documents of vital significance in a transparent document cover so the suspect cannot mutilate them; never leave a suspect alone in a room with important documents.

There are two major categories of questions interviewers can ask:

- ***Open-ended questions*** require the subject to give a detailed reply. For example:

  "What did you do next?"

  "How could this have been done?"'

- ***Closed-ended questions*** usually call for yes/no replies or suggest a possible answer. For example:

  "And then you threw the papers in the shredder?"

  "And he told you to say nothing?"

Interviewers should be aware of the subject's body language, which might indicate whether the person is hesitant, open, frightened, happy, or sad. The signs of stress that often accompany deception include nervous gestures, closed posture, and failure to make eye contact.

The interviewer should prepare a complete record of each interview. It is also advisable to make an audio recording of the interview, if possible. To ensure admissibility in court, the following procedure for recording interviews is recommended:

- Use a quiet interview room. Air conditioning and other audible noises can ruin a recording. For this reason, it is wise to make a test recording and play it back before conducting an interview.
- Make sure that the recording equipment works properly.
- Purchase new storage devices (e.g., thumb drives) for the interview and retain the receipt for production in court, if necessary.
- Initial and date each storage device immediately before loading it into the computer.

- Make a second working copy of each device with stored information as soon as possible; if necessary, take needed steps to remove background noise.
- Deliver the device with stored information immediately to the organization's lawyers and get a signed receipt showing the date and time that the information was handed over. This should reduce the possibility of accusations that the data were manipulated.
- Transcribe notes from the stored information and check them carefully.

If the subject is uncooperative and refuses to answer questions, there are two recommended options:

- Continue to ask formal questions. Each time the subject refuses to answer, make a notation in a notebook and say: "To that question, Mr. X said nothing." It is extremely difficult for the suspect to remain silent in this situation.
- Temporarily suspend the formal interview and engage the subject in general conversation. The interviewer should gently try to direct the conversation back to the investigation.

Admissions of guilt should not be coerced. Record all statements verbatim. When the interview is completed, any ambiguities should be clarified and corrected. The suspect should read the statement and initial all changes. The person should sign the following declaration: "I have read the above statement and have been told that I can correct or add anything I wish. This statement is true. I have made it of my own free will." The interviewer should note if the subject refuses to sign the declaration. The statement also should include the date(s) and time(s) the interview began and ended, including any time allocated for breaks.

Appropriate Standards for Reporting of Integrity Violations Following an Investigation

Auditors should follow the guidelines listed below after they conclude that an integrity violation has occurred:

- Notify management immediately when it becomes clear that a violation has been committed.
- Determine the fiscal or other impact of the violation.
- Write a report that describes findings, conclusions, recommendations, and corrective actions.
- Consult with legal counsel as necessary regarding the proper handling of evidence, the sufficiency of evidence, and other related matters. Additionally, it is advisable to send a draft of the proposed report to legal counsel for review before it is forwarded to management.

The final investigative report serves three major purposes:

- To provide a format for recording the essential details of the integrity violation.
- To give the investigator a framework for analyzing the case.
- To recommend improved management and security policies.

Final investigative reports usually contain:

- Management overview or a brief summary of the case and details of the people involved and recommended actions.
- Detailed description and chronology of events surrounding the violation.
- A detailed account of steps taken in the investigation.
- An estimate of losses resulting from the violation.
- Detailed explanation of important evidence.
- Description of weak or compromised controls that led to the violation.
- Recommendations for corrective action.

III.G Analytical Skills

Logical Thinking

Auditors must be able to develop appropriate and supportable conclusions based on the evidence they collect. In addition, auditors are sometimes called upon to evaluate the soundness of decisions made by management or to review the adequacy of support for conclusions developed by other auditors.

Written findings are essentially formal arguments made in support of a particular position. To develop the critical thinking skills necessary in developing findings and conclusions, auditors should be familiar with the two major categories of logical fallacies:

- *Inductive fallacies* result when evidence is used incorrectly. For example, after interviewing one dissatisfied employee of an agency, an auditor might incorrectly assume that all employees are dissatisfied with agency management or that the morale of all agency employees is low.
- *Deductive fallacies* result from a failure to follow the logic of a series of statements. Deductive arguments are based on a series of statements or premises. Deductive logic states that if a series of premises is true, then the conclusion also must be true. However, deductive arguments are valid only if a sound relationship exists between the premises.

An example of an invalid deductive argument:

Major premise. All employees who are committing fraud drive luxury cars.

Minor premise. John Doe drives a luxury car.

Conclusion. Therefore, John Doe is committing fraud.

Auditors should be familiar with the principles of argumentation and be able to make judgments based on available information. Auditors may exhibit illogical thinking in their own attempts to support conclusions that are not fully supported by the evidence. In addition, auditors may find flaws in the logic supporting some management decision that was not fully explored before being implemented.

Listed below are some specific types of logical fallacies that auditors need to avoid:

- *Slippery slope.* This is the argument that if a particular action is taken, it will inevitably lead to another, less desirable action. Clients often resort to slippery slope arguments in an effort to resist adopting audit recommendations. For example, a client might make the following statement: "If you make us put property tags and numbers on major equipment, next we will have to put tags on every pen, pencil, and paper clip in the place." One can easily recognize this argument as exaggerated and illogical. Auditors also are prone to these logical fallacies. For instance, an auditor might note that the lack of a standard or recommended control (based on use of an ICQ) will lead to losses. The auditor's supervisor should ascertain whether the auditor has ruled out the existence of any compensating controls or other risk-reduction strategies.
- *Non sequitur.* This means "it does not follow." Again, clients often use non sequiturs to oppose findings. For example, a client might make the following statement: "Our financial accounting system is well controlled; our books always balance." Before accepting this argument in favor of effective controls, determine the extent of adjusting entries that must be made to ensure that the books balance.
- *Post hoc, ergo propter hoc.* This means "after this, therefore because of this" and infers that because one event follows another event, the first event must have caused the second. For example, after implementation of a dropout recovery program, employment rates rose. Before concluding that the dropout recovery program is responsible for increases in employment, look for possible economic or other factors that might have contributed to the rise.
- *Hasty generalization.* These are judgments based on limited information that often reflect a bias or prejudice. For example, a person might incorrectly attribute some negative personal characteristic to all members of a particular race, gender, or ethnic group.
- *Ad hominem.* This means "against the man" and refers to attacks on an individual rather than the issue being debated. For example, it would be illogical for a cat-loving manager to not recommend a qualified auditor for promotion simply because the auditor expressed a dislike of cats.
- *False use of authority.* An auditor might cite support for a finding from an external source such as a book or article. However, it is important to ensure that the auditor presents this evidence fairly, which means presenting not only the author's view but also the opposing or alternative views of other authors. It is not acceptable to present a biased or skewed version of available research.

Distinguishing Between Significant and Insignificant Information

Auditors should base findings and recommendations on significant information. For example, one exception in 1,000 cases is probably not reason enough to recommend overhauling the entire system, although the final answer must be derived from the context and the condition of the related control system. Findings and recommendations should be based on sound logic and evidence.

Auditors should be aware that the concepts of materiality and significance take on different meanings in the public and private sectors. Issues affecting public accountability, equity, and stewardship may have a greater direct impact in the public sector. For example, a manager of a very controversial program may have stolen only $200, but the controversy and public accountability aspects may make the $200 significant, where it would not be material in the private sector financial statement opinion audit. Therefore, during the planning and reporting processes, government auditors may need to consider qualitative factors such as the visibility or sensitivity of the program under audit, or the newness of the program or changes in its condition.

DOMAIN IV
Government Auditing Environment

Domain IV highlights key aspects of government environments primarily in the United States, with limited references to other countries. Many broad principles and approaches are similar, but variations do exist from country to country. Thus, those taking the international version of the CGAP examination should use additional relevant sources to supplement their examination preparation.

Authorities and Responsibilities in Government

Government organizations operate under a structure that differs from the private sector. In the United States, the hierarchy of authorities is as follows:

- *Constitutions* at the national and state levels and *charters* at the local levels.
- *Laws* that address policy and administration (some permanent, some temporary).
- *Executive orders* by CEOs (within parameters).
- *Rules and regulations* by executive agencies that guide daily administration.

Government auditors need to be aware of this hierarchy; they are generally concerned with compliance with laws and regulations.

Government auditors also should be aware of the processes for proposing and enacting laws, and of upcoming changes. In this regard, appendix E provides an example of how the national level of government in the United States establishes legislation. Auditors of other government organizations — in the United States and other countries — should have an awareness of the legislative processes of the programs they audit.

Differences Between Government and Nongovernment Environments

Government auditors work in environments that differ in many ways from nongovernment environments.

Following the exam syllabus for domain IV, differences are highlighted in the following areas:

A. Performance management.
B. Financial management.
C. Implications of various service delivery methods.
D. Implications of delivery services to citizens.
E. Unique characteristics of human resources management.
F. Unique purchasing and procurements requirements.

IV.A Performance Management

As noted in domain III, performance measurement and management laws, regulations, and initiatives have expanded greatly in the past few decades. The material below provides highlights as to these government activities and practices primarily in the United States, but with a few examples from other countries. The material focuses on the status in early 2012, but government auditors need to continuously monitor further developments as government performance is of enormous interest of oversight bodies, the media, and the public who push for improvements.

The Federal Level of Government in the United States[1]

The performance measurement initiatives at the federal level are driven by legislation and related initiatives.

The Government Performance and Results Act (GPRA) of 1993 is often cited as the landmark law on performance measurement and management for the federal government. However, before enactment of the GPRA, the Chief Financial Officers (CFO) Act of 1990, as amended by the Government Management Reform Act of 1994 (GMRA), initiated landmark changes in accounting and financial reporting by the largest federal agencies. While the major emphasis of the CFO Act, as amended, was on preparation and audit of financial statements, the legislation did call for "systematic measurement of performance." Reporting on performance was limited to a "high level" (in the narrative section of the annual financial report) — and performance was not required to be audited like financial data — but the legislation did lay the groundwork for GPRA. The CFO Act is discussed further in domain IV of this manual.

The GPRA requires federal agencies to develop goals and file an annual report of program performance and results achieved.

GPRA requires federal agencies to prepare strategic plans that include:

- A comprehensive mission statement covering major functions and operations of the agency.
- General goals and objectives, including outcome-related goals and objectives for the agency's major functions and operations.
- A description of how the goals and objectives are to be achieved, including a description of the operational processes, skills, and technology, and the resources (e.g., human, capital, information) required to meet those goals and objectives.
- A description of how the performance goals relate to the agency's general goals and objectives.
- A description of key factors external to the agency that could significantly affect the achievement of the general goals and objectives.
- A description of the program evaluations used in establishing or revising general goals and objectives, with a schedule for future program evaluations

GPRA also requires agencies to prepare annual performance plans* that include:

- Performance goals (expressed in an objective, quantifiable form) that define the level of performance to be achieved during the year.
- Brief description of the strategies (operational processes, skills, and technology) to be used and the resources required.
- Performance indicators to be used to measure or assess the relevant outputs, service levels, and outcomes of each activity.
- Basis for comparing actual program results to established performance goals.
- Descriptions of the means for verifying and validating the measured values.

GPRA also requires federal agencies to submit an annual report on program performance for the previous fiscal year. The program performance reports are required to compare actual performance in relation to relevant performance indicators. If any performance goals are not met, the report must indicate:

- Why the goal was not met.
- Those plans and schedules for achieving the established performance goal.
- If the performance goal is impractical or infeasible, why that is the case and what action is recommended.

The GPRA was updated and modernized effective January 4, 2011, when the GPRA Modernization Act was signed. New requirements or emphasis were as follows:

- Amends strategic plan to four years, instead of five.
- Streamlines annual performance planning and reporting to focus on key goals and measures.
- Requires cross cutting goals.
- Requires quarterly review of key measures.
- Establishes an organizational structure for performance, including chief performance officers.

The 2011 legislation is intended to increase the use of performance information in program decision-making by defining a governance structure to oversee performance; providing for a better connection among plans, programs, and performance information; and requiring more frequent reporting and reviews.

Executive Order 13576, dated June 13, 2011, is intended to reinforce the intentions of the GPRA Modernization Act by requiring:

- Federal performance officers work with agencies to ensure that each area identified as critical to performance improvement has robust metrics in place.
- Those metrics are frequently analyzed and reviewed by agency leadership.

* (also termed *performance budget)*

- Agencies' chief operating officer be designated as the senior accountable official accountable responsible for leading the performance and management reform efforts, and conducting frequent data-driven performance reviews of agency progress.

Auditors in the federal level of government are well advised to stay informed on further developments related to improved performance management via laws, regulations, and other initiatives. Auditors may be assigned a variety of responsibilities and roles relating to federal performance management activities.

Performance Measurement at State and Local Levels in the United States[2]

The Governmental Accounting Standards Board (GASB) has been an active advocate for performance measurement by state and local governments in the United States. As discussed below, GASB has issued concepts statements and performed research but not standards, deciding instead in 2010 to call for voluntary reporting. Nevertheless, many states and cities have enacted laws and ordinances requiring performance measurement/management systems. A few examples of state and local governments that have performance initiatives are cited below.

GASB Concepts Statement No. 1 states that governmental financial reporting should provide information to assist users in assessing the service efforts and accomplishments (SEA) of the governmental entity. SEA information brings the issue of accountability to the forefront of financial reporting activities. The GASB has encouraged the reporting of SEA performance information by issuing "Suggested Guidelines for Voluntary Reporting." In Concepts Statement 2 (as amended by Concepts Statement 5), the GASB identified three main elements of SEA performance measures:

- *Service efforts,* which are measures of inputs. These input measures include both financial items, such as salaries and equipment costs, as well as nonfinancial items, such as the number of staff hours allocated to a particular function.
- *Service accomplishments,* which are outputs and outcomes. The GASB defines outputs as measures of the quantity of service provided (e.g., number of arrests) and outcomes as the extent provided services achieve a particular result (e.g., change in the number of violent crimes committed). The purpose of reporting on service accomplishments is to assist users in assessing the performance of government programs.
- ***Measures relating service efforts to service accomplishments*** (i.e., efficiency measures), which relate inputs to outputs (e.g., the cost per ambulance responses or the number of applications screened per staff hour) or inputs to outcomes (e.g., cost per lane-mile of road maintained in good or excellent condition).

Due to the diverse nature of governmental organizations, the GASB does not specify relevant SEA measures for all types of entities. Therefore, each governmental entity is to develop its own SEA measures through information from a variety of stakeholders such as agency or department personnel (e.g., financial managers, program managers, budget staff, and internal auditors), elected officials, and other interest groups.

In issuing its Suggested Guidelines for Voluntary Reporting, GASB modified somewhat the SEA reporting suggested. GASB identifies four essential components of reporting: 1) purpose and scope, 2) major goals and objectives, 3) key measures of SEA performance, and 4) discussion and analysis of results and challenges. GASB also calls for the same six *qualitative characteristics* — comparability, consistency, relevance, reliability, timeliness, and understandability — as those expected in general purpose financial statements.

Examples of States and Local Governments with Performance Management Initiatives[3]

A large number of states and local governments have implemented initiatives for performance measurement and performance budgeting. Approaches vary and also change from time to time. Examples include:

States

- Florida ("Florida Performs" website launched in 2007).
- Idaho (Office of Program Evaluations created in 1994).
- Maryland (first state to use a statewide performance measurement system for the public).

- Oregon (Oregon Progress Board created in 1990, not funded for 2009–2011).
- Virginia ("Virginia Performs" is the performance measurement program).
- Washington (Government Accountability and Performance program award in 2008).

Local Governments

- Austin, Texas (Managing for Results System, 1991-2012). See appendix F for an overview of the effectiveness of this approach.
- New York City ("Mayors Management Report" chartered in 1977.
- Columbus, Ohio (Office of Performance Management/Columbus State).
- Sarasota County, Florida (many transformations over the years).
- Minneapolis, Minnesota ("Results Minneapolis" roots in 2003).
- City of Rock Hill, South Carolina (use of measures in budget since 1995).
- Redmond, Washington ("Budgeting by Priorities" established after others).
- Albuquerque, New Mexico (efforts began in 1994).
- Des Moines, Iowa (history can be traced to 1959).
- Portland, Oregon (20 years of SEA reporting by the city auditor has been discontinued, but city management was considering resumption at the time of this publication).

In their 2010 report titled *A Performance Management Framework for State and Local Governments...,* the National Performance Management Advisory Commission offers the following definition:

"Performance management in the public sector is an ongoing, systematic approach to improving results through evidence-based decision-making, continuous organizational learning, and a focus on accountability. Performance management integrated into all aspects of an organization's management and policy-making processes, transforming an organization's practices so it is focused on achieving improved results for the public."

Further, the Commission identified seven principles of performance management.

Performance Management Initiatives in Countries Other than the United States

At a November 2011 conference in Seattle, Washington, on performance management in state and local governments, one presentation discussed performance management initiative in countries other than the United States. The many countries identified as having initiatives included Canada (discussed below), Australia, the Netherlands, Switzerland, Brazil, Finland, and even one province in China.[4]

Performance measurement and reporting in Canada includes the following:

Canada's federal government has a Treasury Board that establishes and communicates to federal departments government-wide management and administrative policies, ensures that management policies and accountability frameworks are in place in departments, and reviews their effectiveness. Adopted in the 1980s, Canada's Increased Ministerial Authority and Accountability (IMAA) initiative required departments to report results-based program performance information. Departmental ministers developed "memoranda of understanding" with the president of the Treasury Board to define specific departmental responsibilities and related performance criteria and indicators. Specific areas of responsibility addressed in the memoranda of understanding include:

- Resource utilization.
- Service efforts.
- Accomplishments.
- Results, effects, outcomes.
- Compliance with Treasury Board policy/guidelines.
- Administrative, management, and/or program performance.[5]

The Canadian federal government also has a Management and Accountability Framework (MAF), which goes from "Governance and Strategic Directions" to "Results and Performance," based on "Policy and Programs," "People," "Citizen-focused Service," "Risk Management," "Stewardship," and "Accountability," all influenced by "Public Service Values" and "Learning, Innovation and Change Management."

In 2005–2006, the Treasury Board secretariat issued a *Guide for Preparing Departmental Performance Reports* with the following principles:

- ***Principle 1.*** Focus on the benefits for Canadians, explain the critical aspects of planning and performance, and set them in context.
- ***Principle 2.*** Present credible, reliable, and balanced information.
- ***Principle 3.*** Associate performance with plans, priorities, and expected results, explain changes, and apply lessons learned.
- ***Principle 4.*** Link resources to results.

Performance measurement and management and related initiatives are extensive in many countries other than the United States and Canada. Therefore, government auditors in any country are well advised to stay abreast of legislation, regulations, and initiatives related to performance measurement, and to be prepared to carry out all relevant duties.

The 2006 Statement of Recommended Practices on Performance Reporting (SORP-2) of Canada's Public Sector Accounting Board emphasizes the need for:

- Information that is relevant, reliable, valid, fair, understandable, comparable, and consistent.
- Focus on a few critical aspects of performance.
- Identification of strategic direction.
- Comparative information, including comparison of actual and planned results.
- Lessons learned and key factors influencing performance and results.
- Linking financial and nonfinancial information.
- Disclosure of the basis for reporting.[6]

Broad Issues to Be Considered in Performance Management Initiatives in Government

The discussion above is about the specifics of performance measurement initiatives in the United States and includes an identification of a few countries with initiatives. The discussion below is about four broad issues to be considered generally in government performance measurement, reporting, and management.

The four issues are:

- Performance management and reporting, and the challenges in applying them in a government context.
- Difficulty of linking information to results and outcomes.
- Framework of performance initiatives.
- Challenge of measuring certain government programs.

Performance Management and Reporting and the Challenges in Applying Them in a Government Context

Effective performance management establishes programs and resources within the organization that address its agency-wide objectives and administers them through four phases: plan, do, check, and act." Guiding principles include long-range planning, collaborative input, a results orientation, decisions based upon measurable data, and continuous improvement in outcomes. The first step in managing performance is a structured, cohesive planning approach. During the plan phase, managers set performance expectations based upon objectives and available resources. In the planning phase of any project, needs are assessed, goals and objectives are established, appropriate strategies for meeting the needs are determined, and resources such as funding and staffing are defined or developed. Employees should be involved in the process to ensure they understand the goals. Employee insight is valuable when defining the actual steps of what needs to be done, why it needs to be done, and how it will be done. Planning should define the programs, desired results, and related program goals and performance indicators. During the planning phase, managers must determine how they will measure the spectrum of performance for which they are responsible. Appropriate outcome measures and targets are developed.

During the do phase, the program is implemented and operations commence. Employees are trained to ensure not only competence but also to get assurances that they understand and agree to comply with policies and procedures designed to make the program successful. During the implementation, the work environment should be a results-oriented climate. Throughout this phase, predetermined data is collected congruent with the performance measures developed in the plan. Sample measurement data can include the number of persons served, timeliness, and whether the issue was satisfactorily resolved.

During the check phase, the data are aggregated and formatted to facilitate management oversight of key measures. Managers review the results to determine whether the program is effective in achieving the desired results. Managers also review employee performance and identify and investigate any reasons for variances from the original plan. Rewards, either on an individual or department-wide level, can be used to motivate employees who return positive results and achieve goals.

The act phase involves management decision-making based upon the program evaluation. Managers should regularly evaluate performance and communicate findings and improvement plans throughout the organization. Actions or decisions can affect any of the other phases. Either plans are revised (whether budgets are adjusted, outcome measurements are revised, programs are redesigned, or procedures are changed, etc.) to address any variances or operational flaws are corrected. Additional training or instructions are provided or reports are revised to improve performance monitoring.

Performance measurement is an evaluation of how well an organization achieves its goals using available resources. Variables that can be measured or defined are inputs of resources, procedures and activities undertaken to achieve goals, outputs from those procedures, and eventual outcomes. Table IV.1, Program Model for Performance Expectations and Measurement, describes the phases of a government program (inputs, processes, outputs, and outcomes) together with the aspects of performance that public-sector managers are responsible for at each phase: economy of inputs; efficiency of processes; effectiveness and quality of outputs; and effectiveness and quality of outcomes. Below these rows are types of measures that might be used to measure the aspects of performance. Finally, at all phases of the process, managers are responsible for crosscutting goals of compliance (at the input stage, for instance, managers must comply with budget constraints, full-time employee caps, etc.; at the process stage, they might be responsible for complying with eligibility rules and other policies/procedures; etc.).

Table IV.1. Program Model for Performance Expectations and Measurement[7]

Inputs	Process	Output	Outcome
(Economy)	(Efficiency)	(Effectiveness)	(Effectiveness)
Financial • Amounts • Timing **Physical** • Quantity • Quality • Timing	**Productivity** • Output/input **Unit Cost** • Input/output **Operating Ratios**	**Level/Quantity** **Timeliness** **Quality** **Price/Cost** **Customer Satisfaction**	**Mission and Goal Achievement** **Financial Viability** **Customer Satisfaction**
	Crosscutting Performance Goals		
	Compliance with Laws and Regulations **Reliability, Validity, and Availability of Information** **Maintaining Underlying Values** • Individual Ethics and Integrity • Societal Equity • Cooperation and Partnership **Continuous Improvement**		

Source: This table was adapted from Public Sector Governance and Accountability Series, "Performance Accountability and Combating Corruption," p. 328. The World Bank, 2007.

Inputs are the measurement of efforts or economic resources that are put into a program activity. This category includes both financial and nonfinancial information. Financial measures might include the cost of salaries, employee pensions, health care, and other benefits. Beyond human resource expenses are costs attributed to office supplies, equipment, and any contractual services needed to support a program.

Information can be reported in its totality or broken down by the average cost of each unit. For example, the total human resource cost for all teachers in a school district is $5.6 million, where the per unit human resource cost is $40,000 for each employee. Nonfinancial measurement of input can be quantified physically in terms of the number of full-time personnel or building square footage, acres of land, etc., used in providing a service.[8] Breaking down the measurement can further delineate this information by type or quality. For example, there are 140 full-time equivalent employees who teach in the school district. Job function, educational background, or years of service can further categorize these 140 people.

Processes are the measurements that relate efforts to accomplishments, generally reporting on efficiency and cost of providing a specific unit of service. This type of data is useful for making comparisons to previous years or other jurisdictions. In a school system that is producing students, one measurement of process would be the annual cost of each student attending. Cost measures also are useful and further categorize efforts so that policy makers and users of information can begin to assess value on certain services. For example, one indicator of higher academic test scores shows that smaller class sizes are generally better learning environments. Although the cost associated with providing a lower student-to-teacher ratio (hiring more staff, requiring more classroom space) would increase, so would the value of education within the school district.

If the objective is to obtain better scores on standardized tests, both efficiency and value have to be considered when developing efforts to achieve the desired outcome. If smaller teacher-to-student ratios are not feasible, other indicators for higher test scores such as curriculum can be measured and assessed. If a school district researches the possibility of changing its mathematics curriculum, for example, costs for textbooks and teacher orientation would have to be considered.

Output refers to accomplishments of services provided. Output is generally measured by quantity and quality. Quantitative indicators of effective output at a school district would include the number or percent of students graduated or promoted in a school year. Qualitative indicators are vital when measuring effectiveness. This would include the number or percent of students graduating on time or with honors, or meeting other standards. Timeliness in providing a service is a key component of accountability.[9] If it takes more than four years, or requires summer attendance for the majority of district students to complete high school, the academic program may be at risk. Of course, other societal factors, which the school district has little effect upon, could explain low performance measurements. However, timeliness in providing a service is an important component of effective output and instills customer satisfaction.

Outcome refers to results that occur because of services provided. Outcome measures are particularly useful when making comparisons to previous years, to other similar organizations, or to established missions and goals. Outcome results can be based upon output effectiveness. For example, if a school district's mission is to prepare students for higher education and then proceeds to graduate (output) a high percentage of honor students, an expected outcome would be a generally healthy acceptance level of students at colleges and universities.

There are secondary effects to outcomes that are not easily measured due to intangible factors. These measures are difficult to identify and correlate back to the service provided because there are so many causes affecting results. Many qualified students, for various reasons, do not choose a college path. They may, however, find very successful and/or meaningful careers and become productive citizens. The degree of impact that quality education has upon their life can be difficult to assess.[10]

Crosscutting performance goals are other factors that managers are responsible for across all phases of the service provision process. These concerns need to be considered when reporting service efforts and accomplishments. While these factors cannot always be measured in quantifiable terms, they definitely impact how and why services are provided. Factors to consider are:

- Compliance with laws and regulations.
    - Reliability, validity, and availability of information.
- Maintaining underlying values.
    - Individual ethics and integrity.
    - Societal equity.
    - Cooperation and partnership.
- Continuous improvement.

Difficulty of Linking Information to Results and Outcomes

To assess whether a government agency is accountable, decision makers, auditors, and other interested parties must measure beyond whether appropriations are being spent as intended by the fiscal budget. They must assess whether, in spending these funds, the agency achieved its desired results.

There are limitations associated with the use of performance information. Methods to measure the effectiveness of programs are hard to ascertain and assessment may have to rely on surrogate factors. Fire departments can have educational programs, yet how effective they are at preventing actual fires is not always apparent. The number of home fires may increase or decrease in any given period, but the effect the prevention program had on the community is hard to gauge. How would someone determine the number of fires that did not occur due to a program? Surrogate measures that can be used to measure a fire prevention program's success can be documented by the number of classes and students, or a test or survey identifying knowledge gained from the class. Other prevention programs that are challenged by linking programs to surrogate outcomes are:

- Drug and alcohol prevention programs.
- Early education intervention programs.
- Teen pregnancy prevention.

Sometimes there are too many difficult-to-measure dimensions of what programs are trying to achieve. For instance, the main goal of an early-intervention program such as Head Start is to provide development skills to children at risk of educational failure. After attending the program, a child would be prepared to enter kindergarten. Would a child's chances at success in school be linked to the Head Start program? At what point would any advantages gained though Head Start even out?

To evaluate this, comparisons between Head Start students and non-Head Start students might provide an answer. If the two populations differ in exercising the abilities required at the kindergarten level, is the difference (positive or negative) attributed to the program? One might be able to directly link carryover curriculum (colors, numbers, letters, or shape recognition) and measure the difference between the two populations. However, one must consider the likelihood that both populations of children were exposed to these subject matters at home or elsewhere. Also, if there is a wide difference, at what point would one population catch up to the other? There are innumerable variables that can relate to educational success such as intelligence, attitude, family support structure, and self-confidence that would need to be adjusted to determine the overall success of the early intervention programs alone.

In certain instances, a onetime or periodic program evaluation, rather than ongoing performance measurement, is the most effective way to measure impacts of government programs. However, onetime evaluations still require reliable performance measurements to determine whether a program is successful or not.

Framework of Performance Initiatives[11]

The integrity and validity of data reported on efforts and accomplishments is a crucial component if decision makers and any interested public group or individual are to assess the value of an organization. Information used in reporting should be reviewed for accuracy and contain the following characteristics:

- Relevance.
- Understandability.
- Comparability.
- Timeliness.
- Consistency.
- Reliability.

Information should be **relevant** and provide the reader with an understanding of the performance measures

used to assess the service efforts and accomplishment of goals and objectives of the agency. Performance information should be management's representations of the agency and its programs and services. To ensure that a single aspect of performance is not being emphasized to the detriment of other aspects of performance, a variety of performance measures should be used to meet the various needs of the decision makers, auditors, and any interested body or individual.

Performance information should be easy to **understand**. It should be able to convey in a clear and concise yet comprehensive manner the performance of the agency to any reasonably informed party. Because government services are so broad, information should be provided at the most appropriate level to achieve a balance among the number of services reported, the performance measures reported, and the capability of users to understand and act on the information. Underlying factors and existing conditions (environment, demographics) that affect performance that are substantially (or partially) outside the control of the agency.

Information should be consistent and provide a clear frame of reference for assessing the performance of the agency when making **comparisons** to previous years, to other similar organizations, or to established industry standards. When presented alone, performance measures do not provide a basis for assessing service efforts or accomplishments. Efforts should also be made to ensure that the information is reported in a **timely** manner so that it is available before it loses its capacity to be of value when assessing accountability and making decisions.

Performance measurements should be reported **consistently** from period to period to allow users a basis for comparing performance over time and to gain an understanding of the measures being used. For instance, it would be useless to compare test scores by one school administered under strict guidelines (i.e., scheduled test days, no interruptions permitted) with scores from another school administered as a surprise with numerous interruptions for announcements and school programs permitted during the examination period.

If information is to be useful, it must be **reliable**. Performance measurements should be verifiable and free from bias, and should represent what they purport to represent. Strong internal controls should be in place when calculating information. Since 1994, the Office of the State Auditor in Texas has performed reviews of performance measures at various state agencies. The reports find some agencies had certified, reliable data, while other agencies used performance data that was unreliable. Reliability is based upon whether controls to ensure accuracy are in place for collecting and reporting data. Measurement definitions can vary from agency to agency, and calculations can be inaccurate or not consistently applied. Numbers can be miscounted due to lack of documentation. Policies and procedures should be developed that address the collection, review, and approval of performance data.

Auditors can encourage performance measurements by auditing existing performance measurement systems. When auditing performance measures, auditors should learn how measurements were calculated and compare them to predefined criteria, determining whether the relevant data and correct calculations are followed. An auditor can review additional controls to determine how measurement data is maintained (automated or manual) and whether adequate controls exist to ensure consistent reporting. Finally an auditor will check all of the information about the process and test it against sample data for accuracy and instances of compliance.

Challenge of Measuring Certain Government Programs

When governments are met with implementing new initiatives and programs, performance measurement standards are undefined. Management is challenged to develop standards that can assess whether a project is meeting its objectives. Examples of new programs could include comprehensive health care, the privatization of education using vouchers as tuition payments, or the investment of public funds into the stock market. All of these experimental programs would need extensive planning to create relevant measures for performance management.

Circumstances that contribute to the difficulty of measuring (experimental) programs include:

- The program may not be large enough to draw useful inferences from the results.
- Lack of baseline data with which to compare program results. The existence of intervening variables may not have been well measured in experimental programs. After a new program is in place, it may struggle to define itself as accountable to the public because there is no standard of comparison. There might be some value in comparing different or older systems to a new system; however, there might be too many differences between the two to draw any relevant conclusions. Additionally, a new program might be able to compare its performance measurements from year to year.
- Some outcomes can be hard to measure either from the lack of measurement instruments, such as changes in self-esteem, or from the logistical difficulty in measuring. Examples are logistical difficulties presented by efforts to measure long-term drug/alcohol usage, or to count homeless populations to identify the impact of services.

IV.B Financial Management

IV.B.1 Unique Requirements in Accounting for and Reporting on Government Financial Operations

Budgeting, financial management, and accounting in the public sector differ significantly from its private-sector counterpart. First and foremost, government budgets are *legal documents* and, thus, agencies must be in legal *compliance.* Second, government budgeting is unique in that its revenue source is based on taxation (or other sources) and subsequent redistribution to accomplish specific objectives. One major difference between public-sector and private-sector financial management is that in the public sector, there is no direct relationship between what a taxpayer pays and the cost of services received by the same taxpayer. For example, the amount of school taxes paid by an individual will not be affected by the number of children, if any, that individual has attending the local public schools.

Broad Principles of Public Management Systems

In the United States and some other countries, the foundation of the public financial management system is based on the following six principles:[12]

1. ***Democratic consent.*** Taxation and spending should not be done without the explicit consent of the governed.
2. ***Equity.*** Governments should be equitable (treat people in similar circumstances similarly) in raising and spending taxes.
3. ***Transparency.*** What governments do in raising and spending funds should be open to public knowledge and scrutiny.
4. ***Probity.*** There must be honesty in dealing with public funds; the stewards (legislators and officials) are not the owners of the funds.
5. ***Prudence.*** The stewards should not take undue risks with public funds.
6. ***Accountability.*** Those who deal in public funds should be regularly called to account for their stewardship through legislative review and audit processes.

The audit process helps ensure transparency, probity, prudence, and, of course, accountability in public financial management. Transparency and accountability have a significant impact on public financial management as management activities are continually reviewed and the results are publicly displayed.

IV.B.2 Principles of Taxation and Revenue Generation

Governments must have a way to finance public services, taxation being primary. There are four primary ways to generate revenue in public administration:

- ***Taxation.*** This includes federal and state income taxes, along with sales and property taxes.
- ***Transfer payments (grants).*** State and local governments receive transfer payments from the federal government. Additionally, state governments often

transfer funds to local governments such as state aid to local schools.

- *User charges.* As individuals become increasingly less receptive to taxes, user fees or charges have been used to finance some services. User charges are intended to cover either the full cost of selected services, such as utilities (water, sewer, etc.), or a portion of the cost for services, such as recreational facility or park use.
- *Fines, fees, and permits.* Fines are imposed as penalties for violating laws or regulations. Permits and fees are required for certain regulated activities, such as restaurant licenses.

Taxation is the most common form of revenue generation for governments. Some of the common forms of taxation include:

- *Income tax.* Income taxes that are paid as a percentage of income. Usually the tax rate is a function of the income level and those with higher incomes pay a higher income tax rate. Some governments do not have income taxes, whereas other governments generally have a standard tax rate that applies to all income levels over a minimum threshold.
- *Property tax.* This is the mainstay of most local governments and is a tax on land and improvements such as buildings. In some cases, personal property such as cars and jewelry are also taxed. Many jurisdictions face constitutional/charter/legal limitations on the ability to raise property tax rates without resorting to a referendum.
- *Sales tax.* This is a tax on consumption rather than income. It is generally a fixed tax rate and generally applies to all items, with the exception of medicine and food. Although widely used, it is considered a regressive tax (higher income groups pay a smaller percentage of their income). However, some governments restrict the application of sales tax to items such as food and pharmaceuticals for public policy reasons. Other specific tax revenues (tobacco, liquor) may have portions designated to go to specific programs, such as anti-smoking or driving under the influence of alcohol prevention programs.

IV.B.3 Unique Aspects of Governmental Budgeting

Process of Governmental Budgeting

Governmental budgets establish *legal authority* for providing services, operating programs, and allocating resources. Although the details and timetables vary from unit to unit, the budgeting cycle generally incorporates the following phases:

- Executive preparation (formulation).
- Legislative consideration.
- Execution.
- Audit and evaluation.

All budgets, whether national, regional, or local, should be tied to achieving objectives. In other words, a projected outcome is an expected result of the expenditures. All government revenue raising and spending should fall into one of the following objectives:

- *Allocation.* Ensuring that an appropriate level of funding flows into sectors of the economy where it is required.
- *Distribution.* Ensuring the balance in public funding between regions, classes of people, and between business and government reflects public policy.
- *Stabilization.* Using public spending to stabilize the macro-economy.
- *Growth.* Using the power of government spending to facilitate economic growth and wealth creation.[13]

Legal Restrictions

The adoption of budgets typically requires enactment of legislation passed by the legislative branch and signed by the executive branch. In the United States, this is called the appropriation act or (at the local level) ordinance, but is commonly thought of as the budget. The appropriation act sets limits on spending that are legally binding.

For example, in the United States, three broad areas of restriction in appropriation acts relate to the *purpose, time, and amount* of spending. In addition, the appropriation act, and other legislation, can establish a wide range of other restrictions. At the national level in the United States, another type of legislation that is influential is so-called *authorizing* legislation, which establishes or continues programs, and may include the appropriation.

In addition to legislation, the formulation and execution of government budgets is often subject to regulation. For example, at the national level in the United States, the Office of Management and Budget (OMB), a central management agency, issues OMB Circular A-11 annually, providing guidance to federal agencies formulating and executing budgets.

The budget processes are complex, vary among government organizations, and can require many technical terms. Therefore, this manual does not attempt to provide detailed coverage. Auditors need to review specific budgetary processes as required to complete their audit work.

From an audit and control perspective, auditors must review enabling legislation, other budget-related legislation, and applicable rules and regulations to ensure that expenditures are made within the confines of the approved authority. Also, they should understand the consequences of poor budget planning or inadequate expenditure control — the political, public, and administrative consequences of making midterm emergency funds requests, or having to implement midterm program cutbacks.

Types of Budgets

The type of budget may have an impact on the implementation and review of controls over the budget process. To this end, the following section addresses seven different budget types:

- Performance-based (performance).
- Line-item/object class.
- Program.
- Executive.
- Zero-based.
- Integrated.
- Multiyear.

Performance Budget

Performance-based budgeting is being increasingly adopted by government entities in the United States. For example, the federal government now develops annual performance budgets to meet a statutory requirement in two laws on results — one enacted in 1993 and the other in 2010, discussed in domain III. In addition, more than half the states have adopted some form of performance-based budgeting or have pursued initiatives to do so.[14]

Performance budgets are the entity's efforts to tie the results of the activities or programs to the cost of operating the programs. This approach provides a mechanism to measure the performance of government services. For example, a transit authority might link proposed advertising expenditure increases to changes in ridership (workload or outputs) and percent of capacity used (efficiency), and tie its maintenance activity to percent on time performance (effectiveness) in its annual budget. Performance budgeting uses the budget process as a tool to assess efficiency and provides management with essential information. The problem with both line-item and performance budgets can be the lack of planning dimensions, identification of global resource allocation, and assessment of effectiveness.

Performance-based budgeting attempts to use strategic planning to set the mission, goals, and objectives of programs, measure programs' outcomes, and set benchmarks. This process is intended to hold agencies accountable for performance, provide flexibility in using resources within programs, and encourage management innovation. Performance-based budgeting can be a valuable agency management tool.

Performance-based budgeting provides a mechanism for systematic review of an agency's organization and purpose, helps identify those parts of government that are performing well, and encourages long-term planning. It also gives legislators new, and possibly better, types of information and helps them focus on program outcomes.

The integration of performance-based budgeting into traditional budget processes is not easy. This method of budgeting requires a focus on activities and outcomes rather than on line-item expenditures. To accommodate this method, agency structures may have to change to put responsibility for a given activity in one agency.

Line-item Budget/Object Class

In the line-item/object class budget, each specific budgetary account is allocated to a narrow purpose (such as travel, supplies, or personnel). It is an effective way to determine whether expenditures comply with budget allocations (legality of expenditures); however, it generally gives no indication regarding the ultimate purpose or objective of the expenditure. A line-item budget is still used by local governments as the baseline for more detailed and specific budgets. From a control perspective, a line item makes it very easy to track the propriety of expenditures; they must stay within the narrow confines of the lines. Although it is easier to ensure compliance with budget/expenditures, a line-item budget does not organize the information in a manner that enables comparison of operational efficiency and effectiveness. Line items per se are not relevant segments for measuring program efficiency or effectiveness (e.g., the effectiveness of travel expenditures).

Program Budget

The primary purpose of program budgeting was to promote planning activities. Instead of budgets being primarily a control and management tool, they became a planning tool and tied budget to agency missions (programs). Thus budgets were looked at from a much broader perspective and provided the opportunity to tie broad goals and objectives to expenditures.

Executive Budget

Representative forms of government were traditionally built on the clear authority of legislatures to determine budgets. However, this approach where each agency received individual appropriations without regard to other agencies lacked overall coordination and promoted inefficient use of resources. Executive budgets are an outgrowth of these problems and are basically the submission of a single budget document that incorporates all executive agencies. Individual agency budgets are submitted to a budget office where they are reviewed and revised to form a single budget document that takes into account executive priorities, projected revenues, and expenditures. This approach provides an overall picture of projected expenditure activities and is open to legislative and public scrutiny.

Zero-based Budget

Public budgets tend to rise incrementally as additional percentages are placed into existing budgets annually to reflect inflation and other factors. Zero-based budgeting was developed to alleviate this problem by reevaluating the complete budget and starting from zero on each new budget year. Zero-based budgeting was used in the federal government in the late 1970s, but is no longer in use. Some states and local governments may still use this concept.

Integrated Budget

The underlying principle for an integrated budget is that all revenues and expenditures for a period should be brought into a single document and framework. An integrated budget provides the mechanism to review spending activities and make judgments on the appropriateness of those expenditures. These budgets also include expenditures from other funds (for example, trust funds and Social Security) and provide a more accurate picture of complete spending activities. An integrated budget approach attempts to ensure that all public spending activities are available for public scrutiny.

Multiyear Budget

Some programs, such as entitlement programs, have financing arrangements that span multiple years. Capital budgeting for construction projects also spans fiscal years, as do long-term financing arrangements (bonds). Some people believe there are advantages with multiyear budgeting for all budgets, such as a reduction in political fights in the budget process, a longer view of government programs, and better matching of available funds with programs. The disadvantages include a diminished ability to institute changes in the annual budget process and the alignment of long-term goals with changes in the political landscape.

IV.B.4 Government Accounting

In the United States, authoritative bodies set establish Generally Accepted Accounting Principles (GAAP) to be followed, which varies depending on the type of entity. For example, the Financial Accounting Standards Board (FASB) establishes GAAP for private sector entities. For government entities, there are two GAAP-setting bodies:

1. The Federal Accounting Standards Advisory Board (FASAB) establishes GAAP for federal agencies. These principles apply to so-called *proprietary* or *financial* accounting; agencies are required by law to follow GAAP. As stated above, separate from GAAP, OMB establishes rules for *budgetary* accounting related to formulation and execution of budgets.
2. The Governmental Accounting Standards Board (GASB) establishes GAAP generally followed by state and local governments. Because state and local governments are *sovereign,* they technically are not required to follow GAAP, but, for a variety of reasons, most do so. As with the federal level, budgetary accounting rules vary among state and local governments.
3. In addition to GAAP, as established by FASAB and GASB and used in preparing external financial reports (generally subject to audit), government units at all levels employ a third type of accounting — cost or managerial — which varies and has more of an internal focus.

The standards established by FASAB and GASB are very relevant in financial statement audits, as one reporting requirement for auditors is to state whether the audited statements conform to GAAP. Auditors also use cost accounting information in other audits, so they may need to understand cost accounting policies and practices.

Presented below is a brief overview of each of the above three types of governmental accounting and reporting. Detailed coverage is beyond the scope of this manual. Thus, if government auditors need a comprehensive understanding of these accounting standards, they should refer directly to the documents of the authoritative bodies.

FASAB Sets GAAP for the Federal Level[15]

The Federal Accounting Standards Advisory Board (FASAB) was established in 1990 by three central financial management agencies — the Office of Management and Budget (OMB), the Government Accountability Office (GAO) and the Treasury Department. FASAB establishes Generally Accepted Accounting Principles (GAAP) for proprietary (financial) accounting by federal agencies. Taken together, two federal laws (the Chief Financial Officers Act of 1990, as amended, and the Accountability for Tax Dollars Act) now require annual financial statements to be prepared and audited for essentially all federal agencies. These statements are to be prepared following GAAP, and the 24 largest agencies that constitute most of the federal budget are statutorily mandated to follow GAAP.

As of January 2012, FASAB issued 41 Statements of Federal Financial Accounting Standards (SFFAS) and seven Statements of Federal Financial Accounting Concepts (SFFAC). In addition to these standards (GAAP) and concepts (not GAAP) statements, FASAB issues other pronouncements. In general, FASAB's standards use the accrual basis but there are variations. FASAB identifies its *FASAB Handbook of Accounting Standards and Other Pronouncements.* To keep current on FASAB activities, visit www.fasab.gov.

The FASAB standards are used in accounting for assets, liabilities, equity (called net position), revenues, expenses, gains, and losses. Entities use proprietary accounting to prepare periodic financial statements; the annual statements are subject to audit under the two laws cited above. The form and content of these financial statements are established by the OMB in Circular A-136, which is updated annually. Entities can be an entire department (e.g., Department of the Interior [DOI]) or components (e.g., DOI's National Park Service).

The financial statements generally required from federal entities include:

- Balance sheet (displays assets, liabilities, and net position at a specific date).

- Statement of net cost (displays earned revenues minus costs for the period).
- Statement of changes in net position (how net position changed in the period).
- Statement of budgetary resources (in budgetary terms, for the period).

For some entities, other financial statements (not discussed in this manual) are required.

The focus of the general purpose financial statements required by law, and based on proprietary accounting standards from FASAB, is on entities. On the other hand, for budgetary accounting in the federal government, the rules are based on rules issued by OMB, and the focus is on appropriation accounts (more than 1,000) and funds, rather than entities. For each appropriation and fund, federal entities are required to track and report on their budgetary resources and the status, notably on what amount of the resources has been obligated (legal commitments to make expenditures).

> **Note:** The Statement of Budgetary Resources cited above is the aggregation of all the appropriation accounts and funds by entity.

GASB Sets GAAP for the State and Local Levels[16]

GAAP for state and local levels of government is established separately from GAAP for the federal level. However, it should be recognized that, while 24 large federal agencies are statutory, state and local governments are sovereign entities and not subject to single uniform law. Nevertheless, many state and local governments have enacted legislation requiring the preparation of financial reports following GAAP from GASB. Also, to receive an unqualified audit opinion, they must prepare financial reports in accordance with GAAP. In short, state and local governments have sound rationale to follow GAAP.

A general discussion of GAAP from GASB is presented here. As with GAAP from FASAB for the federal level, auditors of financial statements for state and local governments should refer to GASB pronouncements directly for details.

Although there were predecessor organizations, since 1984, the GASB is the organization that establishes GAAP for state and local governments in the United States. Starting in 1934, for 70 years, accounting and financial reporting at the state and local level was primarily fund-based, focusing on legal compliance and fiscal accountability. However, GASB Statement 34, Basic Financial Statements — and Management's Discussion and Analysis — for State and Local Governments, introduced a new model, added a new (operational) dimension of accountability, and looked at the government as an entity. Under GASB 34, fund-based accounting and reporting continues, but entity reporting has been added.

Presented below are brief discussions of:

- The definition of a fund and a discussion of the types of funds.
- The definition of a "reporting entity" for financial reporting.

GASB's Fund Categories and Types

GASB (section 1300) defines a fund as:

> A fiscal and accounting entity with a self-balancing set of accounts recording cash and other financial resources, together with all related liabilities and residual equities or balances, and changes therein, which are segregated for the purpose of carrying on specific activities or attaining certain objectives in accordance with special regulations, restrictions, or limitation.

GASB identifies three categories and types within each.

Governmental funds (five types):

1. ***General fund.*** The chief operating fund for a government is called the general fund. GASB's codification (Section 1300.104) states that the general fund is used "to account for all financial resources except those to be accounted for in another fund." Unless there is a compelling reason, such as a legal requirement, all financial activities should be accounted for in the general fund. The general fund is usually the most interesting fund to the users of the financial statements.
2. ***Special revenue fund.*** These funds are used when the revenue sources are earmarked for a specific purpose

(special tax or grant requirement); for example, a gas tax that may be invoked for the express purpose of building and maintaining roads. GASB's codification (Section 1300.104) states that the special revenue fund type may be used "to account for the proceeds of special revenue sources (other than expendable trusts or for major capital projects) that are legally restricted to expenditures for specified purposes."

3. ***Debt service fund.*** Money set aside to meet current and future debt service requirements are placed in debt service funds. GASB's codification (Section 1300.104) states that the debt service fund type may be used "to account for the accumulation of resources for, and the payment of, general long-term debt principal and interests." Unless required legally, the use of debt service funds is generally optional.
4. ***Capital projects fund.*** Governments often prefer to account for significant capital expenditures separately from their regular operations. GASB's codification (Section 1300.104) states that the capital projects fund type may be used "to account for financial resources to be used for the acquisition or construction of major capital facilities (other than those financed by proprietary funds and trust funds)." Similar to the other fund types, the use of capital project funds is optional and not generally required. In addition, even if a capital project fund is used, not all capital acquisitions (e.g., computer, copiers, police cars) need be accounted for in this fund type.
5. ***Permanent fund.*** Endowment-like arrangements available to support the operations or programs of the government (e.g., cemetery perpetual care funds). These types of arrangements will be accounted for in the newly created fund type, the "permanent fund."

Proprietary funds (two types):

1. ***Enterprise fund.*** Enterprise funds are used when a government wants to recoup all or a portion of the cost of providing a service (i.e., utility charges, mass transit fees). GASB's codification (Section 1300.104) states that the enterprise fund type may be used "to account for operations (a) that are financed and operated in a manner similar to private business enterprises — where the intent of the governing body is that costs (expenses, including depreciation) of providing goods or services to the general public on a continuing basis be financed or recovered primarily through user charges; or (b) where the governing body has decided that periodic determination or revenues earned, expenses incurred, and/or net income is appropriate for capital maintenance, public policy, management control, accountability, or other purposes."
2. ***Internal service fund.*** Internal service funds are used to allocate and account for the costs associated with providing a centralized service, such as printing, data processing, or motor pools. GASB's codification (Section 1300.104) states that the internal service fund type may be used "to account for the financing of goods or services provided by one department or agency to other departments or agencies of the governmental unit, or to other governmental units, on a cost-reimbursement basis."

Fiduciary funds (four types not addressed in detail in this manual):

1. Pension (and other employee benefit).
2. Investment trust funds.
3. Private-purpose trust funds.
4. Agency funds (for custodial roles).

For the three major classifications of funds, GASB establishes different accounting principles. These differences relate to 1) the measurement focus (*what* is measured in recognition of transactions and events), and 2) the basis of accounting (*when* transactions are recognized in the accounting process). The two measurement foci are 1) current financial resources, and 2) economic resources. The three bases of accounting are 1) cash, 2) accrual, and 3) modified accrual. The cash basis is not GAAP and modified accrual is used only in state and local governments. The current financial resources focus and modified accrual basis are used in Governmental fund category. The economic resources focus and accrual basis are used in the other two categories of funds; this "model" more closely approximates the accounting in the private sector, with some variations.

Identifying the Financial Reporting Entity under GASB 34

The primary impact of GASB Statement 34 is the requirement for reporting about the government as an economic entity. In the previous model, reporting was

by fund type and did not focus on the government as a whole. Under that model, two factors were a barrier to analyzing the government as a whole:

- As mentioned above, the measurement focus and basis of accounting are not the same for all fund types.
- There were no interfund eliminations.

Under GASB 34, the central focus of the government-wide statements is on the primary government — not on the funds.

The determination of what constitutes an "entity" is more complex at the state and local levels than it is at the federal level. More than 80,000 governments exist at the state and local level. More than 39,000 are general-purpose governments (e.g., states, counties, cities, towns) with the remainder (more than half) being special-purpose governments. One characteristic of general-purpose governments is that they perform multiple functions (e.g., public safety) whereas special-purpose governments generally perform only one or two functions (e.g., education).

Under GASB 34, the financial reporting entity consists of:

- A primary government.
- Components units, for which the primary government is financially accountable, or for which exclusion would be misleading.

A general-purpose government is generally considered a primary government, and a special-purpose government *may* be, if it meets GASB criteria. GASB provides several criteria for determining which component units should be included in the entity and how the component units should be displayed. Discussion of the criteria regarding components is beyond the scope of this manual.

In the government-wide statements, the financial reports display two types of activities — governmental and business. A relationship exists between types of funds and where the fund activities are displayed. For example, the governmental activities on the government-wide statements reflect primarily the transactions of governmental funds. The business activities reflect primarily the transactions of enterprise funds.

The government-wide statements are prepared using 1) the economic resources measurement focus, and 2) the accrual basis of accounting. These are the same as two (proprietary and fiduciary) of the three categories of funds, so minimal conversion is required. However, governmental funds use 1) the current financial resources measurement focus, and 2) the modified accrual basis of accounting. So, to have the statements on the same measurement focus and basis of accounting, the transactions in governmental funds are converted to 1) the economic resources measurement focus, and 2) the accrual basis of accounting.

Financial Reporting at the State and Local Levels

The financial reports for state and local government, as prescribed by GASB, are identified below. A detailed discussion of these reports is beyond this manual. Thus, auditors of financial statements of state and local governments should do further research to fully understand these statements. The purpose herein is to provide a general awareness.

Reporting at the Fund Level

For governmental funds, the following statements are to be prepared:

- Balance sheet.
- Statement of revenues, expenditures, and changes in fund balance.
- Reconciliation of governmental funds balance sheet to (government-wide) statement of net assets.
- Reconciliation of the statement of revenues, expenditures, and changes in fund balance of governmental funds to (government-wide) statement of activities.

For proprietary funds, the following statements are to be prepared:

- Statement of net assets or balance sheet.
- Statement of revenues, expenses, and changes in funds net assets.
- Statement of cash flows.

For fiduciary funds, the following statements are to be prepared:

- Statement of fiduciary net assets.
- Statement of changes in fiduciary net assets.

Reporting at the Government-wide Level

Financial reports at the government-wide level are:

1. Management discussion and analysis (narrative).
2. Statement of net assets (assets – liabilities = net assets).
3. Statement of activities (net cost format).

GASB establishes requirements for presentation of component units in the financial reports. However, discussion of presentation of the component units is beyond the scope of this manual.

GASB Recommends Comprehensive Annual Financial Reports (CAFRs)

GASB recommends (but does not require) that state and local governments prepare a comprehensive annual financial report (CAFR). Specific standards can be found in GASB Codification Section 2200. Although not a requirement, many governments prepare CAFRs, which provide important information to the investment community when governments issue bonds.

CAFRs consist of three sections:

- Introductory.
- Financial.
- Statistical.

Introductory Section

This section includes the cover, title page, table of contents, list of principal officials, organization chart, letter of transmittal, and certificate of achievement (if received). The letter of transmittal is considered the most important element and includes:

- Formal transmittal of the CAFR.
- Profile of the government.
- Discussion of the local economy.
- Long-range planning information.
- Cash management discussion.
- Discussion of how risk is managed.
- Scope of the audit engagement.
- Awards and acknowledgments.

Financial Section

This section includes:

- Auditor's report.
- Management discussion and analysis (MD&A).
- Basic financial statements — government-wide and for the three fund categories.
- Required supplementary information (RSI) other than the MD&A.
- Combining statements and individual fund statements.

Statistical Section

This section provides users of financial statements with additional historical perspective, context, and detail to assist in using the information in the financial statements and notes, and to understand and assess a government's economic condition. Information is to be presented in five categories:

- Financial trends.
- Revenue capacity information.
- Debt capacity information.
- Demographic and economic information.
- Operating information.

The information is very extensive, some for a 10-year period or more.

IV.B.5 Legal Restrictions on Sources and Uses of Funds

Governments use the following methods to finance public services: Direct taxation, indirect taxation, user charges, grants, profits from enterprise activities, borrowing, innovations such as public-private partnerships, franchises, licensing of private sector providers (e.g., cable television providers), or earnings from investments.

In some cases, funds raised are restricted based on the source or proposed use of the funds. There is a difference between spending earmarked revenues (e.g., hunting licenses) and general revenues. For instance, capital budgets, particularly in input-based budgeting processes, can restrict the use of funds. Most funds gained through grants are restricted to the specific purpose of the grant. Insurance trust revenue, such as employee/employer

assessments for retirement and social insurance purposes, are usually restricted and can only be used as intended.

The following are considered abuses of public debt:

- Borrowing to finance operating expenditures.
- Borrowing beyond ability to repay.
- Borrowing to finance no-return projects or speculative facilities.
- Borrowing where corruption is widespread.

IV.B.6 Investment Restrictions for Public Funds

Policy Factors

Investment decisions in the public sector are impacted by several factors, including:[17]

- Legal.
- Non-economic.
- Financial.

Legal requirements place restrictions on government financial managers. A prime concern for investments of public funds is the safety of the principal. Since public funds are derived from taxpayers, there is a legal tradition that restricts investments to only the safest instruments. Even when investment risk can be reduced through diversification, certain investment types are restricted. Although this principle reduces the risks for public investments, it makes it very difficult for public entities to achieve a high rate of return. Additionally some governments face geographical restrictions regarding investment choices. For example, a state may be required to invest a percentage of its investment dollars in state or local investment vehicles. The government's desire to reduce risk also translates into reduced returns.

Policy considerations also have an impact on investment policy. For example, in the past, many governments divested investments related to South Africa before the end of apartheid. Therefore, for policy reasons, the governments were willing to accept a reduced rate of return in order to make a public statement about an internal policy of another sovereign nation.

Local governments sometimes make investment decisions based on constituent pressures as local entities vie for the limited investment dollars. Additionally, socially acceptable investments are encouraged. A certain percentage of investments may be made in minority or environmentally conscious businesses, for example.

Financial factors also impact investment decisions. Investing has become a highly technical endeavor where knowledge and sophistication can increase returns. A wide variety of investment options exists, and the selection of the right mix coupled with economic factors can significantly impact returns.

Investment Concerns

There are four types of concerns with investments:[18]

1. Risk.
2. Yield.
3. Liquidity.
4. Size.

Investment risk refers to the likelihood of a loss. There are three types of investment risk.

1. ***Market risk.*** The possibility of a loss resulting from choosing a relatively poor investment from a large pool of investments.
2. ***Default risk.*** The possibility of a loss resulting from the bankruptcy of an organization in which funds were invested.
3. ***Liquidity risk.*** Losses resulting because invested dollars cannot be accessed. Losses may occur from penalties for early withdrawal, for example.

Yield is the return the investor receives over and above the amount of principal invested. Yield is often called the rate of return. In most cases, there is relationship between risk and return (yield). Generally, the higher the risk, the higher the return, and the lower the risk, the lower the return.

Liquidity refers to how easily an investment can be converted to cash. The investment can range from high liquidity (savings account) to low liquidity (commercial real estate). Long-term debt instruments (bonds) have become more liquid due to the secondary market where investors buy and sell debt investments.

Size refers to the relationship between the size of an investment and the return. With larger investments a favorable rate may be provided and the transaction cost is generally reduced. For example, some extremely safe and higher yielding (in a relative sense) overnight investment vehicles may have minimum thresholds of $1 million or $10 million.

Concerns, Investment Strategies, and Controls

The administration of investments must be done in accordance with the investment policies of the public organization. Thus, the policies must be clearly articulated and should include specific investment criteria.

In a public organization, the "prudent man rule" is often applied. In effect this rule states that those investing funds must apply the same care, discretion, and intelligence when investing public funds as they would exercise in managing their own funds. Additionally, many strategies depend on the goals and objectives of the organization, and investment decisions are impacted by projections of inflation, liquidity, and safety.

In public agencies, investment decisions are often made by boards or commissions that were created to oversee investments. Although a board may oversee investments, the basic responsibility to implement investment decisions rests with management, staff, or contractors responsible for investment execution. Whether internal staff or contractors are used, the board and auditors must review investment practices to ensure that they comply with legal and other requirements.

Some basic guidelines for investment decisions include:

- Adhere to legal requirements.
- Adhere to policy requirements.
- Adhere to investment mix criteria.
- Ensure that an acceptable level of knowledge is available for all investment types.
- Avoid high-risk situations.
- Ensure an appropriate level of investment safety and liquidity.

The complexity of investing often necessitates the use of contractors to support the investment process. It can be difficult to hire and retain internal staff who possess the necessary investment skills, but the board cannot abdicate its responsibilities and assume that the contractor is investing funds within the prescribed guidelines. The amount of funds coupled with the importance of fund safety necessitates frequent and thorough audits.

IV.B.7 Activity-based Costing (Cost or Managerial Accounting)[19]

In addition to the accounting used for preparation of general purpose external financial statements (generally subject to audit), governments also use cost or managerial accounting for a variety of management purposes. A single uniform set of principles (like GAAP) does not apply to cost accounting, so the details differ. Yet there are common purposes and some similar characteristics.

Purposes for using cost accounting in governments in the United States include:

1. Monitoring programs to ensure they are operating efficiently and effectively, and within legal constraints.
2. Establishing user fees; although a policy decision, cost information is useful.
3. Assisting in allocation in the budget process, particularly when resources are tight.
4. Making comparisons over time and with other organizations (benchmarking).
5. Making economic choice decisions (e.g., competition with the private sector).
6. For state and local governments in the United States, determining reimbursable amounts to be reported under grant agreements and contracts.

Some of the above purposes would likely be similar to how cost accounting is used in other countries.

For the federal level of government in the United States, FASAB has issued a Statement of Standards and Concepts (Statement #4, amended by Statement #30). FASAB noted that procedures to accumulate and report costs allow agencies to support legislative actions, including the CFO Act of 1990 and the Government Performance and Results Act, discussed elsewhere in this manual.

FASAB's concepts on cost accounting are summarized as:

"Managerial cost accounting should be a fundamental part of the financial management system and, to the extent practicable, should be integrated with other parts of the system. Managerial costing should use a basis of accounting, recognition and measurement *for the intended purpose.* Cost information developed for different purposes should be drawn from a *common data source,* and output reports should be *reconciliable* to each other."

The five FASAB standards can be viewed as somewhat high level, but they are intended to bring a level of consistency in the use of cost accounting across the federal government. The five standards, briefly described below, are aimed at providing reliable and timely information on the full cost of federal programs, activities, and outputs.

1. ***Requirement for cost accounting.*** "Each reporting entity should accumulate and report the cost of its activities on a regular basis for management information purposes. Cost may be accumulated through the use of cost accounting systems or through the use of cost finding techniques." FASAB describes the general characteristics of cost accounting.
2. ***Responsibility segments.*** "Management of each reporting entity should define and establish responsibility segments. Managerial cost accounting should be performed to measure and report the costs of each segment's outputs. Special cost studies, if necessary, also should be performed to determine the costs of outputs." FASAB states that the responsibility segments usually possess the following characteristics: 1) their managers report to the entity's top management directly, and 2) their resources and results of operations can be clearly distinguished from other segments.
3. ***Full cost.*** "Reporting entities should report the full costs of outputs in general purpose financial reports. The full cost of an output produced by a responsibility segment is the sum of 1) the costs of resources consumed by the segment that directly or indirectly contribute to the output, and 2) the costs of identifiable services provided by other responsibility segments within the reporting entity, and by other reporting entities." It should be noted that the standard does not require full cost reporting in the entity's internal reports or special purpose reports.
4. ***Inter-entity costs.*** "Each entity's full cost should incorporate the full cost of that it receives from other entities. The entity providing the goods or services has the responsibility to provide the receiving entity with information on the full cost of such goods and services through billing *or other advice."* Full implementation of this standard was not required until SFFAS #30 was issued by FASAB.
5. ***Costing methodology.*** "Costs of resources consumed by responsibility segments should be accumulated by type of resource. Outputs produced by responsibility segments should be accumulated and, if practicable, assigned to outputs. The full costs of resources that directly or indirectly contribute to the production of outputs should be assigned to outputs through costing methodologies or cost finding techniques that are *most appropriate* to the segment's operating environment and should be followed consistently." FASAB notes that the standard is intended to be a principle, rather than a methodology, for cost assignment. The standard does not require the use of a particular type of costing system or costing methodology, but discusses four — namely, activity-based costing, job order costing, process costing, and standard costing.

In recent years, studies have been made of the use of managerial cost accounting at federal agencies. For example, the Association of Government Accountants (AGA) released a report in 2009 titled *Managerial Cost Accounting in the Federal Government: Providing Useful Information for Decision-making.* The AGA report discussed managerial cost accounting systems at federal entities, including the Social Security Administration and five components of the Interior Department. The AGA report concluded that all the entities had achieved success in implementing managerial cost accounting and are benefiting. GAO has also issued a number of reports on cost accounting practices at selected federal entities.[20]

Practices in cost accounting vary among states and local government in the United States. The Spring 2007 issue of the AGA's *Journal of Government Financial Management* included an article titled *Activity-Based Costing in Large Cities: Costs and Benefits.* A survey was sent to 234 cities, of which 49 replied — a 21 percent response rate. Only 16 percent of the responding cities used activity-based costing; about half of those agreed that the information was useful and that the benefits covered the costs.[21]

How Cost Information is Presented in General Purpose Financial Statements

At the federal level, one of the general purpose financial statements prepared and audited annually is the Statement of Net Cost. That statement displays the gross cost, from which exchange (earned) revenue are deducted. These statements further report net costs by responsible segments and/or components, and by program or program goals, on the face of the statement, in the notes, or separate reports by sub-organization.[22]

At the state or local level, the Government-wide Statement of Activities can be viewed as a close comparison to two federal statements (the Statement of Net Cost and the Statement of Changes in Net Position). One purpose of the Statement of Activities is to identify the extent to which a particular function requires financial support from the taxpayers.

IV.C Implications of Various Service Delivery Methods

The delivery of services has been an area of intense debate in the past decade. The key question revolves around government's emphasis on the delivery method (process) rather than the outcomes. Strategic management in government is often far more difficult due to factors outlined below.

Some of the issues that impact the delivery of services are:[23]

- Government managers share power and have less flexibility and authority to make instant decisions to enhance the delivery of services (in other words, government red tape impedes the delivery of services).
- Governments function as political rather than rational organizations. As a result, there is often no concurrence as to acceptable performance measures. In addition, it is often prohibitively difficult to measure effectiveness (for example, with social services such as substance abuse recovery programs, or prevention programs such as highway or fire safety activities).
- Private-sector management has more autonomy and control, which make it easier to coordinate and implement a plan of action.

IV.C.1 Direct Delivery by Government Employees

The most common form of service delivery is via government employees. It is this approach that has created bureaucracies at the national, regional, and, in some cases, local level. Under this approach, a bureaucracy is created and supported by management and staff to carry out specific objectives. There are numerous fixed and variable costs associated with this approach. Some types of costs include:

- Personnel compensation (salary, retirement, insurance, accident compensation, etc.).
- Facility costs (workplace, equipment, office supplies, etc.).
- Administrative costs (travel, training, employee relations, etc.).

These costs can be significant, so government organizations also look at less costly alternatives to provide the same level of services.

Some of the advantages and disadvantages of direct delivery of services by government employees are listed below.

Advantages

- Existing government employees might be expected to have a more thorough understanding of program objectives than a private-sector contractor hired for a one-year contract.
- Existing government employees might be expected to have increased knowledge of government regulations and requirements and the environment surrounding the program.
- Existing government employees would be more likely to have been involved in the development and design of the program.

- Often viewed as a more economical approach (for example, a new program is assigned to existing staff and indirect costs are not included in the analysis).

Disadvantages

- Increased lead time for deployment of new programs as internal staff resources are allocated among current and proposed programs.
- Decreased flexibility to make changes/reductions (due to constraints on hiring, layoffs, and position reclassification).
- Indirect (hidden) costs to programs (pension, benefits, training, etc.).

IV.C.2 Grants[24]

Grants are used by governments to operate programs and provide services. GASB Statement No. 24 defines grants and other financial assistance as:

- Transactions in which one government entity transfers cash or other items of value to (or incurs a liability for) another governmental entity, individual, or organization as a means of sharing program costs, subsidizing other governments or entities, or otherwise reallocating resources to the recipients.
- Pass-through grants, which are grants or other financial assistance received by a governmental entity to transfer or spend on behalf of a secondary recipient.

Common types of grant classifications include:

- *Formula grants.* Legally mandated funding levels and restrictions on eligible grantees, with little or no discretion being exercised by the grantor.
- *Project grants.* Similar to contracts because grantors agree to pay the grantee for services, performance, or a specific project.
- *Construction grants.* Awarded only for construction of permanent facilities.
- *Categorical grants.* Offer funding for programs proposed to address specific policy goals. For example, categorical grants may fund programs to construct new, multifamily, or low-income housing or specify funding for rehabilitation and repairs to existing low-income housing stock. Or, categorical grants may offer funding for programs designed to achieve a specific targeted amount of reduced air pollution in a region.
- *Block grants.* Consolidation of funds for broad purposes into a single funding action, typically issued with fewer expenditure restrictions to governments.
- *Noncompetitive grants.* Awarded to all applicants meeting specified legal or other criteria.
- *Competitive grants.* Awarded to a selected number of grantees having similar qualifying characteristics after an evaluation of proposals.

Accounting and control considerations for grants include:

- A formal and objective review process to assess and evaluate grant proposals.
- Adherence to prescribed negotiation practices before the award and execution of a grant agreement.
- Development and approval of a pre-award form to ensure unobligated funds equal to the estimated amount of the grant.
- Execution and issuance of the grant agreement with timely notification to parties.
- Periodic assessments or evaluations to ensure the purpose or objective of the grant is being achieved, that client eligibility and other requirements are being complied with, and the services are being provided in accordance with program specifications.
- Review of the recipient's accounting and management control systems.
- Evaluation of the recipient's management personnel, personnel practices, and intent to comply with various federal laws.
- Conduct a prepayment audit to ensure that expended funds are consistent with the grant conditions.
- Prompt and accurate payment of all invoices submitted by grantees.
- Settlement of any advances of money and inventories of property in a manner consistent with agency policy and grant conditions.
- A final audit of the recipient.
- Timely settlement of grant debts and prompt closeout and final accounting and reporting at the conclusion of the grant program.

Some of the advantages and disadvantages of using grants are listed below.

Advantages

- Increased control over program design and types of services, because specific requirements can be included in grant agreements.
- Increased control over expenditure categories, since only specific expenditures may be permitted in the grant agreement.
- Ability to place limits on costs (such as overhead costs) that will be reimbursed.
- Ability to establish specific reporting requirements.

Disadvantages

- Use of resources for monitoring compliance with grant terms.
- Decrease in control over specific program activities.
- Limitations on consistency of program implementation and leadership.

IV.C.3 Contracts

Definition of contract:[25]

> Contracts are written agreements (in most cases) that obligate the government to an expenditure of money upon delivery of goods or performance of services. Contracts may be used by government to procure a variety of services or products, such as transportation, printing, supplies, equipment, etc.

Types of Contracts

There are various contract types available to ensure cost-effective delivery of services.[26]

- *Fixed-price.* A contract that provides for a firm price or, in appropriate cases, an adjustable price. Fixed-price contracts providing for an adjustable price may include a ceiling price, a target price, or both. Unless otherwise specified in the contract, the ceiling price or target price is subject to adjustment only by operation of contract clauses providing for an equitable adjustment or other revision of the contract price under stated circumstances. Building construction provides an example of a fixed-priced contract in which completion of the building as specified is contracted for a specific ceiling price. The contract also would require that any changes requested by the purchaser during construction would be payable in addition to the fixed price. Such a contract protects the service provider in the event that initial specifications did not fully anticipate the client's needs.
- *Firm fixed-price.* A contract that provides for a price that is not subject to any adjustment on the basis of the contractor's cost experience in performing the contract. This type of contract is appropriate in circumstances where there is little risk that the client's needs will change during the contract period.
- *Cost-plus-award-fee.* A cost-reimbursement contract that provides for a fee consisting of:
  - A base amount fixed at inception of the contract.
  - An award amount that the contractor may earn in whole or in part during performance and that is sufficient to provide motivation for excellence in such areas as quality, timeliness, technical ingenuity, and cost-effective management. The amount of the award fee to be paid is determined by the government's judgmental evaluation of the contractor's performance in terms of the criteria stated in the contract. This determination is made unilaterally by the government and is not subject to the disputes clause.

This type of contract is useful when time, design innovations, or other variables add risk to the successful fulfillment of contract terms.

- *Cost-plus-fixed-fee.* A cost-reimbursement contract that provides for payment to the contractor of a negotiated fee that is fixed at the inception of the contract. The fixed fee does not vary with actual cost but may be adjusted as a result of changes in the work to be performed under the contract. This contract permits contracting for efforts that might otherwise present too great a risk to contractors, but it provides the contractor with only a minimum incentive to control costs.
- *Cost-plus-incentive-fee.* A cost-reimbursement contract that provides for the initially negotiated fee to be adjusted later by a formula based on the relationship of total allowable costs to total target costs. This contract type specifies a target cost, a target fee, minimum and maximum fees, and a fee adjustment formula. After contract performance, the fee payable to the contractor is determined in accordance with the formula. The formula provides, within limits, for

increases in fee-above-target-fee when total allowable costs are less than target costs, and decreases in fee-below-target-fee when total allowable costs exceed target costs. This increase or decrease is intended to provide an incentive for the contractor to manage the contract effectively. When total allowable cost is greater than or less than the range of costs within which the fee-adjustment formula operates, the contractor is paid total allowable costs, plus the minimum or maximum fee.

- *Cost-reimbursement.* A contract that provides for payment of allowable incurred costs to the extent prescribed in the contract. These contracts establish an estimate of total cost for the purpose of obligating funds and establishing a ceiling that the contractor may not exceed (except at its own risk) without the approval of the contracting officer.
- *Cost sharing.* A cost-reimbursement contract in which the contractor receives no fee and is reimbursed only for an agreed-upon portion of its allowable costs. This can be used when the contractor agrees to absorb a portion of the costs in the expectation of substantial compensating benefits.
- *Delivery order.* A contract for supplies that does not procure or specify a firm quantity of supplies (other than a minimum or maximum quantity), and that provides for the issuance of orders for the delivery of supplies during the period of the contract.
- *Indefinite quantity.* A contract that may be used to acquire supplies and/or services when the exact times and/or exact quantities of future deliveries are not known at the time of contract award. There are three types: definite quantity, requirements, and indefinite quantity.
- *Time-and-materials.* A contract that provides for acquiring supplies or services on the basis of:
  - Direct labor hours at specified fixed hourly rates that include wages, overhead, general and administrative expenses, and profit.
  - Materials at cost, including, if appropriate, material handling costs as part of material costs.

Contract Control Considerations

Government entities generally have the authority and responsibility to issue and require adherence to their policies and regulations relating to contracts. However, the design of a system of controls to ensure that control objectives are achieved to protect the government adequately in procurements is the sole responsibility of the contracting entity. Accounting and control considerations for contracts include:[27]

- Development and approval of a pre-award form to ensure unobligated funds equal to the estimated amount of the contract.
- Adherence to the prescribed process for procurements that must be competitively awarded.
- Specifications or statement of work describing goods and services to be obtained (including quality standards).
- A formal and objective review process evaluating all sealed bids and proposals received by the agency, both solicited and unsolicited.
- Adherence to prescribed negotiation practices.
- Execution and issuance of the contract with timely notification to the appropriate parties.
- Positive assertion of the receipt and satisfaction of services or performance received.
- Conduct of prepayment audits.
- Prompt and accurate payment of all invoices.
- Settlement of any advances of money and inventories of property in a manner consistent with agency policy or contract conditions.
- Periodic assessments or evaluations to ensure that the purpose or objective of the contract is being achieved.
- Review of the recipient's accounting and management control systems.
- Evaluation of the contractor's management personnel, personnel practices, and intent to comply with relevant laws.
- Evaluation of the recipient's management personnel, personnel practices, and intent to comply with relevant laws.
- Prompt and accurate payment of all invoices submitted by contractors.
- Settlement of any advances of money and inventories of property in a manner consistent with agency policy and grant conditions.
- A final audit of the contractor.

Some forms or documents that may assist in the contracting process are:

- Procurement request or authorization prepared by internal managers.
- Request for proposal prepared by internal procurement personnel.
- Proposal submitted by interested, prospective contractors.
- Contract document executed only by authorized internal procurement personnel.
- Financial expenditure reports and invoices submitted by the contractors.

Some of the advantages and disadvantages of this approach are listed below.

Advantages

- Increased flexibility to make changes and/or reductions in services, since provisions to change or curtail the program may be included in the contract.
- Ability to distribute revenue to private/nonprofit sector.
- Increased control over program design and types of services, since specific requirements can be included in contracts.
- Ability to place limits on specific categories of costs (such as overhead costs).
- Ability to establish specific reporting requirements.

Disadvantages

- Use of resources for monitoring compliance with contract terms.
- Use of resources for the development of specifications to protect government.
- Potential for uncontrolled or increased costs due to single source privatized government services (government may be subject to unreasonable prices with an extremely high cost replacement alternative).
- Decrease in control over specific program activities.
- Limitations on consistency of program implementation and leadership.

Additional Requirements in Government Contracting

Basic contract agreements contain provisions to protect both contracting parties. Standard guidelines, or boilerplate, are generally established in contracts to clarify the legal responsibility of each party. Examples of standards language in contracts cover:

- Conflict of interest disclosure.
- Anti-kickback or non-bribery clause.
- Staff qualifications.
- Wage reporting.
- Payments/billings procedures.
- Right to audit.
- Property rights of the end product.
- Confidentiality.
- Contract termination.

Conflict of interest disclosure. Contractors are obligated to disclose any potential conflict they might have in the execution of the contracts. Examples include recommending policies or actions that might result in additional benefits for them, family members, or other business affiliates.

Anti-kickback or non-bribery clause. No monetary payments were made or other services rendered to influence the evaluation or contract award process.

Staff qualifications. The staff should possess the skill(s) required to perform the work. This clause may include a requirement that each staff member's educational background, professional designations, applicable training hours, or years of experience be documented. Professional qualification clauses promote the quality of the product and promote its timely delivery.

Wages. The contractor must report wages paid, total hours worked, actual travel expenses, and a reasonable itemization of other expenses incurred for the work performed.

Payments/billings. To protect the contractor and ensure funds exist, the contractor should send billings or invoices within the appropriate time frame and within the designated fiscal year or associated lapse period. Once appropriate billing information and supporting documentation are received, the contractor should be paid within a reasonably prompt period. If the period between billing and payment is delayed, the contractor could be entitled to interest payment on the amount billed.

Right to audit. The contractor shall maintain adequate accounting records and supporting documents to verify the amounts, recipients, and uses of all payments and funds received in conjunction with the contract for a designated period of time. All related records shall be available for review and audit.

Property rights of the end product. All items produced in the performance of a contract is the sole property of the government. Contractor agrees that any work or deliverable created during and in connection with or as a result of the contract shall be a work for hire and cannot assert or claim any rights to the end product. Conversely, if the product, such as software, was developed before the contract, the contractor merely gives license to the government for the use of the product.

Confidentiality. Except for its own internal use, the contractor cannot disclose information during the performance of the contract without the written consent of the government agency. Information that is specified as confidential, including any data produced by, derived from, or acquired during the course of the contract, shall be held confidential at all times by the contractor.

Contract termination. Contractual agreements can end either naturally (i.e., by reaching the termination date or delivery of the final product) or by other means. When one party fails to perform in accordance with the contract, it can be nullified. For example, a breach of contract can occur if a construction company uses substandard or non-specified materials. In instances where contracts are terminated, the contractor can be compensated for all productive hours worked and relevant expenses incurred at the specified contractual rate. However, the government has a right to demand compensation for faulty work.

In addition to standard boilerplate clauses such as those described above, contract terms have become another means (besides legislation and regulation) by which public policies can be expanded to the private sector. When government contracts with private sector or non-governmental organizations, the public policy control over how government funds are spent does not stop because the contractor is a private entity. Contracts may require contractors to pay at a prevailing wage rate, provide equal opportunity hiring protections, and otherwise ensure that the government's equity and stewardship requirements are also fulfilled in the private company performing government-funded work.

IV.C.4 Joint Ventures/Partnerships/ Authorities/Special Operating Agencies/Quasi-governmental

The search for a means to reduce duplication among different governments providing the same services in overlapping jurisdictions is ongoing. Innovative methods to combine entities (both public and private) and develop alternate methods for service delivery have evolved.

Cooperative efforts (such as joint ventures, partnerships or alliances, authorities, and special operating or quasi-governmental agencies) have been used to aggregate capabilities and increase the efficiency and effectiveness of service delivery. These cooperative efforts may reduce administrative costs as they are shared and also provide economies of scale. These alliances have been used extensively in local government as cities and towns have combined to form school districts, water districts, sewer districts, etc. in an effort to provide services more economically.

Authorities are an example of innovative method to provide government services. Authorities are often organizations established to manage resources or infrastructure that cross multiple governmental jurisdictions. They can be governed by a body appointed by the jurisdictions' elected officials, by separately elected officials, or by a combination. Examples of authorities are:

- Public housing authorities established as a subunit of a local government legislative body responsible for setting policy and overseeing the expenditure of low-income housing grant and matching expenditures.
- Water authorities responsible for setting policy and fee structures for access to and use of a regional body or bodies of water.
- Power authorities that establish fees and govern deployment of electric generation capacity within a region.

Advantages

- Increased control over program design and types of services, since specific requirements can be included in legislation.
- Reduced individual government costs as infrastructure costs are shared between jurisdictions.
- Ability to establish specific reporting requirements.

Disadvantages

- Use of resources for developing and maintaining authority.
- Decrease in control over specific program activities by individual jurisdictions.
- Limitations on consistency of program implementation and leadership.

IV.C.5 Privatization

There are those who believe the most effective means to enhance the efficiency and effectiveness of government is through privatization. Privatization can be defined as the process of returning to the private sector property or functions previously owned or performed by government. There are three basic forms of government privatization:

- Sale of government assets (such as selling public housing units to tenants).
- Private financing of public facilities (examples are toll highways in various states).
- Private provision of services (such as trash collection, prisons, or auditing).

The move for privatization places a burden on public managers to develop performance measures that demonstrate the effectiveness of the service delivery method.

Some of the advantages and disadvantages of privatization are listed below.

Advantages

- Access to specialized services.
- Avoidance of expensive startup costs by contracting governments.
- More flexibility to obtain services, since multiple contractors may exist.
- More responsiveness to service consumers and more metrics to measure performance as profit incentives are introduced.

Disadvantages

- Increased potential for corruption and fraud as services are outsourced to multiple firms.
- Reduced control over services as services are outsourced to multiple firms.
- Poor performance by some contractors.
- Limited numbers of potential vendors (increased costs).
- Possibility of political influence over contract selection.

Privatization will continue to be debated as legislators, managers, service providers, and constituents try to find the best alternatives to deliver the necessary services to the public.

IV.D Implications of Delivering Services to Citizens

The government, by its very nature, has distinct differences and requirements from its private-sector counterparts. Government is required to provide certain services to all eligible parties without regard for the costs or identified benefits for those services.

This section provides insights into issues that auditors need to address. These issues force auditors to look beyond the opportunities for safeguarding assets (inventory controls, segregation of duties) and to review some of the more complex issues that impact and cause program performance problems.

IV.D.1 Due Process Rights of Clients/Citizens

The rights of clients/citizens vary significantly in the public and private sectors. Table IV.2, Differences Between Public Sector and Private Sector, on the following page illustrates the basic differences between the two sectors.

The public sector and private sector are generally at opposite ends of the spectrum in the requirement to provide due process to those served or denied service. In the private sector, there is the philosophy "We reserve the right to refuse service to anyone." In fact, until the government intervened, this approach was very common and pervasive and even applied to specific groups of people (denial of service to members of particular ethnic groups).

In the public sector, there are extensive protections in place to prohibit service provision from being distributed inequitably. In other words, if someone is eligible for a service, the government will provide the service regardless of the class membership of the client. This government philosophy has become a mainstay in the American culture. A quick look at emergency room use will illustrate this point. All hospitals (not just government-operated hospitals) are federally restricted (if private hospitals were not restricted by government, patients would be refused) from refusing emergency service based on ability to pay. Nevertheless, more indigent clients end up at the emergency rooms of the publicly funded hospitals in almost every community. This occurs because private-sector providers have a financial interest in rationing services to the minimum required, compared to public-sector providers who will continue to receive funding regardless of the patient's ability to pay.

Table IV.2. Differences Between Public Sector and Private Sector

Issues	Public Sector	Private Sector
Equity of Services	Equity means public-sector organizations cannot "reserve the right to refuse service to anyone" based on their membership in a class.	Increasingly, government and civil rights laws are forcing the private sector to guarantee equity, but a good deal of discretion still exists.
Eligibility Requirements	Services are equivalent for all eligible parties. Distinctions are based on eligibility requirements and other objective measures.	Services are provided based on the ability to pay or other objective or subjective criteria defined by the private organization.
Appeals Process	An objective appeals process must be in place in case services are denied.	Appeals process is at the discretion of the private organization until formal legal action is taken.

Government resources are limited and more and more taxpayers are less enthused about the costs of supporting government. If a client is eligible for a government service, the key question becomes, "Can the government properly deny the service?" If the person is eligible for the service, it is difficult to deny service; however, eligibility limitations that restrict services to those most in need (poverty-level standards are an example of this) is a means to restrict access and reduce costs. A key element in this discussion is eligibility — eligibility for particular services can be modified to reflect changes in funding levels and public support. For example, the welfare-to-work program has changed eligibility standards and placed limits on the length of time public assistance can be received for certain client types. Another means of rationing services is the use of sliding-fee scales, in which fees are based on income levels.

Another factor impacting the cost of government services is the appeals process. Governments generally have higher overhead in service provision, because there must be administrative appeals processes or other due process protections to ensure that rejected clients can have a fair hearing. An example of an appeals process (and the process itself) that illustrates the administrative costs is the U.S. Freedom of Information Act. Any citizen can request public records (with generally little or no regard to purpose, volume, or cost of the request), and government must comply with the request or deny the request for just cause. If the request is denied, an appeals process (ultimately a court battle, if desired by the citizen) is invoked in which the law is applied to the merits of the request. This appeals process can be costly and time-consuming; however, the citizen's rights must be protected. In effect, it is the cost of doing government business.

IV.D.2 Confidentiality/Privacy/Rights of Clients/Citizens

The privacy conflict — conflict between the organization's right to obtain and use information to make decisions (marketing, eligibility) — will be one of the most important issues of the 21st century. As computer processing and storage capacity have increased, the ability to cost-effectively store huge amounts of data for processing and review has become commonplace in both the public and private sectors. While making itself more accessible to its citizenry, the challenge of government is to strike a balance between the right of the publics' need to know and the privacy rights of any individuals or organizations.

Some of the key issues are:

- ***Information security.*** The means to protect information from unauthorized disclosure, modification, or destruction.
- ***Distinguishing public versus private information.*** Defining what information is considered to be public versus private information. For example, medical records are clearly private; however, the distinction between public and private information blurs for general information such as the number of doctor visits in a particular time frame.
- ***Combining data.*** The volume of data on each individual is staggering. Even if privacy is emphasized in individual databases, combining information from multiple sources can create private data from public records.
- ***Intergovernmental communications.*** Transmission of confidential or sensitive data for authorized purposes via non-secure media can jeopardize the security of the information.

There is an inherent conflict between the confidentiality rights of clients and citizens being served and transparency of government. For example, should the public have access to the case notes of social workers serving families of developmentally delayed children? As a general rule, the public should be able to request government records to determine whether services were provided as authorized. However, some confidential documents such as medical records must remain private, even though services are provided in a publicly funded family planning clinic. As another example of this inherent conflict, in the past, state departments of transportation have made driver's license information (citizens' home addresses, eye color, age, and weight) accessible to the public through open records requests. Because this information has been employed in instances of stalking and other invasions of privacy, most states have restricted access to legitimate law enforcement uses.

Some examples of the intersection of public information with privacy include:

- Private-sector contractors' proposals or unit cost information (proprietary information related to a business that was disclosed in a proposal to provide services to a unit of government).
- Mental health data, medical records, and social services provided to clients (personal information retained for specific government programs).
- Income levels of clients to determine eligibility for a service (for example, free and reduced-price lunch programs).
- Availability of private individuals' home addresses and income/asset information from public records like driver's license agencies, tax assessor, etc. (For example, some states permit the sale of driver's license information to the private sector.)

IV.D.3 Issues Arising from the Methods of Funding/Delivering Services

There is an increased burden for demonstrating prudent and effective stewardship of public funds, because taxpayers' money is being used to help individuals or groups whom the giver (taxpayer) might not have chosen to help.

In many social service programs, the client receiving the services is only paying for a portion of the service or not at all. Since the services are being subsidized, there are financial and other limitations for the services. Some key issues that need to be addressed are:

- Limitations on services available or numbers served.
- Eligibility versus entitlement.

There are generally limitations on the services available. Although the government has tremendous resources, all

needs cannot be met. Planning, program designs, and budgeting processes are affected by these limitations and lead to debates about fee-for-service participation by clients and even the propriety of cost shifting. An example of cost shifting is the use of funds (excess revenues or profits) from a publicly owned water and electric utilities to support the general obligations of a local government. As more services are desired, alternative methods such as cost shifting will be developed to pay for such services.

Entitlement programs (such as Social Security and Medicare) guarantee the payment of benefits and are backed by the government. When entitlement programs are created, should they be budgeted based on actuarial probabilities or available revenues? The expanding role of entitlement programs in the U.S. federal budget is a growing risk, and is sometimes passed through to the states in the form of required matching funds.

IV.D.4 Reality of Conflicting Missions

There are frequently compromises that must occur as government tries to carry out its responsibilities. Governments have duties/responsibilities for ensuring the safety and well-being of a variety of constituencies. Accordingly, the means for achieving that can sometimes conflict.

In government, there are often conflicts between the rights of private individuals versus programs for the common good. A common example is the government purchase of private land for a public purpose, such as for roads or parks. A private individual can be forced to sell based on the eminent domain principle, because the purchase is determined to be in the public's interest.

Other arenas where conflicting missions of government have collided include:

- The need to protect the natural environment versus the need to support economic development.
- Child protective agencies' mission to keep families together sometimes conflicts with their role in keeping children safe (if from an abusive family member).
- Regulators/inspectors of nursing homes often face concerns about the community's limited capacity to absorb clients should the regulator close an inadequate facility.
- Correctional officials are often charged with the dual responsibility of rehabilitating and holding accountable the inmates in their care.

In addition to the inherent conflicts of mission these issues raise, legal liabilities can also hamper decision-making. For instance, governments can establish restrictive zoning laws that limit development in environmentally sensitive areas, which can create the risk of a lawsuit claiming that the government is taking the property of private citizens without due process of law. In essence, the government is limiting a citizen from building or developing a tract of land however he or she pleases and potentially reducing the value of the land.

Governments are increasingly avoiding these risks by innovative means, such as acquiring dedicated land for parks or requiring land set-asides for parks and green space by developers in return for allowing more dense usage of the remaining property.

The struggle between what is best for the public versus private rights and interests of individuals is ongoing. Suburban communities in large metropolitan areas address this issue continually as they determine whether dense developments will adversely affect the infrastructure (water, sewer), traffic flow, the environment, etc. In today's litigious society, government must devise ways to influence public policy while reducing legal costs. As a result, innovative compromises that help governments avoid the liabilities associated with their conflicting duties include:

- Tax incentives for fuel-efficient vehicles, etc.
- Public funding (through bonds, etc.) of industry or economic development in target areas.
- County funding of school nurses (to avoid conflicts in the school district over social issues like birth control).

IV.D.5 Issues Associated with At-risk Populations

Governments often serve the hardest-to-serve populations. Moreover, in these populations, needs are typically multiple, overlapping, and interactive. For instance, recipients of low-income housing are more likely to have unmet health-care needs, require job skills training, and be unable to afford childcare in order to go to work. Homeless populations suffer from mental health problems, hunger, and malnutrition, as well as a higher incidence of substance abuse. The typical government program is designed to address one, possibly a few, interactive problems comprehensively. The likelihood of effectiveness is hampered by the variety and interactive nature of the challenges faced by the recipients of government services.

Moreover, it is often more difficult for government to provide the services because eligibility is guaranteed and not optional. For example, a public school system is required to take all students within its district. Students with learning disabilities or behavioral problems must be provided with the service. Private schools can impose requirements that limit the student population and ease the educational process. By contrast, government is required to provide all students with the necessary education, and this philosophy makes it more difficult and more expensive to provide services.

A program designed to prevent school dropout may have funding requirements that restrict its ability to address the true cause of the problem. Funds may be restricted to tutorial and after-school programs when the root cause for the problem may be the lack of adequate food and shelter for the students. If the funds are used to address food and shelter issues, the program may violate the funding terms. If the root cause is not addressed, then the expenditures on tutorials, etc. will most likely not resolve the problem. Ultimately, the program may be terminated due to violations or ineffectiveness.

This is a complex issue and an area where government needs to refocus its efforts. Some issues that limit program effectiveness are:

- Services address symptoms but not causes.
- Tracking of outputs, but impacts are not measurable.
- Considerable lead time for results to become observable.
- Different organizations responsible for services to the same population, policy differences, eligibility differences, lack of communication/coordination, and lack of reporting.

These issues complicate the effectiveness and the efficiency of providing government services. As auditors, we may not be doing our jobs effectively if we only address the basic compliance issues and never provide information to improve program effectiveness. Auditors should try to identify the variables and factors that impact program effectiveness beyond the control of program management. And if they cannot audit the variables, they should consider recommending program evaluation, or include it as an issue for further study in routine or special audits.

IV.E Unique Characteristics of Human Resources Management

This section concentrates on the roles of public service in national and regional administrative systems, specifically:

- Formal hiring and promotion processes designed to ensure fairness and competition.
- Formal constraints on compensation and benefits.
- Constraints on procedures for sanctions and firing.

Formal Hiring and Promotion Processes Designed to Ensure Fairness and Competition

Employment based upon a person's merit rather than political affiliation has two benefits. Civil service merit-based systems not only organize and structure government services, they also lend credibility to the integrity of government. Employees now have to exhibit predetermined qualifications to prove they are competent for specific jobs. As the system gained popularity, most burgeoning governments followed suit and formalized their personnel procedures.

In the United States, civil servants are civilian government employees in nonelected positions. Significant legislation and policies include the Pendleton Act of 1883, which created the U.S Civil Service Commission providing for open competition for federal jobs, standardized testing, and de-politicized hiring practices. The Veterans' Preference Act of 1944 added five points to the scores of honorably discharged veterans. Ten points are

added if the veteran suffered a disability during his or her term of military service. The Civil Service Reform Act of 1978 split the Commission into two bodies: the Office of Personnel and Management (OPM) and the Merit Systems Protection Board (MSPB). OPM serves as the hiring arm of the federal government while the MSPB provides an arena for employee grievances.[28]

To ensure consistent human resource practices throughout the various departments that make up a national government, all civil service job positions are defined and classified in a similar manner. Position classifications are formal descriptions that categorize all jobs in terms of duties, responsibilities, and salary schedules. The basic principles of position classification are:

- Positions and not individuals should be classified.
- The duties and responsibilities pertaining to a position constitute the outstanding characteristics that distinguish it from, or mark its similarity to, other positions.
- Qualifications in respect to education, experience, knowledge, and skill necessary for the performance of certain duties are determined by the nature of these duties. (Therefore the qualifications for the position are an important factor in the determination of the classification of the position.)
- The individual characteristics of an employee occupying a position should have no bearing on the classification of the position.
- Persons holding positions in the same class should be considered equally qualified for any other position in that class.[29]

Once a position is categorized and qualifications are defined, human resource managers advertise for potential candidates for prospective employment. Top candidates are interviewed and reference checks are made with previous employers. Finally, a formal job offer is made to the successful candidate.

Opportunities for advancement within the civil service structure are based upon a person's ability to take on more responsibility, continue to sharpen his or her skills, and increase productivity. While seniority in a position may give a person more experience in that role, it cannot determine whether a person is truly more qualified for a promotion than his or her junior coworker. When an opportunity for promotion exists, factors besides length of service are considered before the appointment is made. Factors such as supervisory appraisals, educational background, and examination scores are all scrutinized by human resource personnel.

Formal Constraints on Compensation and Benefits

Theoretically, the concept of a civil service based on a true merit system would succeed if all aspects of human resource management were able to be defined uniformly and remain consistent over a reasonable period of time. While the system assists in the administration of government by defining roles and structure and filling job openings, it can be restrictive to top managers when trying to reorganize their departments based on actual needs. The following factors have constrained management:

- Inaccurate position classification.
- Noncompetitive salary ranges.
- Demands of unions and collective bargaining organizations.
- Weak incentive structures.

Position classification is premised upon the ability to define qualifications associated with job duties. In large organizations, position structures change slowly and may not be responsive enough to meet the needs of a particular department or division. If a public hospital has an opening for a nurse but does not need another person in that position, it might fill the position and have the individual perform different duties altogether. To avoid this situation, human resource managers have to be aware of the needs of their departments and adjust the staffing numbers of position classifications regularly.

Human resource managers also need to be aware of critical changes in qualifications. With the exponential growth of computer technology, position classifications become outdated quickly as desirable qualifications change from innovation to innovation. Conversely, some existing clerical positions can be eliminated as their jobs become automated.

In some locations, certain government employees such as teachers or police officers negotiate contracts as a single body through collective bargaining between union representatives and management. Beyond wages, many aspects of employee benefits are open to negotiation. These include, and are not limited to, working conditions, work schedules, pension benefits, health insurance, training, childcare, bonus pay, and educational reimbursements. While workers can use these organizations to barter for higher salaries or better working conditions, union pressure can create another constraint on human resource management.

Constraints on Procedures for Sanctions and Firing

To protect employees from arbitrary termination, government personnel structures have given workers rights so they cannot be deprived of their jobs, or their quest for promotion, without due process. Supervisors must demonstrate that an employee's work performance is so poor, or that they purposely violated employment policy, to the degree that sanctions such as a demotion or termination are warranted.

One aspect of a performance appraisal is to evaluate an employee's quality of work. Some employees have had to pass a probationary period to prove they can do the job within the first few months of their employment or promotion. However, an annual appraisal is generally the most common method used to commend or award an employee for good performance. If the work is inadequate, the appraisal can be used as a documented record for disciplinary and separation actions.

IV.F Unique Purchasing and Procurement Requirements

As stewards of public funds, governments are responsible for spending taxpayer money prudently and in the interests of their constituency. Like the private sector, governments use budgets and performance measurements to assist them in planning and allocating monies for various projects. Unlike the private sector, governments do not use their own assets and are accountable to the public. Therefore, spending should be transparent, equitable, undertaken with care and integrity, and regularly reviewed. The opportunity to do business with the government is based upon an individual's or an organization's potential to provide a necessary service at a competitive or negotiated price. It is open to all qualified entities, with some weighting in the interest of social equity and fairness.

As governments spend large sums through contracts for commodities and services, regulations have been written to assist government personnel, potential vendors, and the general public to understand and organize the process of how billions of dollars are dispersed. Qualified individuals and businesses are potential recipients of government contracts if they can provide a needed service at a market price. In the United States, the Federal Acquisition Regulation defines how purchases are made within the federal government. According to the U.S. Federal Acquisition Institute, a contract is:

> A mutually binding legal relationship obligating the seller to furnish the supplies or services (including construction) and the buyer to pay for them. It includes all types of commitments that obligate the Government to an expenditure of appropriated funds and that, except as otherwise authorized, are in writing. In addition to bilateral instruments, contracts include (but are not limited to) awards and notices of awards; job orders or task letters issued under basic ordering agreements; letter contracts; orders, such as purchase orders, under which the contract becomes effective by written acceptance or performance; and bilateral contract modifications.[30]

Requirements to Ensure Adequate Competition

In general, government procurement officers should always try to create a competitive environment when offering contracts. Individuals or teams deciding who will receive the contract awards evaluate all proposals, comparing the similarities and the differences in product, materials, timeliness, and price. The best environment for full and open competition occurs when all responsible bidders are allowed to compete for business. Some ways to ensure competition are through sealed bids and competitive proposals.

Sealed bids are a contracting method employing competitive undisclosed bids, public bid opening, and awards.

The award is made to that responsible bidder whose bid, conforming to the requirements specified in the bids, will be most advantageous. Sealed bids should be considered for all fixed fee contracts when:

- Time for bid solicitation permits.
- The award is based solely on price-related factors.
- It is not necessary to discuss offers before opening the bids.
- A reasonable expectation of receiving more than one sealed bid exists.[31]

Important elements to be reviewed when auditing a sealed bid contract are:

- ***Preparation of invitations for bids.*** Invitations must describe the government's requirements in a clear, accurate, and complete manner. Unnecessarily restrictive specifications or requirements that might limit the number of bidders are prohibited. The invitation should include all necessary documents (whether attached or incorporated by reference) to prospective bidders for the purpose of bidding.
- ***Publicizing the invitation for bids.*** Invitations must be publicized to prospective bidders by posting in public places; advertised in major newspaper, industry publications, government data interchange sites, or agency websites; and such other means as may be appropriate. Publicizing must occur over a sufficient time before public opening of bids to enable prospective bidders to prepare and submit bids.
- ***Submission of bids.*** Bidders must submit sealed bids to be opened at the time and place stated in the solicitation for the public opening of bids.
- ***Evaluation of bids.*** Bids shall be evaluated without discussions. Evaluations should be fairly apparent since price and price-related factors are the prevalent criteria.
- ***Contract award.*** After bids are publicly opened, an award will be made with reasonable promptness so that the responsible bidder whose bid, conforming to the specified requirements, will be most advantageous to the government, considering only price and the price-related factors included in the invitation.
- ***Non-responsiveness.*** If none of the bids are deemed to meet the requirements in terms of price and/or delivery of service, they can be rejected.

Competitive proposals should be built into the selection process when sealed bids cannot be used. Contracts for professional or artistic services fall into this category, where the end product is not always as definitive as commodities, such as office supplies. They do not lend themselves to a pure sealed bid process. Due to complexities that might require communications between the government agency and prospective bidders, sealed bids will not work. Pre-bid conferences may need to be conducted to enhance the potential bidders' understanding of the procurement requirements.

Competition should still exist in the acquisition process. Invitation for bids (IFBs) and request for proposals (RFPs) should still be prepared clearly and describe all the requirements as well as the evaluation criteria. They should be advertised in media that will reach prospective bidders. Once received, bids should be opened, compared, and evaluated based upon predetermined criteria and prudent economical procurement practices. Contracts should be awarded to the lowest responsible and responsive bidder whose bid meets the specified requirements and established criteria. Criteria to be considered should include items in the proposal, such as:

- Supplies.
- Services.
- Prices/costs.
- Statement of work.
- Quality assurance.
- Timeliness of delivery.

Successful bidders should be notified of the award in a timely manner. After notification, they must decide whether to accept or reject the award in a predefined time frame. If accepted, the contracting process begins. If rejected, the selection committee can review the existing bids to determine whether one is responsive enough to be considered for an award. If none are, all of the bids can be rejected.

To build confidence into the contracting and acquisition process, recourse procedures should exist for those who protest the bid award. Interested parties should be able to protest any part of the process. The protest should include a detailed statement of the legal and factual grounds for the protest, formally request a reply by the agency, and list the recourse if the protest has merit.

Recourse can include repeating the bidding process or monetary rewards to unsuccessful injured parties. The agency should respond to all protests quickly to remedy any incorrect bidding processes. If necessary, they can halt the work of the contracting process of the original successful bidder. If the protest is unsuccessful within the agency, the objecting party should have the right to have an independent party review the protest. In the federal government, the U.S. GAO can review protests.[32]

Purchasing Requirements Vary by Type of Purchase

Governments purchase a multitude of services from the private sector. Certain types of purchases lend themselves to open competition more than others. Projects that can be easily or clearly defined and have a large population able to comply with contracting requirements will get more responses (e.g., competition) than a project defining complex provisions from a smaller population. For example, a public works construction project calling for road repairs will receive bids by several asphalt or cement companies (depending upon road material), while a contract to maintain a complex traffic light system for a large metropolitan area might only produce a handful of responsible offers. There are many arenas of services into which a government might enter:

- *Architect-engineer services.* Professional services of an architectural or engineering nature performed by contract that are associated with research, planning, development, design, construction, alteration, or repair of real property.
- *Building service contract.* A contract for recurring services related to the maintenance of a public building (i.e., janitorial, custodial, security, window washing, housekeeping).
- *Construction.* Construction, alteration, or repair (including dredging, excavating, and painting) of buildings, structures, or other real property. Also includes all types, such as bridges, dams, plants, highways, parkways, streets, subways, tunnels, sewers, mains, power lines, cemeteries, pumping stations, railways, airport facilities, terminals, docks, piers, wharves, lighthouses, buoys, breakwaters, levees, canals, and channels.
- *Facilities contract.* Government facilities are provided to a contractor or subcontractor by the government for use in connection with performing one or more related contracts for supplies or services. It is used occasionally to provide special tooling or special test equipment.
- *Health/social welfare services.* Providing health care at public hospitals, veteran centers, home health care, and social services.
- *Investments.* Qualified persons or financial organizations possessing skills and knowledge regarding short- and long-term money management services.
- *Professional and consultant services.* Services rendered by persons who are members of a particular profession or possess a special skill and who are not officers or employees of the contractor. Examples include those services acquired by contractors or subcontractors to enhance their legal, economic, financial, or technical positions. Professional and consultant services are generally acquired to obtain information, advice, opinions, alternatives, conclusions, recommendations, training, or direct assistance, such as studies, analyses, evaluations, liaison with government officials, or other forms of representation.
- *Transportation term contracts.* Indefinite delivery requirement contracts for transportation or for transportation-related services. They are particularly useful for office relocations within a metropolitan area.

  If the cost of the services is reduced by economic factors during the duration of the contract, the government may be entitled to the lower costs. Prevailing costs are determined by the Consumer Price Index.

Including Disadvantaged Businesses in Procurement

The sheer size of government and the volume of business it can do in one particular project or contract can preclude certain vendors from competing for resources. Smaller organizations simply would not have the resources to supply contracts. Rather than government narrowing the scope of its projects so that all qualified businesses can compete for work, several measures have been taken to open up the contracting process to more populations:

- ***Set-aside programs for small or disadvantaged businesses.*** To allow greater access to government contracts, portions or whole contracts are set aside specifically for small businesses. Factors that determine whether a business can be categorized as small can include net worth, annual sales, and number of employees. Ownership defines disadvantaged businesses. Traditionally, these are companies owned, at least by 51 percent, by minorities or women. Set-aside programs can address affirmative action issues as they can remedy past discriminations to minorities and women.
- ***Multi-award contracts.*** Multiple awards are given for certain contracts to more than one responsible bid. Generally, the contracts are similar in conditions and amounts. Agencies should divide proposed acquisitions of supplies and services into reasonably small lots to permit offers on quantities less than the total requirement.

  This type of award can be advantageous to the government in that if several entities are producing or supplying a product or service, future costs may be more easily controlled and additional supply chains are created. Traditionally, contracts are awarded to suppliers for a certain dollar amount. Once that amount is realized, the government has to use a different supplier whose award limit has not been reached.

- ***Subcontracting opportunities.*** A subcontract is a contract or contractual action entered into by a prime contractor or subcontractor for the purpose of obtaining supplies, materials, equipment, or services of any kind under a prime contract. Prime contractors should be encouraged to subcontract with small business concerns.
- ***Equal opportunity.*** Contractors should be in compliance with applicable provisions of state and federal constitutions, the U.S. Civil Rights Act, the Federal Rehabilitation Act, the Public Works Employment Discrimination Act, the Americans With Disabilities Act, and any other applicable laws, regulations, and policies regarding human rights or the prohibition of discrimination, including sexual harassment and sexual orientation.

One of the limitations of these practices occurs because smaller businesses are often not able to take advantage of economies of scale. Accordingly, unit prices paid to disadvantaged businesses may not be the most economical choices for a government. Conversely, the target businesses may not realistically be able to participate in the government opportunities because their bids cannot be competitive. These limitations highlight the controversial balance between government's responsibility for economical use of public resources and the public policy issues of equitable participation and opportunities for all citizens.

APPENDIX A
Sample CGAP Exam Questions

The 15 sample questions shown here are provided to give candidates and other interested parties a preview of the format and content of CGAP exam questions. These questions may not have been pretested and may therefore vary in difficulty from the pretested questions used on the CGAP exam. While these sample questions are intended to be generally representative of those on the CGAP exam, your results on this small group of questions should not be taken as a guarantee of your performance on a future CGAP exam.

1. In a financial statement audit, the *Standards* require that the scope of the review of compliance and internal control over financial reporting be specifically communicated to all of the following EXCEPT the:

   A. Audit client.
   B. Audit committee.
   C. Requestor of audit services.
   D. Funding agency.

2. It is important that an internal audit department's statement of purpose, authority, and responsibility detail:

   A. The delineation of responsibilities between the internal and external auditors.
   B. The organizational status of the internal audit function.
   C. Whether the agency head will present audit findings to the oversight committee.
   D. Under what circumstances the internal audit director may have confidential access to the oversight committee.

3. A meter-reading audit for a municipal utility includes the following audit program steps:

   - Determine whether meter readings used in customer billings are free of significant error.
   - Analyze the average read time per day for each meter reader.
   - Review controls over the accurate transmission of meter-reading data from handheld devices to the organization's computer.

   Which of the following types of audit services are included in these audit program steps?

   I. Efficiency audits.
   II. Information technology audits.
   III. Financial statement audits.
   IV. Quality audits.

   A. I only.
   B. I and IV only.
   C. II and III only.
   D. I, II, and IV only.

4. An internal auditing department plans to begin an audit of a city's highway maintenance department. One of the audit objectives is to determine whether fixed assets employed in highway maintenance are properly reflected in the accounting records. In meeting this objective, which of the following audit approaches is likely to be most effective?

   A. Inspecting fixed assets used in the highway maintenance process and tracing to the asset subsidiary ledger.
   B. Scanning the asset subsidiary ledger for credit entries.
   C. Selecting items from the asset subsidiary ledger and recalculating depreciation.
   D. Examining documentation concerning the cost of fixed assets used in the highway maintenance process.

5. Which would be part of the compliance segment of a performance audit?

   A. Performance reports comply with reporting guidelines.
   B. Laws and regulations significant to the entity are being followed.
   C. Activities required by law or policy are being carried out.
   D. Laws and regulations significant to the audit objective are being followed.

6. Which audit procedure has the best chance of detecting fraud committed by agency procurement managers who receive kickbacks from vendors in exchange for contracts awarded at higher than market rates?

   A. Reviewing signatures on purchase orders to ensure they are properly executed and meet all of the agency's approval guidelines.
   B. Comparing itemized charges on invoices received from vendors to industry averages for similar goods.
   C. Comparing the number of contracts issued to a list of qualified vendors to determine whether there is an even distribution.
   D. Reviewing the procedures vendors used when bidding on contracts to ensure they adhered to agency guidelines.

7. An agency suspects that its supplemental food program for low-income persons has a high rate of fraud due to food vouchers being sold to individuals for cash instead of being redeemed for food at a certified vendor. The following controls are currently in place:

   - Photo identification cards are issued to qualified participants.
   - Participants write their name and address on each voucher in the presence of an agency counselor.
   - Vendors are evaluated and certified under strict agency guidelines.

   Which of the following additional controls would best help prevent the possibility of voucher fraud?

   A. Matching vouchers issued by the agency to those redeemed by vendors.
   B. Assigning participants to a select group of certified vendors.
   C. Enacting a law that ensures swift prosecution of anyone buying or selling the vouchers for cash.
   D. Requiring vendors to match a participant's photo identification card to the information on the voucher.

8. Outcome measures are the foundation of any good performance measurement system. An outcome is defined as the:

   A. Amount of resources that are put into a program.
   B. Strategies, processes, and activities used by a program.
   C. Accomplishments or results achieved by a program.
   D. Quantity of goods and services provided by a program.

9. Which of the following analysis techniques would be most useful to determine if the time to process disability claims has increased?

   A. Run chart.
   B. Aging schedule.
   C. Histogram.
   D. Pareto analysis.

10. An internal control that may be useful in the detection of integrity violations is:

   A. Segregation of incompatible duties.
   B. Periodic surprise cash counts.
   C. Regularly scheduled site visits.
   D. Properly designed forms.

11. In the public sector, one impediment to ensuring accountability for program effectiveness is the:

    A. Presence of restrictive government regulations.
    B. Requirement to ensure equal treatment to all beneficiaries.
    C. Fragmentation of governmental functions.
    D. Existence of bureaucratic controls.

12. Which of the following represents a formal control to ensure that legal restrictions for a governmental entity are met?

    A. Citizens use a government hotline to report waste, fraud, and abuse.
    B. Encumbrances are used to prevent over-expenditure of the budget.
    C. Citizen hearings and open forums are held so that citizens can provide input and register complaints.
    D. Part of the fund balance is specified as a designated fund balance.

13. Which contract type should be used for acquiring a commercial item?

    A. Firm-fixed-price.
    B. Cost-sharing.
    C. Cost-plus-incentive-fee.
    D. Cost-plus-award-fee.

14. Which of the following is NOT an example of a government program to assist at-risk populations?

    A. Requirements to purchase goods and services from historically underutilized businesses.
    B. Regulations requiring compliance with access to facilities for disabled citizens.
    C. Programs to provide early education to eligible children.
    D. Requirements that financial institutions make loans to a representative number of local agricultural entities.

15. The government issued multiple-award contracts for a program. Each contract contained a minimum guarantee of $200,000. As of June 30, the government had ordered $225,500 from contractor A, $175,750 from contractor B, and $201,000 from contractor C. The government is planning to issue one more order for $25,000. Under these circumstances, the government:

    A. Should award the order to contractor A, based on a superior performance record.
    B. Must compete the order among all three contractors.
    C. Can award the order to contractor B without informing the other contractors.
    D. Should split the order equally among all three contractors.

APPENDIX B
Suggested Solutions to Sample CGAP Questions

Question 1

(From Domain I: Standards, Governance, and Risk/Control Frameworks)
Solution: D

A. Incorrect. Specific communication with the audit client is one of the required communications.

B. Incorrect. Specific communication with the audit committee is one of the required communications.

C. Incorrect. Specific communication with the individuals contracting for or requesting the audit services is one of the required communications.

D. Correct. Specific communication with the funding agency is not a *Standards* requirement.

Question 2

(From Domain II: Government Auditing Practice)
Solution: B

A. Incorrect. Proper planning and coordination between internal and external auditors should provide efficient audit coverage of the entity, but this can change from year to year and is not addressed in a more nearly permanent document such as a charter.

B. Correct. Independence is a key aspect of the internal audit charter.

C. Incorrect. The director of internal audit should share audit results directly with the audit committee.

D. Incorrect. The internal audit director's access to the audit committee should not be restricted.

Question 3

(From Domain II: Government Auditing Practice)
Solution: D (I, II, and IV only)

I. Correct. Determining the average read time per meter reader relates to efficiency.

II. Correct. Reviewing controls over the accurate transmission of meter-reading data relates to information technology (IT) auditing. These controls are part of application controls over the IT system.

III. Incorrect. Financial statement auditing relates to the accuracy of the financial statements. Although the auditor is testing the accuracy of meter readings, there is no mention of testing the accuracy of the billings or tracing the billed amounts to the ledger entries. Since the ledger is not tested, the audit program steps listed do not relate to financial statement auditing.

IV. Correct. Quality auditing includes the quality of information, which is included in testing the accuracy of meter readings and the accurate transmission of meter-reading data to the main computer.

Question 4

(From Domain II: Government Auditing Practice)
Solution: A

A. Correct. This objective is likely to be effective because it requires sampling from the population of existing assets and tracing to the accounting records.

B. Incorrect. The issue is completeness of financial records (that is, whether existing assets are recorded in the accounting records). The write-down or removal of recorded assets is not relevant.

C. Incorrect. The issue is completeness, not valuation, so this approach would not be relevant.

D. Incorrect. The issue is not valuation, but rather the appropriate inclusion of assets in the records.

Question 5

(From Domain II: Government Auditing Practice)
Solution: D

A. Incorrect. This would be a compliance audit of all performance reports to verify that they comply with reporting guidelines.

B. Incorrect. This would be a compliance audit of the entity's actions in relation to significant laws and regulations.

C. Incorrect. This would be a compliance audit of the entity's procedures in performing activities required by law.

D. Correct. This would be part of the compliance segment of a performance audit. Unlike the other answer choices, this is not a full audit of compliance, but rather it focuses only on compliance with laws and regulations as they apply to a specific performance audit objective.

Question 6

(From Domain II: Government Auditing Practice)
Solution: B

A. Incorrect. An examination of authorization controls would not detect fraud perpetrated by a properly authorized employee.

B. Correct. A comparison of itemized charges on vendor's invoices to average rates for similar goods should enable the auditor to find prices out of the normal range, also known as "higher than market." This is a basic audit tool for detecting potential fraud.

C. Incorrect. This procedure would not have the best chance of detecting this type of fraud, because an even distribution of contracts is not particularly expected, and the comparison does not take into account the dollar value of the contracts.

D. Incorrect. Although this procedure may help detect fraud in the vendor selection process, it does not address the specific fraud in the question and is not likely to detect fraud committed by procurement managers who have received kickbacks from vendors.

Question 7

(From Domain II: Government Auditing Practice)
Solution: D

A. Incorrect. Matching vouchers issued to those redeemed is only a control over outstanding vouchers, not over fraud perpetrated by participants.

B. Incorrect. Assigning participants to a select group of certified vendors would not prevent participants from selling their vouchers to unauthorized persons.

C. Incorrect. Swift prosecution takes place after the fraud has been committed and is therefore less of a preventive control.

D. Correct. If vendors were required to match a participant's photo I.D. card to the name and address written on a food voucher, there would be little opportunity for fraud during that phase of voucher redemption.

Question 8

(From Domain III: Government Auditing Skills and Techniques)
Solution: C

A. Incorrect. The amount of resources that are put into a program is referred to as the inputs or efforts.

B. Incorrect. The strategies, processes, and activities used by a program are the operations used to convert inputs into outputs.

C. Correct. The accomplishments or results that occur because of a program's services are referred to as outcomes. Outcomes can be categorized as immediate to long-term.

D. Incorrect. Outputs are the quantity of goods and services provided by a program.

Question 9

(From Domain III: Government Auditing Skills and Techniques)
Solution: A

A. Correct. A run chart displays changes in a particular event over a given period of time.

B. Incorrect. An aging schedule is used to show the distribution of time to complete a given task (for example, collection of receivables) relative to a desired time period. It would not be most useful in determining whether a change has occurred.

C. Incorrect. A histogram is used to show the frequency distribution around an average. This would not particularly determine whether a change has occurred.

D. Incorrect. Pareto analysis involves the ranking of data to focus on the few things (or people) that make the biggest impact on a situation. It cannot be applied to display changes of a particular event over time.

Question 10

(From Domain III: Government Auditing Skills and Techniques)
Solution: B

A. Incorrect. Segregation of incompatible duties is a deterrent to wrongdoing, not a detective control.

B. Correct. Periodic surprise cash counts can act as a deterrent and can actually detect integrity violations.

C. Incorrect. Regularly scheduled site visits will not necessarily detect problems because the individual who is perpetrating a fraud can prepare for the visit.

D. Incorrect. Properly designed forms can act as a deterrent, but they do not constitute a detective control.

Question 11

(From Domain IV: Government Auditing Environment)
Solution: C

A. Incorrect. Regulations can also be a means of ensuring accountability for achieving program objectives.

B. Incorrect. Equality is intended to ensure access to services and does not impact accountability for results.

C. Correct. Fragmentation of functions among government entities responsible for a specific policy often prevents a program from having control over the full continuum of services being provided. This can lead to poor accountability.

D. Incorrect. Bureaucracy may be an impediment to achieving effectiveness, but one of its underlying purposes is to ensure accountability.

Question 12

(From Domain IV: Government Auditing Environment)
Solution: B

A. Incorrect. A citizens' hot line may or may not be effective as a watchdog mechanism for legal restrictions, and it would certainly come after the fact.

B. Correct. By law, the budget cannot be overspent. The use of encumbrances ensures that sufficient money remains to cover outstanding purchase orders.

C. Incorrect. Citizen hearings may or may not be effective in ensuring that legal restrictions are met.

D. Incorrect. The use of a designated fund balance only indicates that management would prefer to use an amount for a specific purpose. It does not indicate a legal requirement restricting the funds.

Question 13

(From Domain IV: Government Auditing Environment)
Solution: A

A. Correct. Firm-fixed-price contracts are suitable for acquiring commercial items.

B. Incorrect. Cost-sharing is a cost-reimbursable contract, which is prohibited for acquiring commercial items.

C. Incorrect. Cost-plus-incentive-fee is a cost-reimbursable contract, which is prohibited for acquiring commercial items.

D. Incorrect. Cost-plus-award-fee is a cost-reimbursable contract, which is prohibited for acquiring commercial items.

Question 14

(From Domain IV: Government Auditing Environment)
Solution: D

A. Incorrect. Historically underutilized businesses, such as businesses owned by women or minority individuals, are generally considered an at-risk population.

B. Incorrect. Disabled citizens are generally considered an at-risk population.

C. Incorrect. Children from low-income families are generally considered an at-risk population, and they are usually eligible to benefit from early education programs.

D. Correct. Programs that benefit local agricultural entities may be instituted for various reasons, including economic reasons, but the agricultural entities would not generally be considered an at-risk population.

Question 15

(From Domain IV: Government Auditing Environment)
Solution: C

A. Incorrect. The minimum guarantee for contractor B should be met before orders are awarded to the other contractors.

B. Incorrect. The government is not required to compete the order since the minimum guarantee has not yet been met for contractor B.

C. Correct. All contractors under a multiple-award contract do not have to be given an opportunity to compete on orders above $2,500 if the contracting officer determines that it is necessary to place the order with a specific contractor to satisfy a minimum guarantee.

D. Incorrect. Splitting the order would not be appropriate, especially since the minimum guarantee for contractor B still needs to be met.

APPENDIX C
CGAP Exam Syllabus

> **Note:** Exam topics and/or format are subject to change as approved by The IIA's Professional Certification Board (PCB).

The one-part CGAP exam includes 115 multiple-choice questions, covers four domains, and requires a completion time of two hours and 55 minutes. The following standards are tested:

Standards Tested on all CGAP Exams

- The IIA's International Professional Practices Framework (IPPF) (P) (Includes the Code of Ethics, *International Standards for the Professional Practice of Internal Auditing* (*Standards*), Practice Advisories, and Development and Practice Aids).
- INTOSAI Standards and Code of Ethics (International Organization of Supreme Audit Institutions (INTOSAI) Government Auditing Standards) (A).

Additional Standards for CGAP Exams Administered in the United States

- Generally Accepted Government Auditing Standards (GAGAS/Yellow Book) (P).

CGAP Exam Domains

The CGAP exam core content covers is divided among four domains according to the following percentages:

Domain I: Standards, Governance, and Risk/Control Frameworks (10–20 percent).

Domain II: Government Auditing Practice (35–45 percent).

Domain III: Government Auditing Skills and Techniques (20–25 percent).

Domain IV: Government Auditing Environment (20–25 percent).

See below for a more detailed breakdown of the contents of each domain. The topics are marked with a (P) or (A) according to whether the exam requires proficiency (P) or simply awareness (A).

(P) = Proficiency: thorough understanding; ability to apply concepts in these topic areas.

(A) = Awareness: knowledge of terminology and fundamentals in these topic areas.

Domain I: Standards, Governance, and Risk/Control Frameworks (10–20%)

I.A Standards

I.A.1 Role of a Comprehensive Set of Auditing/Evaluation Standards (A)

I.A.2 Application of Appropriate Standards in All Assignments (P)

I.A.3 Role and Impact of Other Auditing Standards (Standards of Public Accounting Bodies, Quality Assurance Bodies, etc.) and Their Relationship with the Above Standards (A)

I.B Governance

I.B.1 Governance in the Public Sector (e.g., Audit Committee, Code of Conduct, Open Government, Public Scrutiny, Equity, Accountability) (P)

I.B.2 Role of Audit within the Governance Structure (P)

I.C Risk/Control Frameworks (e.g., COSO, CoCo)

I.C.1 Role of Frameworks (A)

I.C.2 Elements of a Risk/Control Framework (P)

I.C.3 Application of Frameworks (P)

I.D IIA Code of Ethics (P)

Domain II: Government Auditing Practice (35–45%)

II.A Management of the Audit Function
II.A.1 Need for a Formal Document of Purpose, Authority, and Responsibility (P)
II.A.2 Policies and Procedures (A)
II.A.3 Quality Assurance (A)
II.A.4 Planning (A)
II.A.5 Staffing (A)
II.A.6 Marketing the Audit Function (A)
II.A.7 Mission/Role/Outcome of the Audit Function within Government (A)

II.B Types of Audit Services
II.B.1 Audits of Compliance (P)
II.B.2 Audits of Performance/Value-for-Money/ Operations (e.g., Economy, Efficiency, Effectiveness) (P)
II.B.3 Audits of Financial Statements (A)
II.B.4 Audits of Financial Systems (P)
II.B.5 Audits of Information and Related Technology (P)
II.B.6 Consulting/Assistance Services (e.g., Nonaudit Advisory Services) (A)
II.B.7 Integrity Services (e.g., Fraud, Waste, and Abuse) (P)

II.C Processes for Delivery of Audit Services
II.C.1 Management of Individual Projects (P)
II.C.2 Planning (the Role of Laws, Regulations, Rules, and Ordinances in Your Planning Process Should Be Considered in the Planning Process) (P)
II.C.3 Risk and Control Assessment Practices (P)
II.C.4 Performing the Engagement (P)
II.C.5 Communicating Results (P)
II.C.6 Monitoring Results (Follow-up) (P)

Domain III: Government Auditing Skills and Techniques (20–25%)

III.A Management Concepts and Techniques (A)

III.B Performance Measurement (P)

III.C Program Evaluation (A)

III.D Quantitative Methods (e.g., Statistical Methods and Analytical Review) (P)

III.E Qualitative Methods (e.g., Questionnaires, Interviews, and Flowcharts) (P)

III.F Methods for the Identification and Investigation of Integrity Violations (P)

III.G Research/Data Collection Techniques (P)

III.H Analytical Skills (e.g., Distinguish between Significant and Insignificant Information) (P)

Domain IV: Government Auditing Environment (20–25%)

IV.A Performance Management (P)

IV.B Financial Management
IV.B.1 Unique Requirements in Accounting for and Reporting On Government Financial Operations (P)
IV.B.2 Principles of Taxation and Revenue Generation (P)
IV.B.3 Unique Aspects of Governmental Budgeting (e.g., Encumbrances, Earmarking) (P)
IV.B.4 Government Accounting (e.g., Fund Accounting, Resource Accounting) (P)
IV.B.5 Legal Restrictions on Sources and Uses of Funds (e.g., Voted Funds, Conditional Grants, Revenues) (A)
IV.B.6 Investment Restrictions for Public Funds (A)
IV.B.7 Activity-based Costing/Cost Allocation (A)

IV.C Implications of Various Service Delivery Methods

IV.C.1 Direct Delivery by Government Employees (P)
IV.C.2 Grants (P)
IV.C.3 Contracts (P)
IV.C.4 Joint Ventures/Partnerships/Authorities/Special Operating Agencies/Quasi-governmental (A)
IV.C.5 Privatization (A)

IV.D Implications of Delivering Services to Citizens

IV.D.1 Due Process Rights of Clients/Citizens (P)
IV.D.2 Confidentiality/Privacy/Rights of Clients/Citizens (P)
IV.D.3 Issues Arising from the Methods of Funding/Delivering Services (Condition that Client Receiving Service May Mot Be Party Paying for the Services; Ability-to-pay Principle; User Pay; Eligibility Requirements; Limitations On Services Available; Entitlements; etc.) (A)
IV.D.4 Reality of Conflicting Missions (e.g., Satisfy Both Developers and Environmentalists, Keep Families Together and Kids Safe) (A)
IV.D.5 Issues Associated with At-risk Populations (e.g., Multiple, Interacting Causes and Conditions; Difficulty of Measuring Prevention) (A)

IV.E Unique Characteristics of Human Resources Management (A)

IV.F Unique Purchasing and Procurement Requirements (P)

Exam Nondisclosure

The CGAP exam is a nondisclosed examination, which means that current exam questions and answers will not be published or divulged.

CGAP® Exam Administration Information

> **Note:** This document reflects CGAP examination information as of date of publication. Visit The IIA's website for current information at http://www.theiia.org/.

The Certified Government Auditing Professional® (CGAP) designation was launched in 2000 to serve the areas of specialized knowledge required for those working in federal, state/provincial, local, quasi-governmental areas or authority/crown corporations. The CGAP certification program is designed for auditors working in the public sector at all levels — federal/national, state/provincial, local, quasi-governmental, or crown authority.

The CGAP exam is offered in the following languages: Chinese (unsimplified), English, Polish, Spanish, and Turkish.

Countries with Additional CGAP Certification Requirements

Candidates from the following countries must refer to their local IIA institute website or contact their local representative for more information about local certification processes:

Argentina	Germany	New Zealand
Australia	Greece	Norway
Austria	Indonesia	Philippines
Belgium	Italy	Singapore
Brazil	Japan	South Africa
Bulgaria	Korea	Spain
China	Malaysia	Sweden
Chinese Taiwan	Mexico	Switzerland
Czech Republic	Morocco	Thailand
France	Netherlands	Turkey

The information presented in this book regarding CGAP pertains only to those countries that are not listed above).

Computer-based Testing

Before scheduling an exam, you must apply and register in The IIA's Certification Candidate Management System (CCMS) (https://www.globaliia.org/).

The CGAP exam is available through computer-based testing, allowing you to test year-round at more than 500 locations worldwide. Candidates are able to sit for exams at any IIA-authorized Pearson VUE testing center worldwide, regardless of whether the testing center is located in your hometown or country. To locate the testing centers nearest you, visit the Pearson VUE website (http://pearsonvue.com/iia/).

Eligibility Requirements

By applying to become a candidate in the CGAP program, an individual agrees to accept the conditions of the program. These include eligibility requirements, exam confidentiality, Code of Ethics, Continuing Professional Education (CPE), and any other conditions enacted by The IIA's Professional Certification Board (PCB).

CGAP candidates must meet the following eligibility requirements:

Education

The candidate must have a post-secondary (four-year) or equivalent degree. A two-year degree plus three years of general business experience may be substituted. For further details, please refer to the Certification Candidate Handbook (https://www.globaliia.org/).

Character Reference

The candidate must exhibit high moral and professional character and submit a completed character reference form signed by a CIA, CGAP, CCSA, CFSA, or the candidate's supervisor. This one-page form is included in the Certification Candidate Handbook (https://www.globaliia.org/).

Work Experience

The candidate must acquire two years of auditing experience in a government environment (federal, state/provincial, local, quasi-governmental areas, authority/crown corporation). A completed Experience Verification Form is required. Candidates may apply to the program and sit for the exam before satisfying the professional experience requirement, but will not be certified until all program requirements have been met. This one-page form is included in the Certification Candidate Handbook (https://www.globaliia.org/).

Eligibility Period

Effective November 2010, the certification program's eligibility requires candidates to complete the program certification process within four years of application approval. If a candidate has not completed the certification process within four years, all fees and exam parts will be forfeited.

Confidentiality

The CGAP certification exam is a nondisclosed exam. Candidates agree to keep the contents of the CGAP exam confidential and therefore may not discuss the specific exam content with anyone except The IIA's Certification Department. Unauthorized disclosure of exam material will be considered a breach of the Code of Ethics and could result in disqualification of the candidate or other appropriate censure.

Code of Ethics

CGAP candidates agree to abide by the Code of Ethics established by The IIA.

Continuing Professional Education

Upon certification, CGAPs are required to maintain their knowledge and skills and stay abreast of improvements and current developments in government auditing by satisfying CPE requirements.

IIA Membership

In most cases, you do not have to be a member of The IIA to take the CGAP exam or become a CGAP, but we encourage you to consider its advantages. There are some countries, however, that do require candidates to be IIA members to take the CGAP exam. See the section above with the heading, "Countries with Additional CGAP Certification Requirements" for more details.

IIA members receive discounts on CGAP review materials and courses and have access to the latest exam preparation resources, networking opportunities, and current CGAP news and information. In addition, CPE reporting for CGAPs who are IIA members is free.

Sample CGAP Exam Questions

The IIA provides a limited number of sample CGAP exam questions (with answers) to give candidates an understanding of the types of questions that typically appear on the CGAP exam (see globaliia.org).

In addition, The IIARF offers more than 200 CGAP Exam Study Questions in book form and on CD as a sample, timed test. (See the IIARF bookstore for ordering information.)

APPENDIX D
Supplementary Study Materials

Applicable Audit Standards

The Institute of Internal Auditors (IIA) International Professional Practices Framework (includes the *International Standards for the Professional Practice of Internal Auditing*).

Generally Accepted Government Auditing Standards (GAGAS/Yellow Book) — U.S. version only.

International Organization of Supreme Audit Institutions (INTOSAI) Code of Ethics and Auditing Standards.

IFAC's International Standards on Auditing.

Relevant IIA Publications

Tom O'Connor, *CGAP Exam Study Questions*, 2010.

Stephen L. Morgan and Ronell B. Raaum, *Performance Auditing: A Measurement Approach*, 2nd edition, 2009.

Paul D. Epstein, Stuart S. Grifel, and Stephen L. Morgan, *Auditor Roles in Government Performance Measurement: A Guide to Exemplary Practices at the Local, State, and Provincial Levels*, 2004.

Optimizing Public Sector Audit Functions, Supplementary Guidance, 2012.

Public Sector Definition and the Role of Auditing in Public Sector Governance, 2012.

Topics Where Other Publications May Provide In-depth Coverage*

Performance measurement and management is extensively covered in public administration publications of many types. Examples are:

- National Performance Management Advisory Commission, *A Performance Management Framework for State and Local Government: From Measurement and Reporting to Management and Improving*, 2010.
- Association of Government Accountants, *Using Performance Information to Drive Performance Improvement,* 2011.

Risk assessment, internal control, and governance are the subject of many publications from both the private and public sectors.

Certified internal auditor (CIA) exam preparation publications provide relevant coverage of material that is included in the CGAP examination.

Other issues where CGAP candidates may find other literature relevant include specialized areas, e.g. fraud, information technology, statistics, and analytics.

* Note: The intent of citing issues where supplementary references may be advisable is not to suggest that a large amount of added research will be needed to prepare for the CGAP examination. For many, if not most, CGAP candidates, especially those with sufficient experience, this manual should allow sufficient preparation. However, the list of issues is cited to assist those candidates who conclude that they need further elaboration in some areas of preparation.

Internet Resources

The Institute of Internal Auditors (IIA)

http://www.theiia.org/

U.S. Government Accountability Office (GAO)

http://www.gao.gov

International Federation of Accountants (IFAC)

http://www.ifac.org

INTSOAI

http://www.intosai.org/

Governmental Accounting Standards Board (GASB)

http://www.gasb.org/

Federal Accounting Standards Advisory Board (FASAB)

http://www.fasab.gov

American Institute of Certified Public Accountants (AICPA)

http://www.aicpa.org/index.htm

Canadian Institute of Chartered Accountants (CICA)

http://www.cica.ca/

Association of Certified Fraud Examiners (ACFE)

http://www.cfenet.com

APPENDIX E
An Example of the Legislative Process

> **Note:** This example uses the U.S. House of Representatives as a model to demonstrate the legislative process. The following information was taken from the U.S. House of Representatives website and other relevant literature.

The chief function of the Congress in the United States is making laws. There are many aspects and variations of the process, which are not addressed in the following text.

Using U.S. processes as an example, the following three distinct processes of creating laws are discussed in this section. All three processes impact the audit process as auditors must understand and be aware of applicable laws and regulations to effectively test for compliance. The three processes are:

1. Legislative.
2. Regulatory.
3. Judicial.

Legislative Process

Federal, state, and local legislative processes vary depending on the political structure; however, there are general similarities. Regardless of the specific form (Congress or state legislature (bicameral) or city council (unicameral)), laws are created by elected representatives of the citizens (democracy). Since there are general similarities in the basic legislative process, the U.S. House of Representatives process is outlined in this section.

"All Legislative Powers herein granted shall be vested in a Congress of the United States, which shall consist of a Senate and House of Representatives." (Article I, Section 1, of the United States Constitution)

Forms of Congressional Action

The work of Congress is initiated by the introduction of a proposal in one of four principal forms: bill, joint resolution, concurrent resolution, and simple resolution.

- *Bills.* A bill is the form used for most legislation, whether permanent or temporary, general or special, public or private. Bills are presented to the president for action when approved in identical form by both the House of Representatives and the Senate.
- *Joint resolutions.* Joint resolutions may originate either in the House of Representatives or in the Senate. There is little practical difference between a bill and a joint resolution. Both are subject to the same procedure, except for a joint resolution proposing an amendment to the Constitution. On approval of such a resolution by two-thirds of both the House and Senate, it is sent directly to the administrator of general services for submission to the individual states for ratification. It is not presented to the president for approval. Joint resolutions become law in the same manner as bills.
- *Concurrent resolutions.* Matters affecting the operations of both the House of Representatives and Senate are usually initiated by means of concurrent resolutions. On approval by both the House of Representatives and Senate, they are signed by the clerk of the House and the secretary of the Senate. They are not presented to the president for action.
- *Simple resolutions.* A matter concerning the operation of either the House of Representatives or Senate alone is initiated by a simple resolution. They are not presented to the president for action.

Introduction and Referral to Committee

Any member in the House of Representatives may introduce a bill at any time while the House is in session by simply placing it in the "hopper" provided for the purpose at the side of the clerk's desk in the House chamber. The sponsor's signature must appear on the bill. A public bill may have an unlimited number of cosponsoring members. The bill is assigned its legislative number by the clerk and referred to the appropriate committee by the speaker, with the assistance of the parliamentarian.

An important phase of the legislative process is the action taken by committees. It is during committee action that the most intense consideration is given to the proposed measures; this is also the time when the people are given their opportunity to be heard. Each piece of legislation is referred to the committee that has jurisdiction over the area affected by the measure.

Consideration by Committee

Usually the first step in this process is a public hearing, where the committee members hear witnesses representing various viewpoints on the measure. Each committee makes public the date, place, and subject of any hearing it conducts.

After hearings are completed, the bill is considered in a session that is popularly known as the "markup" session. Members of the committee study the viewpoints presented in detail. Amendments may be offered to the bill, and the committee members vote to accept or reject these changes.

Committee Action

At the conclusion of deliberation, a vote of committee or subcommittee members is taken to determine what action to take on the measure. It can be reported, with or without amendment, or tabled, which means no further action on it will occur. If the committee has approved extensive amendments, it may decide to report a new bill incorporating all the amendments. This is known as a clean bill, which will have a new number.

If the committee votes to report a bill, the committee report is written. This report describes the purpose and scope of the measure and the reasons for recommended approval.

House Floor Consideration

Consideration of a measure by the full House can be a simple or very complex operation. In general, a measure is ready for consideration by the full House after it has been reported by a committee.

After all debate is concluded and amendments decided upon, the House is ready to vote on final passage. In some cases, a vote to "recommit" the bill to committee is requested. This is usually an effort by opponents to change some portion or table the measure. If the attempt to recommit fails, a vote on final passage is ordered.

Resolving Differences

After a measure passes in the House, it goes to the Senate for consideration. A bill must pass both bodies in the same form before it can be presented to the president for signature into law. If the Senate changes the language of the measure, it must return to the House for concurrence or additional changes. This back-and-forth negotiation may occur on the House floor, with the House accepting or rejecting Senate amendments or complete Senate text. Often a conference committee will be appointed with both House and Senate members. This group will resolve the differences in committee and report the identical measure back to both bodies for a vote. Conference committees also issue reports outlining the final version of the bill.

Final Step

Votes on final passage, as well as all other votes in the House, may be taken by the electronic voting system, which registers each individual member's response. Votes in the House may also be by voice vote, and no record of individual responses is available.

After a measure has been passed in identical form by both the House and Senate, it is considered "enrolled." It is sent to the president who may sign the measure into law, veto it and return it to Congress, let it become law without signature, or at the end of a session, pocket-veto it.

Regulatory Process

Another lawmaking process is the regulatory process where an executive agency promulgates rules or regulations in accordance with applicable requirements. Political executives such as presidents, governors, and mayors often use their policymaking power to mandate requirements or regulations. There is often a debate regarding the constitutionality of mandating actions and bypassing the legislative process. An executive's ability to enact regulations is often a function of his or her political strength. The process of enacting regulations generally includes a public comment period where the public is informed of the regulation and comments are solicited. These administrative regulations are often promulgated based on legislative requirements, which establish a public policy and direct an executive agency to implement "all necessary rules and regulations" to carry out the policy. Other times, agencies will base their authority to enact regulations on a "broad construction" of their own enabling legislation. If administrative regulations are implemented in accordance with the government's established process and are not reversed, they have the same "force and effect" as any other law. The implementation process requires publishing rules for public comment during a specified time before they take effect. Administrative regulations may subsequently be reversed either by new legislation or through a court challenge.

Judicial Process

The constitutional independence of the judicial branch provides an opportunity for courts to interpret the law and set precedents. Judicial precedents are based on case law (the results of judicial decisions) and can have extensive impact on governments. Since the application of laws and regulations is ultimately subject to judicial interpretation, courts have a powerful presence in government.

APPENDIX F
Managing for Results System (Austin, Texas)

This is a PowerPoint presentation was created by coauthor Stephen Morgan, March 2012, to give the history of the Managing for Results System used by the city of Austin, Texas, from 1992–2012.

History of Austin's Managing for Results (MFR) System—1992-2012

Source: AGA National Audio Conference, March 21, 2012, "A Systems Approach to Implementing Performance-Based Management and Budgeting"

1992-1998: Where We've Been (in the City of Austin) ...

- 1992 – Council Resolution on Performance Measurement and Reporting
- 1994 – First Performance Measurement & Reporting System Audit
- 1996 – Second Performance Measurement and Reporting System Audit; Program Budgeting implemented
- 1998 – Third Performance Measurement and Reporting System Audit

2

1998-1999: Where We've Been...

- **1998 Corporate *Managing for Results* Initiative Defined**
  - Simplify our System
  - Clarify the Information We Provide
  - Develop Measures that are Meaningful to our Employees
  - Focus on Cost
- **1999 Corporate Partnership Implements CMO Initiative**
  - Developed a Standard manual--The Resource Guide
  - Trained over 200 managers
  - Developed a Single Accounting System
  - Identified Key Performance Measures for Executive SSPRs
  - Corporate Review Team

1999-2008: Where We've Been...

- **2002 Fourth Audit of the Performance Management System**
  - Ongoing Integrated System
  - Information Used for Operational Management
  - Measures Are Relevant and Reliable
  - Budgets Are More Data and Results Driven
- **2003-2008 Continuous Improvement**
  - Managers and Supervisors Fully Trained
  - Performance Measures Supported by More Robust Technology
  - Improvements Made to City's Website and Stakeholder Access to Performance Information
  - Citizen and Employee Surveys Provide Data for Selected Performance Measures

4

2008-2012: Where We Are Now...

- **2008-Current**
  - Website Robust with Capacity to "Drill Down" and Search" through Performance Measures Database
  - "Managing for Results" Used as Business Planning and Performance Monitoring Model for More than a Decade--Now Part of City Culture
  - Performance Report on Website tracks 115 Key Departmental Measures, of these 21 are Designated Citywide Key or "Dashboard" Measures
  - Performance Comparisons Presented in Graphics with Goal/Targets and Measures Tracked Over Five Years
  - Performance Report for 2009-2010 Received "Certificate of Excellence" from ICMA in October 2010
  - Annual Citizen Surveys Strengthened to Include Focus Groups and Presentations to City Council
  - "Best Practice Citizen Centric" External Performance Accountability Report Is Needed

5

NOTES

DOMAIN I
STANDARDS, GOVERNANCE, AND RISK/CONTROL FRAMEWORKS

1. Summarized from the International Professional Practices Framework (IPPF) issued by The Institute of Internal Auditors (IIA), www.theiia.org.

2. Summarized from the December 2011 *Government Auditing Standards* issued by the U.S. Government Accountability Office (GAO), www.gao.gov.

3. *Professional Guidance: IIA International Standards for the Professional Practice of Internal Auditing (Red Book)* and *The Government Accountability Office Government Audit Standards (Yellow Book): A Comparison,* 2nd Edition (Altamonte Springs, FL: The Institute of Internal Auditors), June 2012.

4. Summarized from documents on two websites — www.intosai.org and www.issai.org, as of 2011.

5. Summarized from *Handbook of International Standards on Auditing, Assurance, and Ethics Pronouncements,* 2008, and later information on www.ifac.org.

6. Email, August 24, 2011, from James Gunn, director of the International Auditing and Assurance Standards Board (IAASB) of the International Federation of Accountants (IFAC), to Thomas F. O'Connor, coauthor of this study guide.

7. International Professional Practices Framework (IPPF), Glossary (Altamonte Springs, FL: The Institute of Internal Auditors).

8. *Government Auditing Standards,* Chapter 1, December 2011 Revision, Government Accountability Office (GAO).

9. Summarized from *Internal Control – Integrated Framework,* Committee of Sponsoring Organizations of the Treadway Commission (COSO), 1992.

10. Exposure Draft, November 2011, Committee of Sponsoring Organizations of the Treadway Commission (COSO) website, www.coso.org.

11. Summarized from *Enterprise Risk Management – Integrated Framework,* Committee of Sponsoring Organizations of the Treadway Commission (COSO), September 2004, and other enterprise risk management sources.

12. The IIA's Position Paper, Internal Audit Role in ERM, September 2004.

13. Email, September 6, 2011, from Gigi Dawe, principal, Canadian Institute of Chartered Accountants (CICA), to Thomas F. O'Connor, coauthor of this manual.

14. Code of Ethics (Altamonte Springs, FL: The Institute of Internal Auditors).

15. Chapter 1, GAO's *Government Auditing Standards,* December 2011 Revision.

16. Code of Ethics, International Organization of Supreme Audit Institutions (INTOSAI), www.intosai.org, 2012.

17. Code of Ethics, International Federation of Accountants (IFAC), www.ifac.org.

ADDITIONAL SOURCES FOR DOMAIN I

Listed by Domain Number and Subhead

A.1 The Institute of Internal Auditors' (IIA) *Standards*

International Professional Practices Framework (IPPF) (Altamonte Springs, FL: The Institute of Internal Auditors), updated for 2012.

A.2 GAO's Generally Accepted Government Auditing Standards

Generally Accepted Government Auditing Standards (GAGAS) (U.S. Government Accountability Office, 2011), www.gao.gov.

A.3 International Standards of Supreme Audit Institutions

International Organization of Supreme Audit Institutions (INTOSAI), www.intosai.org, and International Standards of Supreme Audit Institutions (ISSAI), www.issai.org, 2011.

A.4 Auditing and Assurance Standards issued through the IFAC's IAASB

Email, August 2011, from James Gunn, director of the International Auditing and Assurance Standards Board (IAASB) of the International Federation of Accountants (IFAC), www.ifac.org/IAASB, September 2011.

B. Governance

Generally Accepted Government Auditing Standards (GAGAS) (U.S. Government Accountability Office), Chapter 1 (paragraphs 1.01-1.03).

C. Risk/Control Frameworks (e.g., COSO, CoCo)

Report of the National Commission on Fraudulent Financial Reporting (New York: National Commission on Fraudulent Reporting, October 1987).

Internal Control – Integrated Framework (New Jersey: Committee of Sponsoring Organizations of the Treadway Commission, 1994), 13.

Enterprise Risk Management – Integrated Framework (New Jersey: Committee of Sponsoring Organizations of the Treadway Commission, 2004), excerpts from Executive Summary.

Relevant excerpts from The IIA's *International Standards for the Professional Practice of Internal Auditing (Standards)*, Generally Accepted Government Auditing Standards (GAGAS), International Standards of Supreme Audit Institutions (ISSAI), and the International Federation of Accountants (IFACs) and International Auditing and Assurance Standards Board (IAASB) standards.

Email, August 4, 2011, from Gigi Dawe, principal, Canadian Institute of Chartered Accountants (CICA).

D. IIA and Other Codes of Ethics

International Professional Practices Framework (IPPF) (Altamonte Springs, FL: The Institute of Internal Auditors, 2011).

Generally Accepted Government Auditing Standards (GAGAS) (U.S. Government Accountability Office, 2011), Internet version, Chapter 1.

Code of Ethics, International Organization of Supreme Audit Institutions (INTOSAI), www.intosai.org, 2012.

Handbook of International Standards on Auditing, Assurance, and Ethics Pronouncements (International Federation of Accountants [IFAC] 2008).

DOMAIN II
GOVERNMENT AUDITING PRACTICE

1. Lawrence B. Sawyer et al., *Sawyer's Internal Auditing: The Practice of Modern Internal Auditing* (Altamonte Springs, FL: The Institute of Internal Auditors), Various Editions.

2. Governance, risk management, and control are included (with some variation) as areas of audit coverage in the following audit standards: The IIA's *International Standards for the Professional Practices of Internal Auditing (Standards)*, Generally Accepted Government Auditing Standards (GAGAS), International Standards of Supreme Audit Institutions (ISSAI), and International Standards of Auditing (ISA).

3. Financial statement audit standards are included in Generally Accepted Government Auditing Standards (GAGAS), International Standards of Supreme Audit Institutions (ISSAI), and International Standards of Auditing (ISA).

4. Performance audit standards are included in Generally Accepted Government Auditing Standards (GAGAS) and International Standards of Supreme Audit Institutions (ISSAI).

5. Undated table issued by the International Organization of Supreme Audit Institutions (INTOSAI), comparing financial and performance audits.

6. Compliance audit work may be included as either a separate audit category or as an aspect of broader categories under The IIA's *International Standards for the Professional Practice of Internal Auditing* (*Standards*), Generally Accepted Government Auditing Standards (GAGAS), International Standards of Supreme Audit Institutions (ISSAI), or International Standards of Auditing (ISA).

7. Internal control audit work may be included as either a separate audit category or as an aspect of broader categories under The IIA's *International Standards for the Professional Practice of Internal Auditing* (*Standards*), Generally Accepted Government Auditing Standards (GAGAS), International Standards of Supreme Audit Institutions (ISSAI), or International Standards of Auditing (ISA).

8. Attestations are a category of engagement under Generally Accepted Government Auditing Standards (GAGAS). Assurances are a category of engagement under standards from the International Auditing and Assurance Standards Board (IAASB).

9. Summarized information on evaluations is based on a variety of sources, such as standards issued by the American Evaluation Association and the Joint Committee on Standards for Education, which are discussed in chapter 2 of Generally Accepted Government Auditing Standards (GAGAS).

10. *IT Standards, Guidelines, and Tools and Techniques for Audit and Assurance and Control Professionals* and *Control Objectives for Information and related Technology* issued by ISACA. See www.isaca.org.

11. *Federal Information System Control Audit Manual* (FISCAM). See GAO-09-232G at www.gao.gov.

12. Information posted at www.isaca.org.

13. The IIA's Global Technology Audit Guides (GTAGs) and Guide to the Assessment of IT Risk (GAIT).

14. Summarized information from a variety of sources, e.g., The IIA's Practice Guide, Internal Auditing and Fraud.

15. 2010 table, issued by the Canadian Treasury Board, comparing internal audits and fraud investigations.

16. Nonaudit services are addressed in Generally Accepted Government Auditing Standards (GAGAS) and International Standards of Supreme Audit Institutions (ISSAI). The IIA's definition of "internal auditing" includes *assurance* and *consulting*. Some audit organizations may view consulting as a nonaudit service.

DOMAIN III
GOVERNMENT AUDITING SKILLS AND TECHNIQUES

1. Jay M. Shafritz and E. W. Russell, *Introducing Public Administration* (New York: Longman Press, 2000).

2. Ibid.

3. Based on a variety of performance measurement and management publications from professional organizations, government entities, and recognized individual authors and relevant conference presentations, as well as experiences and discussions of the coauthors, over the period of 1977 to the present.

4. Based on a variety of evaluation publications by professional organizations and recognized individual authors.

5. Information for this section is adapted from The IIA's Practice Guide, Internal Auditing and Fraud, and other relevant literature.

DOMAIN IV
GOVERNMENT AUDITING ENVIRONMENT

1. Government Performance and Results Act (GPRA) of 1993, and the GPRA Modernization Act of 2010 and President's Executive Orders cited.

2. Summary of performance measurement documents from the Governmental Accounting Standards Board (GASB), www.GASAB.org.

3. National Performance Management Advisory Commission, *A Performance Management Framework for State and Local Government: From Measurement and Reporting to Management and Improving,* 2010.

4. Coauthor Thomas F. O'Connor's notes from AGA Performance Management Conference, Seattle, November 3–4, 2011.

5. Canadian Treasury Board, *Increased Ministerial Authority and Accountability (IMAA) Initiative of the 1980s.*

6. Canadian Public Sector Accounting Board, *Statement of Recommended Practices on Performance Reporting of Canada's Public Sector Accounting Board,* 2006.

7. Stephen L. Morgan presentation titled "Performance Accountability in Government."

8. Governmental Accounting Standards Board (GASB) Concepts Statement No. 2, Service Efforts and Accomplishments (SEA).

9. Ibid.

10. Ibid.

11. Ibid.

12. Jay M. Shafritz and E. W. Russell, *Introducing Public Administration* (New York: Longman Press, 2000).

13. Ibid.

14. Undated study by the University of Texas circa 2005.

15. Summarized from documents of Federal Accounting Standards Advisory Board (FASAB), www.fasab.gov.

16. Summarized from documents of the Governmental Accounting Standards Board (GASB), www.gasb.org.

17. Shafritz and Russell, *Introducing Public Administration.*

18. B. J. Reed and John Swain, *Public Finance Administration* (California: Sage Publishing, 1997).

19. Statements of Federal Accounting Standards (SFFAS) #4, #5, and #30 (from Federal Accounting Standards Advisory Board [FASAB]) and OMB Circular A-136, and the CFO Act, as amended, and Government Performance and Results Act of 1993.

20. Association of Government Accountants' *Managerial Cost Accounting in the Federal Government; Providing Useful Information for Decision Making,* CPAG 22, September 2009.

21. *Journal of Government Financial Management,* Spring 2007, *Activity-Based Costing in Large U.S. Cities: Cost and Benefits.*

22. Office of Management and Budget (OMB) Circular A-136.

23. Summarized from a variety of sources on delivery methods used by governmental bodies.

24. Cornelius E. Tierney, *Federal Accounting Handbook* (New York: John Wiley & Sons, 2000).

25. Ibid.

26. Federal Acquisition Institute, Glossary of Terms.

27. Tierney, *Federal Accounting Handbook.*

28. Shafritz and Russell, *Introducing Public Administration.*

29. Ibid.

30. Federal Acquisition Regulation (U.S. Government).

31. Ibid.

32. www.house.gov. (USA)

GLOSSARY

> **Note:** Many of the definitions in this glossary are taken from the glossary in The IIA's International Professional Practices Framework, or have been modified as appropriate to conform to the discussions in this exam study guide.

Add Value
Value is provided by improving opportunities to achieve organizational objectives, identifying operational improvement, and/or reducing risk exposure through both assurance and consulting services.

Adequately Designed — See Controls Are Adequately Designed.

Application Systems
Sets of programs that are designed for end users such as payroll, accounts payable, and in some cases, large applications such as enterprise resource planning (ERP) systems that provide many business functions.

Appropriate Evidence
Any piece or collection of evidence gained during an engagement that provides relevant and reliable support for the judgments and conclusions reached during the engagement.

Asset Misappropriation
Acts involving the theft or misuse of an organization's assets (for example, skimming revenues, stealing inventory, or payroll fraud).

Assurance Services
An objective examination of evidence for the purpose of providing an independent assessment on governance, risk management, and control processes for the organization. Examples may include financial, performance, compliance, system security, and due diligence engagements.

Audit Engagement — See Assurance Services.

Audit Observation
Any identified and validated gap between the current and desired state arising from an assurance engagement.

Audit Risk
The risk of reaching invalid audit conclusions and/or providing faulty advice based on the audit work conducted.

Audit Sampling
The application of an audit procedure to less than 100 percent of the items in a population for the purpose of drawing an inference about the entire population.

Audit Universe
A compilation of the subsidiaries, business units, departments, groups, processes, or other established subdivisions of an organization that exist to manage one or more business risks.

Auditee
The subsidiary, business unit, department, group, or other established subdivision of an organization that is the subject of an assurance engagement.

Board
An organization's governing body, such as a board of directors, supervisory board, head of an agency or legislative body, board of governors or trustees of a nonprofit organization, or any other designated body of the organization.

Bottom-up Approach
To begin by looking at all processes directly at the activity level, and then aggregating the identified processes across the organization.

Business Process
The set of connected activities linked with each other for the purpose of achieving one or more business objectives.

Business Process Outsourcing (BPO)
The act of transferring some of an organization's business processes to an outside provider to achieve cost reductions, operating effectiveness, or operating efficiency while improving service quality.

Cause
The reason for the difference between the expected and actual conditions (why the difference exists).

Chief Audit Executive
A senior position within the organization responsible for internal audit activities. When internal audit activities are obtained from external service providers, the chief audit executive is the person responsible for overseeing the service contract and the overall quality assurance of these activities, and follow-up of engagement results. The term also includes titles such as general auditor, head of internal audit, chief internal auditor, internal audit director, and inspector general.

Code of Ethics
The Code of Ethics of The Institute of Internal Auditors contains principles relevant to the profession and practice of internal auditing and Rules of Conduct that describe behavior expected of internal auditors. The Code of Ethics applies to both parties and entities that provide internal audit services. The purpose of the Code of Ethics is to promote an ethical culture in the global profession of internal auditing.

Compensating Control
An activity that, if key controls do not fully operate effectively, may help to reduce the related risk. A compensating control will not, by itself, reduce risk to an acceptable level.

Complementary Control
An activity that, when taken together with other controls, contributes to the overall effective mitigation of risk. Frequently, complementary controls operate across multiple processes and risks.

Compliance
Conformity and adherence to applicable laws and regulations (COSO definition). May also include conformity and adherence to policies, plans, procedures, contracts, or other requirements.

Computer-assisted Audit Techniques (CAATs)
Automated audit techniques, such as generalized audit software, utility software, test data, application software tracing and mapping, and audit expert systems, that help the internal auditor directly test controls built into computerized information systems and data contained in computer files.

Condition
The factual evidence that the internal auditor found in the course of the examination (what does exist).

Conflict of Interest
Any relationship that is, or appears to be, not in the best interest of the organization. A conflict of interest would prejudice an individual's ability to perform his or her duties and responsibilities objectively.

Consulting Services
Advisory and related services, the nature and scope of which are agreed to with the customer, and which are intended to improve an organization's governance, risk management, and control processes without the internal auditor assuming management responsibility. Examples include advice, facilitation, and training.

Continuous Auditing
Using computerized techniques to perpetually audit the processing of business transactions.

Control
Any action taken by management, the board, and other parties to manage risk and increase the likelihood that established objectives and goals will be achieved. Management plans, organizes, and directs the performance of sufficient actions to provide reasonable assurance that objectives and goals will be achieved (also see Internal Control and System of Internal Controls).

Control Environment
The attitude and actions of the board and management regarding the significance of control within the organization. The control environment provides the discipline and structure for the achievement of the primary objectives of the system of internal controls. The control environment includes the following elements:

- Integrity and ethical values.
- Management's philosophy and operating style.
- Organizational structure.
- Assignment of authority and responsibility.
- Human resource policies and practices.
- Competence of personnel.

Control Risk
The potential that controls will fail to reduce controllable risk to an acceptable level.

Controllable Risk
The portion of inherent risk that management can reduce through day-to-day operations and management activities.

Controls Are Adequately Designed
Present if management has planned and organized (designed) the controls or the system of internal controls in a manner that provides reasonable assurance that the organization's entity-level and process-level risks can be managed to an acceptable level.

Controls Are Operating Effectively
Present if management has executed (operated) the controls or the system of internal controls in a manner that provides reasonable assurance that the organization's entity-level and process-level risks have been managed effectively and that the organization's goals and objectives will be achieved efficiently and economically.

Corrective Control
An activity in which detected omissions and errors are corrected.

Corruption
Acts in which individuals wrongfully use their influence in a business transaction in order to procure some benefit for themselves or another person, contrary to their duty to their employer or the rights of another (for example, kickbacks, self-dealing, or conflicts of interest).

Criteria
The standards, measures, or expectations used in making an evaluation and/or verification of an observation (what should exist).

Customer
The subsidiary, business unit, department, group, individual, or other established subdivision of an organization that is the subject of a consulting engagement.

Database
A large repository of data, typically contained in many linked files, and stored in a manner that allows the data to be easily accessed, retrieved, and manipulated.

Detective Control
An activity that is designed to discover undesirable events that have already occurred. A detective control must occur on a timely basis (before the undesirable event has had a negative impact on the organization) to be considered effective.

Directive Control
An activity that gives explicit direction regarding what actions need to take place to cause or encourage a desirable event to occur.

Effect
The risk or exposure the organization and/or others encounter because the condition is not consistent with the criteria (the consequence of the difference).

Engagement
A specific internal audit assignment or project that includes multiple tasks or activities designed to accomplish a specific set of objectives. See also Assurance Services and Consulting Services.

Engagement Work Program
A document that lists the procedures to be followed during an engagement, designed to achieve the engagement plan.

Enterprise Risk Management — See Risk Management.

Entity-level Control
A control that operates across an entire entity and, as such, is not bound by, or associated with, individual processes.

External Auditor — See Independent Outside Auditor.

Framework
A body of guiding principles that form a template against which organizations can evaluate a multitude of business practices. These principles are comprised of various concepts, values, assumptions, and practices intended to provide a yardstick against which an organization can assess or evaluate a particular structure, process, or environment or a group of practices or procedures.

Fraud
Any illegal act characterized by deceit, concealment, or violation of trust. These acts are not dependent upon the threat of violence or physical force. Frauds are perpetrated by parties and organizations to obtain money, property, or services; to avoid payment or loss of services; or to secure personal or business advantage.

Fraudulent Financial Reporting
Acts that involve falsification of an organization's financial statements (for example, overstating revenues, or understating liabilities and expenses).

General Information Technology Controls
Controls that operate across all information technology systems and are in place to ensure the integrity, reliability, and accuracy of the application systems. Also represents a specific example of an "entity-level control."

Governance
The combination of processes and structures implemented by the board to inform, direct, manage, and monitor the activities of the organization toward the achievement of its objectives.

Impairment to Independence or Objectivity
The introduction of threats that may result in a substantial limitation, or the appearance of a substantial limitation, to the internal auditor's ability to perform an engagement without bias or interference.

Independence
The freedom from conditions that threaten objectivity or the appearance of objectivity. Such threats to objectivity must be managed at the individual auditor, engagement, functional, and organizational levels (also see Organizational Independence).

Independent Outside Auditor
A registered public accounting firm, hired by the organization's board or executive management, to perform a financial statement audit providing assurance for which the firm issues a written attestation report that expresses an opinion about whether the financial statements are fairly presented in accordance with applicable Generally Accepted Accounting Principles.

Individual Objectivity
An unbiased mental attitude that allows internal auditors to perform engagements in such a manner that they have an honest belief in their work product and that no significant quality compromises are made. Objectivity requires internal auditors not to subordinate their judgment on audit matters to that of others.

Information Technology Governance
The leadership, structure, and oversight processes that ensure the organization's information technology supports the objectives and strategies of the organization.

Information Technology Operations
The department or area in an organization (people, processes, and equipment) that performs the function of running the computer systems and various devices that support the business objectives and activities.

Inherent Limitations of Internal Control
The confines that relate to the limits of human judgment, resource constraints and the need to consider the cost of controls in relation to expected benefits, the reality that breakdowns can occur, and the possibility of collusion or management override.

Inherent Risk
The combination of internal and external risk factors in their pure, uncontrolled state, or, the gross risk that exists, assuming there are no internal controls in place.

Internal Audit Charter
A formal, written document that defines the internal audit function's purpose, authority, and responsibility. The charter should (a) establish the internal audit

function's position within the organization, (b) authorize access to records, personnel, and physical properties relevant to the performance of engagements, and (c) define the scope of the internal audit function.

Internal Audit Function
A department, division, team of consultants, or other practitioner(s) that provides independent, objective assurance and consulting services designed to add value and improve an organization's operations.

Internal Control
A process, effected by an entity's board of directors, management, and other personnel, designed to provide reasonable assurance regarding the achievement of objectives in the following categories:

- Effectiveness and efficiency of operations.
- Reliability of financial reporting.
- Compliance with applicable laws and regulations.

Key Control
An activity designed to reduce risk associated with a critical business objective.

Key Performance Indicator
A metric or other form of measuring whether a process or individual tasks are operating within prescribed tolerances.

Material Observation
An individual observation, or a group of observations, is considered "material" if the control in question has a reasonable possibility of failing and the impact of its failure is not only significant, but also exceeds management's materiality threshold.

Monitoring
A process that assesses the presence and functioning of governance, risk management, and control over time.

Network
A configuration that enables computers and devices to communicate and be linked together to efficiently process data and share information.

Objectives
What an entity desires to achieve. When referring to what an organization wants to achieve, these are called business objectives, and may be classified as strategic, operations, reporting, and compliance. When referring to what an audit wants to achieve, these are called audit objectives or engagement objectives.

Objectivity — See Individual Objectivity.

Observation
A finding, determination, or judgment derived from the internal auditor's test results from an assurance or consulting engagement.

Operating Effectively — See Controls Are Operating Effectively.

Operating System
Software programs that run the computer and perform basic tasks, such as recognizing input from the keyboard, sending output to the printer, keeping track of files and directories on the hard drive, and controlling various computer peripheral devices.

Opportunity
The possibility that an event will occur and positively affect the achievement of objectives.

Organizational Independence
The chief audit executive's line of reporting within the organization that allows the internal audit function to fulfill its responsibilities free from interference (also see Independence).

Preventive Control
An activity that is designed to deter unintended events from occurring.

Process-level Control
An activity that operates within a specific process for the purpose of achieving process-level objectives.

Professional Skepticism
The state of mind in which internal auditors take nothing for granted; they continuously question what they hear and see and critically assess audit evidence.

Reasonable Assurance
A level of assurance that is supported by generally accepted auditing procedures and judgments. Reasonable assurance can apply to judgments surrounding the effectiveness of internal controls, the mitigation of risks, the achievement of objectives, or other engagement-related conclusions.

Residual Risk
The portion of inherent risk that remains after management executes its risk responses (sometimes referred to as net risk).

Risk
The possibility that an event will occur and adversely affect the achievement of objectives.

Risk Appetite
The amount of risk, on a broad level, an organization is willing to accept in pursuit of its business objectives. Risk appetite takes into consideration the amount of risk that management consciously accepts after balancing the cost and benefits of implementing controls.

Risk Assessment
The identification and analysis (typically in terms of impact and likelihood) of relevant risks to the achievement of an organization's objectives, forming a basis for determining how the risks should be managed.

Risk Management
The process conducted by management to understand and deal with uncertainties (that is, risks and opportunities) that could affect the organization's ability to achieve its objectives.

Risk Mitigation
An action, or set of actions, taken by management to reduce the impact and/or likelihood of a risk to a lower, more acceptable level.

Risk Response
An action, or set of actions, taken by management to achieve a desired risk management strategy. Risk responses can be categorized as risk avoidance, reduction, sharing, or acceptance. Exploiting opportunities that, in turn, enable the achievement of objectives, is also a risk response.

Risk Tolerance
The acceptable levels of risk size and variation relative to the achievement of objectives, which must align with the organization's risk appetite.

Secondary Control
An activity designed to either reduce risk associated with business objectives that are not critical to the organization's survival or success or serve as a backup to a key control.

Significant Observation
An individual observation, or a group of observations, is considered "significant" if the control activity in question has a reasonable possibility of failing and the impact of its failure is significant.

Standard
A professional pronouncement promulgated by the International Internal Audit Standards Board that delineates the requirements for performing a broad range of internal audit activities, and for evaluating internal audit performance.

Strategic Objectives
What an entity desires to achieve through the value creation choices management makes on behalf of the organization's stakeholders.

Strategy
Refers to how management plans to achieve the organization's objectives.

Sufficient Evidence
A collection of evidence gained during an engagement that, in its totality, is enough to support the judgments and conclusions made in the engagement.

System of Internal Controls
Comprises the five components of internal control: the control environment, risk assessment, control activities, information and communication, and monitoring that are in place to manage risks related to the financial reporting, compliance, and operational objectives of an organization. See also Internal Control.

Third-party Service Provider
A person or firm, outside of the organization, who provides assurance and/or consulting services to an organization.

Tone at the Top
The entity-wide attitude of integrity and control consciousness, as exhibited by the most senior executives of an organization. See also Control Environment.

Top-down Approach
To begin at the entity level, with the organization's objectives, and then identify the key processes critical to the success of each of the organization's objectives.

Transparency
Communicating in a manner that a prudent individual would consider to be fair and sufficiently clear and comprehensive to meet the needs of the recipient(s) of such communication.

Work Program — See Engagement Work Program.